FEAR

IN CHILE

FEAR

IN

CHILE

LIVES UNDER PINOCHET

PATRICIA POLITZER

Translated by Diane Wachtell

PANTHEON BOOKS NEW YORK

The translator would like to thank Patricia Politzer, Asa Zatz, and above all George Black, for their much appreciated help.

Library of Congress Cataloging-in-Publication Data

Politzer, Patricia.
[Miedo en Chile. English]
Fear in Chile: lives under Pinochet/by Patricia Politzer.
p.   cm.
Translation of: Miedo en Chile.
ISBN 0-394-56476-6
1. Working class—Chile—Interviews.   2. Fear—Chile —Public opinion.   3. Poor—Chile—Public opinion.
4. Trade-unions—Chile—Public opinion.
5. Chile—Armed forces—Public opinion.   6. Chile— Politics and government—1973–   —Public opinion.
7. Chile—Economic policy—Public opinion.
8. Public opinion—Chile.
I. Title.
HD8296.5.P6513   1989   305.5'62'0983—dc20
89-42678

CONTENTS

CONTENTS

ACKNOWLEDGMENTS

To all the people who were interviewed
and who, for reasons of space,
could not be included in this book.
To the Academy of Christian Humanism,
the Latin American Council
of Social Sciences,
and the World University Service,
institutions without whose support
this work would not have been possible.

FOREWORD

One of the hardest things to convey about dictatorship is the quality of daily life. When one order violently displaces another, the dramatic moment stands out in relief. But later, as the new order continues, so does the life of family, of work or lack of work, of personal aspirations and self-preservation. When we review the course of a regime we focus normally on the large events that signify shifts of policy, or the revelation of uncommonly severe crimes, the beginnings or ends of stages. Yet the experience of dictatorship for each citizen is the sum of the daily choices that define a life's course. And it can be argued that the sum of those choices determines the course of a nation.

In Chile, a nation with a long democratic tradition, military government was unthinkable until the coup. On September 11, 1973, when the presidential palace was bombed by the air force and the soccer stadiums became prison camps, Chile passed into an era for which no one, not even the supporters of the coup, had been prepared. The voices in this book speak of profoundly changed lives. Where there are first no understandable rules, and then the rules bear no relation to life before, each individual must become a new person based on the choices he or she makes—some of them seemingly mundane, some opportunistic, some ethical, many desperate.

Patricia Politzer is interested in those choices, and particularly in how people have defined them to themselves. Because a cardinal fact of dictatorship is isolation, the prevention of open social discourse, each person defines his or her confrontation with the new order through a profound and lonely self-definition, as friend or victim of the new authority, as success or mere survivor. It is through this long, ongoing act of definition that each citizen searches for coherence and a sense of worth.

The personal testaments in this book are Politzer's way of recovering a history of Chile since 1973, under the regime of General Augusto Pinochet. Fourteen of Chile's isolated, complete individual worlds are presented side by side. We learn how a prominent right-wing spokesman opted for the regime in part to please his family; how a Communist woman suffered almost more than one can imagine and emerged with her sense of self intact; how a bank employee experiences his frustrations in work and channels them into the first stirrings of political protest; how the Socialist widow of the former government's minister of defense makes sense of her betrayal by officers who were once her murdered husband's close friends. At the time these interviews were carried out, no dialogue among such varied people was possible in Chile, and few of them had ever spoken out on these subjects before. Yet each is free to emerge here, intimately, as a person of frailties and complex impulses.

Politzer started her interviews in 1983, a year when massive protests broke out against the regime, due in part to an economic crisis and in part to the grievances of victims of human rights abuses and advocates of democracy. The middle class that had supported Pinochet began to abandon him, and in the next five years—despite two periods of state of siege on the one hand, and some economic improvement on the other—the opposition movement grew into a clear majority of the population. On October 5, 1988, in a yes-or-no vote on whether Pinochet should remain as president, he was soundly defeated.

There are clues to the regime's longevity, as well as its defeat, throughout this book. In some cases Politzer's approach permits her subjects to be pedestrian, like the military mayor who considers himself liberal and enlightened while also considering that a possible 5,000 dead after the coup was a small price to pay. Other speakers describe the dedication of their lives to the regime's undoing, like the boy who inches his way into support of armed rebellion. In other cases, modest people reveal a buried eloquence, like the labor leader for whom organizing collective action has been a forced, if moral, choice; he would rather have led a more contemplative life, and feels deeply that "man also has a right to be emotionally thrilled. He shouldn't always be enraged, fighting for a crust of bread."

Although rage is seldom expressed in these pages, it is, like fear, a constant undercurrent. One of the choices these people have faced is how to deal with the polarization of their society, a process which began before the coup, surely, but which accelerated enormously under the strain of both the regime's economic policies and its political war on the opposition. The legacy of a military regime is the military framework of thought, which deals in enemies and in crushing them. Yet no democratic society can survive with such a logic. A few of the speakers here attempt to think about reconciliation, but when most of these interviews were given, the prospect of forgiving the enemy—whatever side one was on—seemed remote.

Since the plebiscite of October 1988, a new passage is under way. Today the question is how to go forward and shape a democracy that can recover from sixteen years of authoritarianism. And how to do so while looking back, learning all that happened, and finding a formula for reparation. In a democracy, the stories of each of the people in this book must be taken into account, along with the stories of millions more, whether on the right or the left; whether survivors, or missing, or dead. Their concerns and their rights must be woven together again, a new definition of normalcy must be created. Just as large events do not tell the whole story of dictatorship, so the process of recuperation is both societal and intimate, and often inconclusive. Immense choices remain to be made in Chile, a life at a time.

Cynthia Brown
Deputy Director, Americas Watch

New York City
May 1989

PREFACE

"Chile was and is afraid. Our fear makes us live half-lives, repressed and suffocated." This is what I wrote when I first published this book in 1984. After the 1988 plebiscite in which Pinochet was defeated, I was tempted to change it until I realized that Chile is still afraid.

Looking around once again, I see that dictatorship is much more than just brutal repression or lack of political freedom. Nowadays, political activity would seem to be almost totally free—except for the Communists, of course—and the worst human rights violations seem to be over. But the dictatorship is still here. It is present day after day, year after year, invading even our most intimate moments. It affects not only those who suffer cruelty or censorship directly but also those who are indifferent to dictatorship, and even those who support and justify it; because they, too, are caught in a system that determines what we can and cannot do, what we think, what we create, what we dream, and what we suppress.

Rather than offering statistics or political analysis in this book, I wanted to give a picture of the Pinochet years through the experiences of men and women who have lived through them, in widely different ways. Each chapter would be the statement of a real person with whom one could identify, and through whom one could discover a part of our history.

As time went by, and as I pried into the hearts of people as different as priests and soldiers, Communist activists and bank employees, I began to realize that fear was something common to almost all of them. Their experiences were as diverse as they could possibly be, ranging from a "Chicago Boy" economist to a copper miner, from a Pinochet diehard to the mother of a "disappeared." Still, at some point in each conversation, fear surfaced more or less explicitly, with more or less profound roots. For some, it was fear of the army; for others, of unemployment; for still others, of poverty, informers, repression, communism, Marxists, chaos, violence, or terrorism. Each person had his or her own.

This list of fears reminded me of September 3, 1970, when I saw my best friend leave for Buenos Aires. If Allende were to win the next day, she would not come back. Her father, a European immigrant who had been victimized first by Nazism, then by Stalinism, had become absolutely irrational about the idea of a leftist government. He was afraid.

My friend didn't come back, and many other people like her packed their bags, sold their houses, and left everything behind in an effort to escape. I didn't understand at the time, but today—although I still believe there was no reason to flee—I believe that fear took control of Chile and transformed everything.

But if fear had become an important variable of our political life before the 1973 military coup, under Pinochet it grew to be the linchpin of the regime. Through fear, the dictatorship infiltrated our daily lives and fastened itself to us like a barnacle.

For many years now, Chile has been divided into two clearly defined countries that don't look at each other, don't touch each other, and don't know each other; but they sense and fear one another. The grave danger of the situation lies in the natural progression from fear to hate, and from hate to aggression—a progression which so often ends in the logic of war, as it did in September of 1973.

It's true that in October 1988 Pinochet lost a plebiscite and that in December 1989 there is to be a free election, but that's not enough to end our nightmare. Now that we are on the verge of a democratic solution, we must recognize that Chile is both ourselves and the others—those whom we don't know but to whom we all too readily attribute our problems.

We have lived through unbelievable horrors in a country that—like Nazi Germany—was supposed to be cultured and civilized. But it was here, in Chile, that two youngsters were burned alive by a military patrol; it was here that three Communist professionals were beheaded, that a journalist was dragged from his bed at midnight to be shot; it was here that thousands were tortured. All this and much more in only the last three years. These are facts and cannot be imputed to the so-called civil war of 1973, which serves the Pinochet supporters to justify the inhuman acts perpetrated between 1973 and 1978.

To assure ourselves of a democratic future, we must all face this horror we have endured. It won't be easy. Some simply want to turn the page; they say we must heal our wounds and stop scratching. But if we want to build a sane society we have to confront the truth and accept it, ugly though it may be. We must recognize that there are many who are guilty because of their actions, but that there are also many others who are guilty for their negligence. There was complicity in the most unexpected social groups, and there were too many who kept silent.

Maybe it's not the free election but rather this painful task of self-recognition which constitutes the first step toward building a true democracy—without imposing absolute ideologies, without killing, denigrating, or discounting others simply because they think differently.

Throughout these fourteen interviews I have tried to give a broad and realistic picture of what has happened to us in the last two decades. There may be historical errors in some of the statements, but that is how those people perceived events, and it is by means of their perception that they analyze the past and predict the future. When we are able to look at each other with all our characteristics, all our defects, our sufferings, our weaknesses, errors, and accumulated experience, we will be able to respect each other without fear. The lives of the people in this book are meant to contribute to the challenge of recognizing what we are: neither as good nor as bad as we believed, neither as black nor as white as we supposed.

PATRICIA POLITZER
SANTIAGO
APRIL 1989

STATEMENT BY
THE CARDINAL ARCHBISHOP OF
SANTIAGO DE CHILE

CHILE IS THE OBLIGATORY THEME OF EVERY DAY. EACH *Chilean feels, profoundly and personally, the problems and the triumphs of our country. We have learned to love it deeply. We sympathize with it. It hurts us.*

Of one thing we were always proud: our diversity. The Spanish conquistadors, the German colonists, the Arab and Italian immigrants all came here. Our families have put down roots here, we have buried our dead here, and here our children have been educated. The Mapuche and the Hispanic, the O'Higginist and the Carrerista, the Pipiolo and the Pelucón, the unbeliever and the believer, have all learned to live together.

Patricia Politizer's work is valuable because it reminds us of what we should never forget: we can think differently without considering each other enemies. Our ideas can diverge, but we needn't seek to destroy our adversaries.

She shows us, at the same time, the courage of our noble and good community. Chile is its community, its people, its workers, businesspeople, fishermen, peasants, young people, and women. I think of Chile with immense confidence in the wisdom of its people. I love Chile. And I pray for it every day.

RAÚL CARDINAL SILVA HENRÍQUEZ

FEAR

IN

CHILE

THE EXECUTED MAYOR

BLANCA ESTER VALDERAS GARRIDO

T HADN'T BEEN AN ACT. THEY SHOT AT HER WITH REAL BUL-
lets on a bridge over the Río Bueno near Osorno. Her husband and three
others died as they fell into the water, but miraculously she survived. "If
God didn't take me," she says, "it was for the sake of my children." Or
perhaps so that someone would be left to tell the story.

It is the story of a country woman who had been named mayor of Entre
Lagos by Allende. And—for her—that's much more important than having
been put before a firing squad.

Her passions become inflamed when she speaks of her role in the town.
Even if it was Allende who created the township, it was she who transformed
it from "a hamlet between a trench and a sewer" into a new town that was to
have everything, including a university.

After several years of living in anonymity, still certain that she had only
done her duty as a citizen, she returned to Osorno to demand justice and to
confront the carabineros who had arrested and "executed" her.

On the seventeenth, at five in the afternoon, they came to get us. A police official arrived from Osorno with sergeants, corporals, and about ten men. They came in those green Bureau of Agricultural Development trucks that don't even belong to the police. They took me, my husband, and some people from a nearby town.

My children were left behind, huddled together, crying. And the sergeant said to my daughter—who had turned six on September 11 —"The others have already cried and now it's your turn." He said that to her—incredibly insolent! It was insolence, nothing else. No man with judgment or delicacy would speak that way to a bunch of children who have no idea what you are talking about! All they saw was that these men were taking away their father and their mother, that's it.

They took us all to jail. They put me in a cell and the men—four, including my husband—in another area. They took us out at about one-thirty in the morning.

Two cars came from Osorno, either dark green or black, I couldn't tell. There were masked men in them, wearing black masks with vampire teeth, with their eyes hidden.

They took us out of the jail at gunpoint; they backed the car up to the doorway and we got in. The four men were tied up, but I wasn't . . . maybe because I was a woman, I don't know.

We left Entre Lagos by the road to Osorno, but they switched onto a road called La Poza that goes to the outlet of the Río Bueno. We got to the suspension bridge over the river; they had exchanged their machine guns for rifles.

There were five of us and about twelve of them, one on either side of each of us, plus one or two leaders. They seemed to be civilians. We knew there was a uniformed corps of Patria y Libertad,* but we had never found out who they were because we didn't want to get involved with them. We got out of the car, and they took us to the bridge. They hit and kicked the men and cursed them. They made us kneel down on the bridge, facing the river, about five or six meters

---

* A paramilitary organization of the extreme right, created to combat the government of Salvador Allende.

apart. They put me at one end and my husband at the other, with the other three men in the middle.

I knew they were going to kill us. I knew because all their movements indicated it. I didn't say anything at all to them. They didn't see me cry or moan or anything else. I had no reason to cry before them. I wasn't afraid. I knew that I hadn't done anything. I hadn't committed any crime. I said to myself, "If it's God's will, I'll have to die and they'll kill me. I haven't done anything. I'm not a murderer. I haven't ordered anyone to be killed nor have I killed anyone." I was completely calm. What hurt me most—and what bothered my conscience—was that they were going to kill my husband. Why him? He wasn't guilty either. I was more guilty, because I was the mayor.

THE SOCIALIST CARD

In '64 my husband was contracted by a man to work at developing the timber industry in the mountains. My husband could look at a log and tell you, This one will yield so many inches of wood, that one's trash, and that one's good for kindling. That was his specialty.

We lived in Osorno—I was born and raised in Osorno—but we went to the mountains because this man offered my husband a good job with good benefits.

"Look, Fierro," he said, "I'm going to have a good house built for you and your family and I'm going to give you all the extras." At first my husband went alone to work for about five months, but the house didn't appear. "It'll come," he thought. "First I have to finish my part of the contract." So he asked for a truck, and we all went up, including the children, the youngest just a month old. We took some things, but we left most of our belongings in Osorno. I was a young woman, ignorant of life in the country, but I went with him anyway.

We got there, where it gets really cold and rainy, and since we didn't have a house, the administrator told us to put together three *monjas*—those makeshift shelters with wheels that are pulled by oxen at harvesttime—while the owner took stock of the situation and came up with a house. The little furniture we'd brought fell apart from the dampness. We started out well dressed, but after three years we were all barefoot and half-naked. There was still no house. We lived in those huts and in a wooden shelter my husband built for two years, waiting for something better.

My oldest daughter was twelve. She had been in her sixth year of school and had a scholarship from President Eduardo Frei* to keep on studying as long as she liked. And we turned it all down for this man's promises! According to my husband, the job was worth three or four times anything my daughter might have amounted to; so we went to the mountains, and she lost her chance. My second son, another smart one, also lost out by going with his father to the mountains. He went to school for a while in the country, but as it became clear that we couldn't make ends meet with my husband's salary and benefits, my husband felt he had to put his son to work.

We couldn't go back to Osorno, because they wouldn't let us have a truck. We were so far away that it would have been very expensive to leave—the little they were paying my husband wasn't enough. Every month my husband would have an argument with his boss, who always managed to cheat him out of something. It was the same story every month! My husband would ask for what he thought was due to him, and the boss would say no.

The truth is that I was the one who began to wake up . . . it was my suffering, my bitterness, the tears of my children that made us see our need, our poverty and humiliation.

"Look, Joel," I said, "he offers you this and promises you that, and look where we are. Because we listened to a scoundrel, my daughter lost her education and the money the government was going to give her. When will you give up?"

My husband spoke up so often that the owner began to hate him. One day he showed up with the police sergeant from Entre Lagos and two other *carabineros* to look for my husband on the mountain. According to the owner, my husband had robbed him. My husband was working with my son, and when they took him away, they tricked my son into staying there alone.

"Don't worry," the sergeant said to him. "Your father will be right

* The Christian Democratic president of Chile from 1964 to 1970.

back. Wait for him—he'll come to get you at three or four this afternoon." So the poor kid stayed there, like an idiot. He told me he had waited, and that when it was dark he got scared and came down the mountain and found only his younger brothers and sisters at home because I was out.

To save money, I shopped far from home. That day I had gone in search of wheat to make cereal, cheese, and chickens, because at that time we weren't even allowed to raise our own fowls. I would leave around seven in the morning and go about forty kilometers away, but I couldn't return the same day because the bus only went every other day. Since I would buy enough food to last a month, my son always took an oxcart and met me at the bus stop.

We had gone about two kilometers when I asked what was the matter, because I saw he was sad, and I had the feeling something was wrong. But I had no idea what had happened!

"Mami," he said and stopped the cart. "Yesterday at about ten they came to get Papi . . ."

"You foolish child!" I said. "Why didn't you say something sooner? Don't keep these things to yourself. They've been holding your father since yesterday without food or water. Think!" I said. "Do you suppose they took him off to sit him down at their table and serve him a roast? It doesn't work like that, my boy. Take these things home and watch out for your brothers and sisters. I'm going back right now!"

I got out of the cart and began to walk. I had no problem walking for kilometers on end, because I was used to hardship. As I walked along, I cried, thinking how humiliated and miserable my husband must be, and how much we would all suffer for this.

I got to the Entre Lagos police station, and an attendant told me that, indeed, some so-and-so named Joel Fierro was there, but that he couldn't do anything for me until the sergeant came. I stopped at a bridge by the front of the building and sat down . . . and suddenly a sadness came over me that made me cry . . . I imagined my husband shut up in a cell without food and my children alone and neglected. I was busy with these thoughts when a small man came up and offered help. He took me to find an instructor from the school, my children's teacher, to speak to the sergeant for me. The teacher's name was Iván Sánchez and he was a member of the Socialist Party of Entre Lagos.

Together we went to look for the sergeant, and we took him back to the police station so he could tell me what kind of crimes my husband had committed that made them lock him up like a horse for an entire night. Seeing how upset I was, the sergeant took the teacher aside and explained to him that my husband wasn't guilty at all, but that his boss had been bothering them for ages to take my husband in, and the arrest was simply a way to shut him up. The teacher advised him to let my husband go, because I wouldn't calm down.

In the pocket of my jacket I happened to have a card that had been given to me by a senator from the Socialist Party named Aniceto Rodríguez. I'd been carrying it around with me, but the truth is, I had no idea how significant it was. Once the senator came to the village from Santiago for a large meeting of farmers, and a friend invited us to attend. My husband wasn't able to go that day, so I went, and they gave me this card with my name on it, signed by Aniceto Rodríguez.

"When you have problems," he said, "remember this card, and look for other people of this sort—they'll help you."

When he said that, I wondered, "Who will these people be? Where will they be?" Then I put the card away in my jacket pocket and never took it out. But when my son told me what had happened to his father, I remembered the card. So when they freed my husband and we were left with the teacher, I told him about this meeting and showed him my piece of paper.

"Ahhhh," he said, "so you're one of us!"

"That's right," I said, "and will you please tell me honestly, because as a teacher you know far more than I, what should I do? I'm not going to remain silent, I can't remain silent, because tomorrow or the next day my husband will be out on the mountain, and the boss will come up with some reason or other to have him picked up again. They'll lock him up forever, and if I'm left tomorrow or the next day without a husband, the boss isn't going to feed my seven children."

The teacher gave me a letter and sent me to Osorno, to someone who was on the farmers' committee of the party.

My husband continued to work, but I made several things clear: "No one is going to stop me—neither you or the boss. I'm fed up with everything I've been through and I'm going to do what I want to do even if it kills me. I've had it!"

In Osorno I recounted everything that had happened to us, and my story appeared in the papers and on the radio. It was heard throughout the province! The speaker was a modest, hard-working peasant woman who spoke the truth. Since I had made this big complaint, and since they mentioned the name of the farm where I lived, peasant women, peasant men, and poor farmers began to come there, wanting to know how I had done it and where they could go to be heard; so I showed them, and from then on I took people almost daily to the labor tribunals.

This whole business of my statement was taken up by the party, and they brought it to Santiago. They made quite a story out of me, and presented it to President Allende upon his election. I didn't know anything about it, but when they announced the appointment of mayors at the national level, I found I had been named mayor of Entre Lagos by the president.

A township was created, and shortly after my appointment we moved into town—it wasn't even a town, but a hamlet between a trench and a sewer. Poor people lived there, who worked the fields and kept their old horses by the edge of the ditches along old cattle trails. These trails had been the streets, but now that it was a township things had to change. We had to make it a town, not a rathole!

We drew up a blueprint. I went to Santiago, went through all the red tape, and about three months later got the plans back with everything approved. We had asked for a grade school, a high school; here a trade school, there a hospital; here a university, there a health center; commercial establishments, a post office, a telegraph office, and three separate residential areas. It was all there on the plan, because it was time to create order, to see that everyone was healthy, that everyone had food and shelter. That was my design: streets, plazas, and a theater that the people could go to. We were dealing with a new town, not just any old thing.

I used my head, and that is what people should do. I didn't have much education, I had only gone through the fifth grade because my father had died and I hadn't been able to continue, but when I was a mayor, I knew what had to be done. But the day of the coup changed my life profoundly. I knew I wouldn't be able to do the things I had envisioned.

On the eleventh, at about seven in the morning, I switched on the radio and we heard about the coup. We knew the president was no longer in command and that things were now in the hands of the military.

A COWARD!

I was thinking how my husband was innocent, when they hit me with the end of a rifle. The man kept pulling the trigger of the gun, but it didn't fire. He put it to my head and trembled and shook. I gave him a look without saying anything, but I think that the look said, "You are a coward," because he shook and trembled.

They had the men in the same position I was, but they hit me with the rifle first to push me into the river. As I fell, I could see bullets passing me on all sides—even going between my legs! And then I began to feel the bullets meant for the others, as well as those they were firing at me. I hit the river and the bullets hit with me. Not one touched me, not even my clothing. The only thing I did was let out a cry as I fell toward the water, because my heart . . . I don't know . . . my heart was bursting. I believe that when I saw I was headed for the river, I prepared myself for the water. Since it was night, I hadn't realized how high up we were, but it was about twenty or twenty-five meters, and I didn't calculate well, so that I went very deep and it took me three strokes to get to the surface. When I was finally able to float, I was about three hundred meters farther down the river, because while I was trying to reach the surface the current had carried me toward the other bank. It was full of trees, and the men couldn't see me when I stuck my head up. They'd heard me cry out as I fell, but after that they didn't see me again. I kept on swimming downriver along the bank, passing below the Pan-American Highway bridge and continuing on about four kilometers.

I knew they had killed the men because they were tied up and so couldn't save themselves. I knew I had lost my husband and three friends. The only thing left was to think what I had to do.

As I was swimming, I listened for the sound of their cars, but they didn't drive off. I stopped awhile until I heard them leave. They started out toward Osorno, and then they came back to see if anyone had come out of the water. After a while I didn't hear them any more. I got partway out of the water and began to pull myself up by the tree branches and roots, which kept me hidden.

When I was out of the water, I knelt and thanked God: "Thank You, Lord, for helping me. You helped me and gave me life." And I started walking.

SHOTS IN THE NIGHT

I was still walking when I heard a rooster crow at dawn and thought it must mean there were people nearby. I went in the direction of the rooster, and there was the house of a tenant on the farm near the suspension bridge. Apparently I'd got confused, or blacked out during the night or when I hit the water, and so I didn't realize that after leaving the river I had gone back in the direction of the bridge. As the new day dawned, I saw that I had ended up not two hundred meters away . . .

I went up to the tenant farmer's house and knocked. "Please," I said to him, "I beg you to take me in for a little while. I'm all wet. I'm running away from La Unión"—that was the name of the next town over—"because my husband wants to kill me."

I had to say that, because if I had said they had thrown me in the river, he would not have opened the door, much less helped me. They had everyone terrorized! There were people who could have been saved, but their own neighbors turned them in out of fear, the fear that they too would die. And many people did die.

The man asked his wife and then let me in.

"I was running, and I tripped and fell into a stream," I told them. I also told them that my husband was a terrible, hateful man, a drunkard and a brawler. I had to say these things!

The woman got up immediately and offered me her bed. I took

off the wettest of my clothing and left on my underthings. They
were very poor people. The woman gave me a cup of tea and told
me to sleep—but who could sleep with all that had happened?

When I felt her coming near, I closed my eyes and pretended to
be asleep so that she wouldn't know the anguish I felt. I cried and
cried, cried and cried—it was the only way to relieve my heart. I felt
there was something hard in my heart, something that wanted to
explode, and I knew that crying would ease it. I spent the entire day
that way.

Then they moved me to a different bed next to a small window; I
sat up and I could see the Pan-American bridge that I'd passed under.
During the night the patrols kept going past. Suddenly, about one-
thirty in the morning, I heard a patrol running like the devil in our
direction. I sat up to look: two men, in their shirtsleeves, with their
hands up, came running down the middle of the road. After them
came the patrol; they got to the bridge and stopped. They turned
both men to face the river, shot them in the back, and then shoved
them into the water. The men had come from near San Pablo, but I
never found out who they were. The man and the woman woke up
when they heard the shots from the machine gun.

The next day, the man came home and began to eat lunch in their
little kitchen. I stayed in bed, because I didn't have the energy even
to swallow, and suddenly I heard the man:

"You won't believe what those gangsters have done. What have we
come to? Those shots we heard the other night—they killed the
mayor of Entre Lagos. They killed her and pushed her into the river.
And damned if they weren't laughing over the story."

"Poor thing!" said the woman. "And all the good things they said
about her. I wanted so much to meet her. They said she would talk
with anyone."

I let them go on, listening to them and trying to adjust myself. My
God, I thought, they think I'm not to blame for what happened.
Because if they thought I was a bad woman, they would be pleased
that I had been killed.

"We must be careful," he told her. "Don't let it get out that we
were talking this way about the mayor. Don't discuss it with anyone!
They're going after anyone who knows anything about the politicians."

I had to try to leave. When he went out, I approached the woman and asked if we could talk a bit.

"Señora," I said, "you didn't know this woman from Entre Lagos?"

"No, I didn't know her. I've wanted to go and see her but I wasn't able to meet her."

"Do you know that you are speaking to her?" I said, and she stood there dumbfounded. "I am the woman they came to kill. And I tell you this because I want you to help me."

The woman went out at once to find her husband, and I asked them if she would go to Osorno to tell my mother to come and get me. The man told her to get ready immediately, to leave right then and return quickly. At about two in the afternoon I gave her a note for my mother and one of my shoes so my mother would know it was me, and I told the woman to ask her for some clothing, because my killers would recognize me in what I had been wearing.

I had always worn my hair very long, so I cut it off with a knife, painted my eyes with heavy make-up, darkened some moles on my face, and put a handkerchief around my neck.

The woman returned promptly with my mother and a suitcase with clothing. We caught the last bus to Osorno, and the next day I went on to Valdivia, where my husband's family lives.

PAIN AND SOLITUDE

I stayed in Valdivia six months. They were very sad, bitter months, full of suffering. I knew that my children were neglected, that they went about aimlessly, and that I couldn't see them because I couldn't let them know I was still alive.

At one point they seized one of my boys and gave him such a going over that if he had known I was alive, with all that torment, all the things they put him through, he would have told them. That's why they couldn't know.

At that time my son was eighteen and working at the Agrarian Reform Agency, driving one of those Rumanian jeeps. The police showed up and threw about fifteen workers into a van, kicking and punching them, and carried them off.

My oldest daughter, the only one who knew I was still alive, tried to find her father. She asked in the municipal offices, in the jails, in the stadiums, wherever they said people were being held. She knew that I was in Valdivia, but she would always inquire about both of us and then about her brother who had also disappeared. They denied everything and told her that they didn't know.

My son was missing about two weeks before they let him go. They wanted to put him before a firing squad! But they discussed it and, since they had already killed his mother and father, and since he was still a minor, they didn't kill him. He didn't want to admit it, but I think they tortured him a lot, because at that time they didn't let anyone off just like that, least of all the son of the woman who was a mayor! From then on they had him in their files, and if they found he was up to anything, they would kill him at once.

That's how it was with my children. The youngest ones I finally saw five or six years later, when they were already grown. They had grown up being sent from pillar to post, without a mother to look after them. They had nothing, because our entire household was lost; the authorities took over the house, and my children weren't allowed anywhere near it. They went wherever they could: one to Osorno, another to Lanco, another to Chillán, another to the country, wherever someone would take care of them. My oldest daughter was the only one who always came back to where I was, but she had to work to take care of her brothers and sisters.

In Valdivia I just tried to recover, nothing else. The army thought I was dead, and I couldn't get work because I didn't have any papers. So I decided to go to Santiago, where I went to the authorities to get a new identification card.

I became Blanca Ester Céspedes, which had been the name of my true father. He was dead, and I was brought up by Enrique Valderas. I added Pérez also, and I kept those names until, later, I got to the Vicariate* in Santiago.

Since at that time I didn't know Santiago, I took my card and went back south to get work in Temuco. I hired myself out to work in the

* The Vicariate of Solidarity (Vicaría de la Solidaridad), created in 1976 by the Catholic Church to defend human rights.

fields at planting time or in the potato harvest, or I cleaned people's houses. I did whatever there was to do. I moved around so I wouldn't be recognized. I never took a permanent job, because working for a monthly wage would have meant putting myself on the books, and I would have had to go to an office where there were nosy people. I preferred things like this; I felt more secure and calmer.

Always alone, because I didn't trust anyone. I didn't know anyone in Temuco, I had no family, no one. Who could I trust? I made friends, but no one close enough to tell my story. I told them that I lived alone, that my children were with my mother, and that the only thing I wanted was to work. The truth is that the only thing I thought about was work—recovering, and working, and rejoining my children.

At night I didn't sleep much, only for a little while, and when I woke up I couldn't go back to sleep. I did things and undid them, put them together and took them apart. I thought about this, then that; here, then there; everything. Everything swirled in the night. I thought about what had happened, remembering when my husband took me to the country, and, the saddest thing, the loneliness I was carrying with me.

I remember a dream I had. I was in my house in Entre Lagos, seated on a sofa that we had, and I was crying. Suddenly, my husband arrived and entered into my dream!

"Why do you cry so much?" he said.

"How could I not cry," I asked him, "when you left me alone and never came back to look for me?"

Then he spoke these words: "Don't cry any more, because you'll ruin your eyes if you keep crying. I came to leave you this," and he put his hand into his wallet and handed me a fistful of bills, more than I could count. "With this you can buy whatever you need. And be happy, because I am well." He said that, and I woke up. I woke up crying because I didn't want him to leave me all alone. You can imagine how much I suffered and wept. But after this dream, I felt that I could stop crying.

Several years passed that way until one day—in 1979, I think—I met a half-drunken woman waiting on a corner for the bus. She motioned to me and asked me the time.

"I was supposed to go to a meeting, and I forgot," she said. "I'm a worthless good-for-nothing. But those wretches have got to tell me about my husband—where they have him and what they've done to him." The poor woman was quite drunk, and she went on shouting. "In '76," she said, "I lost my husband and I haven't been able to find him. They must have killed him! I never saw him again, and the soldiers must know why."

"And what meeting are you going to?" I asked her, to make conversation. "Can you have a talk with them and get them to tell you where he is?"

"No, señora," she said, "but we women are organized and have a lawyer and an investigator making inquiries. I was supposed to go, but I missed my chance, and now I'll have to wait until Tuesday. If you have some kind of claim, even though you're not one of us, go ahead, because the lawyer will take care of anyone."

I told her that I had a problem in the house where I lived because the mistress treated me badly. So we arranged to meet at that same place the following week.

I had heard about that kind of support group, but I hadn't known how to reach them since I didn't know where their offices were. When we arrived the next week and I saw human rights posters, I realized it was affiliated with the Vicariate. They were waiting for the woman, but it seems she suddenly felt like another drink, because she told me she had to leave. She gave me change for the bus and left. I waited until everyone else was attended to, until they had each had their say and I was the only person left. When there was no one else, I went in and spoke with the social worker.

I had hardly begun to tell her who I was and what had happened to me when she became very excited. She told me that they knew about me, but hadn't known how to find me. She left to get the lawyer and to call the vicar of Osorno, who came to get me in Temuco and took me to the Vicariate in Santiago.

I was in such bad shape after so much suffering and worrying about my children that they had to nurse me back to health. I was terrified that I would suddenly be caught. The doctors understood and gave me the help I needed to recover. Then I was able to get on with the legal proceedings, and I went to Osorno to present my case to the courts. I went to testify five different times. Just the way I am now, unafraid, I calmly went to state my case.

I had nothing to fear, because I was not lying to the people I spoke to; I was telling them the truth. I wasn't inventing anything, but telling them what had actually happened to me, and I had to tell them even if they were going to deny it! That is how I had to rid myself of this enormous injustice.

They did deny it. I felt the lack of moral courage in Chileans. I wasn't fooled—I knew what I saw in them was hypocrisy, cowardice, because I was telling the truth and they were denying it. I know that the judge believed me, that she realized what I said was true, but even judges have limits, and that's as far as it went. I know that she believed me, because when the sergeant raised his voice to me, she reprimanded him.

Furthermore, when we reenacted the execution where it had actually happened, and I knelt down in the same place as before, I moved some earth with my foot and found a used gun cartridge!

"Look," I said to them, "I was here, and this is here. Did they shoot at me, or not?"

"How awful, how awful!" said the judge.

I don't know what state the law is in these days, because the law should be just. I told the truth, but they didn't want to admit it.

A SAD TIME

I suffered greatly. We were like birds without a nest. That is how my children were brought up, living on the edge.

Now at least we've been able to come back here, where I was able to buy this house—these walls and this roof, because I don't own the land. The social worker wrote up my case, and the World Council of Churches sent me the money to buy this house, here in Renca.* But I can't make any improvements, such as putting in running water, because how would I get the money? From where?

* A poor neighborhood in Santiago.

When I first went to Santiago I thought it would be for just a few days and then I would return to Temuco. The only thing that I wanted, that I asked for, that I cried for and begged from God, was somehow to be with my children again. So when we bought this house, I quickly fetched one of my sons who had been left to fend for himself here in Santiago. Poor thing! When I found him, he already had a wife, a child and another on the way. They lived in great poverty.

They came home with me. The house had no ceiling or plaster, only a floor and walls. We began to fix it up. At any rate, our first night here we were all very happy. It was all so hard to believe, since I had spent so many years without a home. This house was one of the greatest satisfactions I have had in my life. I prayed that all my children would come there someday. They began to arrive the next year, and they have been reunited over time.

We have had much happiness here, I, my children, their husbands and wives, and my grandchildren. There are fifteen of us now, and I am able to feel calmer. But things get sadder every day. When the children cry and ask me for a piece of bread, it makes me very bitter. I become ill; I can't stand it.

My daughter is the one who works the hardest. She goes out and makes 360 pesos a day, but 40 of those go for transportation. She is the one who spends her days feeding us. If she gets married, I don't know what will happen to us.

One of my sons found a better job; he makes about 8,000 pesos a month, but it doesn't help us much because he has to send money to his children in the south. Alfredo was in a leather factory, but he had to quit because the conditions were unbearable. Carlos Esteban works in the same factory, and this week he brought home 500 pesos. Some weeks it's only 300. Ernesto recently found a job with a work crew, but we don't know yet how much he will get.

We are always looking for ways to make money because we all prefer to do whatever we can rather than go on the infamous PEM.*

---

* The Minimum Employment Program, established by the government in 1975, which grew to include more than 10 percent of the work force (396,277 people in May 1983). The pay amounted to approximately $15 a month.

Working there is even worse. It's the ultimate joke on the worker, a mockery. My children have never turned to the authorities. I could go, I suppose, but I'd be embarrassed. I'd be ashamed to be Chilean and work at that. I know work isn't offensive, but that kind of work *is* offensive! I would rather die of hunger than work there.

I keep hearing how the Marxists did this or the Marxists did that —the word is on everyone's lips. And what does it mean? I think my way of proceeding, of defending my rights, of protesting for my children and for my husband, I think all of that makes me a Marxist. Because I chose justice: when I was a mayor I said the workers deserved bread. I learned about basic human rights. I don't think it was political. It was simply common sense!

But my children are afraid to stand up for themselves. They have always been afraid. They don't understand their rights; they say they'll lose their lives the way their father lost his. They believe that all politics is a crime, that politicians are responsible for things being bad. Because most leaders, my son says, don't know how to lead. I always listen to him, and I think he is partly right. Because the others, those who are alive, where are they? What are they doing? What have they done for us?

Jesus said that we must forgive, but I think that neither we nor God will ever forgive the men who are governing this way. We cannot judge them, but I know that God will judge them and punish them.

I don't agree that they should be killed, but they should be made to work, because they don't work the way the people work. They should know in their own flesh what suffering is, what hunger means, what it is like to be thirsty, to be ragged, picking up crumbs from the street.

I have been trying for ten years to forget what happened to me, and I cannot. Will the child who was abandoned in the streets without father or mother forget? How could we forget?

A MAYOR OF THE REGIME

COLONEL JUAN DEICHLER GUZMÁN

WANTED TO INTERVIEW SOMEONE IN ACTIVE MILITARY SER-
*vice, but they seem even more fearful than the civilians. I don't know exactly
what they are afraid of, but none of the ones I was able to reach would
agree to talk with me about the past decade. What is clear is that they all
have unlimited confidence in their intelligence agencies: they wouldn't
agree to speak even after being promised strict anonymity.*

*Finally I discovered Colonel Deichler, who, though retired from active
service since 1977, is as thoroughly military as the most active. Having
proved his loyalty to General Pinochet and his government, Deichler was
appointed mayor nine years ago. Convinced of the regime's virtues and of the
many services it has provided his community, he agreed to the interview
immediately and, much to my surprise, never suggested the possibility of cen-
soring any of the text.*

*At fifty-eight he has abundant energy and arrives at his office before eight
each morning. We had two long sessions there, in which he explained to me
the difference between a coup and a "military intervention." He also spoke of*

the professional training and the patriotism of the military; of the Communists, who should be outlawed because they are atheists and have done great harm to the country; of the officials of Popular Unity whom, as mayor, he kept on; of the disappeared; of the secret police, the DINA, and its head, his friend General Manuel Contreras. He also complained about the priests who have not been helpful to the regime and about those politicians who consider this government the most evil in Chile's history. He explained to me what the regime had done for the country and assured me they were moving toward democracy, but he also said that the timetable would not be pushed up any earlier than 1989. Because that is how it is settled in the 1980 Constitution —Pinochet's Constitution.

I knew absolutely nothing about the eleventh. Nothing at all. You could see that things were bad and that we soldiers had to do something, but I thought more time would go by: three months, six months, or maybe a year. And even though I was a colonel in active service, it came as a complete surprise to me since I wasn't housed in the general barracks at that point.

Since March of '73 I had been president of the National Food Distributors (DINAC), because the government had asked military leaders to coordinate provisions. General Bachelet was the national coordinator. We worked with him daily, seeing who needed sugar, potatoes, beets, tea, coffee . . . I loved the work and thought it was very patriotic to supply the people, the barrios, the neighborhood councils, or the JAP,* to help maintain some semblance of order. Uniformed officers are always ready to take on whatever tasks are assigned us. As I always say: when they call me, I go, and when they sing for me, I dance. I fulfilled my official duties with great pleasure.

I was nominated to DINAC by General Pinochet, who at that time was commander in chief of the army, because he was replac-

* The Councils on Provisions and Prices, neighborhood organizations backed by Popular Unity.

ing General Prats,* who had been nominated as minister of the interior.

Don Carlos Prats was my first artillery captain in military school. I looked up to him greatly because he was always first in his class— very studious, very capable, and thoroughly professional. He was also my division general, and we always maintained an excellent professional relationship, because he was a splendid person. During the Popular Unity government they assigned him to be commander in chief and minister of the interior. I don't know about his thoughts or feelings or what his ultimate goals were, but I think that his actions as minister were well-intentioned and altruistic. Still, I think he was wrong; he should not have permitted the army to be manipulated and poorly paid, nor should he have allowed the defense budget to be so severely cut.

Between March and September, things were a mess. Supplies were totally lacking. I felt terrible being at the center of it all, in situations where fights were breaking out over food.

My wife never actually said there should be a military coup, but she made me see the problems that existed—with public transportation, tires being burned in the streets, strikes, and general disorder . . .

And while I was feeling bad, my managers, who belonged to Popular Unity, were coming in with their helmets and packs for a mass demonstration. It was a terrible mess.

Popular Unity was a dreadful thing. Education was bad, distribution was bad, transportation was bad—everything. I speak very frankly: it was a total shambles. That is not a country! They had a lot of useless members. It was painful to see such pompous people in charge, with so little capacity for organization! There were other people—politicians, senators, representatives—who were splendid, but a group must be an organized whole, so that no one part lets the others down.

---

* General Carlos Prats, commander in chief of the army during the government of Salvador Allende, was assassinated along with his wife on September 30, 1974, in Buenos Aires.

There were terrible problems because appointments were made on the basis of politics and not ability. How could a shoemaker be an industrial inspector? Those jobs require engineers or people with training, yet they had someone from the party with a little bit of guts and that's it. But guts don't make a machine go.

The shortages were overwhelming. Everything was stockpiled in the warehouses and was never distributed. It was all hidden by the members of Popular Unity! I have no idea why they did it, but I think they wanted to aggravate the shortages in order to finish everything and start from scratch. I saw what was in my DINAC warehouses, but I couldn't do anything because I was under General Bachelet. If it had been up to me, I would have put it all on the market, but I couldn't. That was a different government, I had a different leader, and I had to obey . . .

Another issue was the way the arms arrived. In my DINAC warehouses I found rocket launchers, antitank cannons, machine guns, and a lot of ammunition. My friends from the former Popular Unity had hidden them in bags of sugar. I, personally, removed eight machine guns, so no one can tell me that this wasn't happening. I remember that I called the admiral,* who at that time was commander of the fleet and was in Valparaíso, to ask him to organize a raid on the DINAC warehouses in the port. He did, and they found seventy or eighty machine guns and ammunition in the bags of sugar. It was lunacy!

On the eleventh of September I arrived at my office as I do every day, and I heard the news that the Junta had assumed power. Since I was in the military, I got in touch at once with my director in the Ministry of Defense. Orders were to control the situation, to help coordinate, and in our case, to guard the DINAC warehouses and see that distribution was not interrupted since they had received word that all the warehouses were to be burned down.

It was a memorable day. Just below the DINAC offices—on Huérfanos and Teatinos streets—was a unit of the Buin regiment that

* Admiral José Toribio Merino, commander in chief of the navy and a member of the Military Junta.

had six fifty-caliber machine guns and a dozen thirty-calibers. They were engaged in combat right there, which created an enormous racket. My DINAC people were all very frightened.

Initially the leaders of Popular Unity joined forces, determined to defend their government, but they came to see that it was just a matter of time, since the military was solidly installed. They had plenty of weapons, but apparently they couldn't rely on their people, because the midlevel supporters saw what was happening and went home. During the afternoon I personally escorted to their homes those Unity leaders who had remained in their offices. Since I was in uniform, I dropped them off one by one to avoid any problems, such as being arrested or being shot for failing to heed a "halt." It seemed right and lawful to take them home.

I think the impact of the coup was so great that they didn't have a chance to use their weapons. They couldn't distribute them in time. They probably thought they would stay in power longer, so they missed their opportunity, but, speaking as a colonel in the army, I am sure they would have used them!

The decree was necessary, because Marxist regimes always act with violence and solve their problems through destruction. The best thing that could have happened to the country, once it realized it was headed for civil war, was the September 11 military intervention. It prevented a lot of deaths. And I say military intervention, because if it had been a military coup, many more people would have died. With a military intervention, you come in and take charge, trying within reason not to hurt anyone and not to declare war; in a coup, the whole military apparatus is called into service, and then there are a lot of deaths.

When they talk about how many people were killed, they make me laugh. I assure you—and I would take an oath on it—that on the eleventh of September and the days after, there were less than 5,000 corpses in Chile on both sides. I've traveled throughout Latin America, and in El Salvador, for example, there are 36,000 deaths in one year. So thinking about it doesn't upset me or make me lose any sleep. In Chile it was very calm. *Very* calm.

· · · · ·

SPLENDID COMMUNISTS

In the following days things straightened themselves out, and General González Acevedo, who had become minister of the economy, named me national president of distribution.

For the first time, on the fourteenth or fifteenth of September, we actually entered the Ministry of Housing and Finance, together with General González and his advisers. The weapons they had not managed to distribute were all over the place: in the closets, in the drawers, in the elevators—machine guns, pistols, revolvers, and unused ammunition.

Despite this, many DINAC officials who had belonged to Popular Unity continued to work with me. They were very professional people and, in a way, you had to respect them. They accepted the idea that there had been a complete change, and I was pleased they stayed on, because there was a lot to be put in order. Many people went into exile, but others stayed with me, and even now on holidays, I get calls from people who were or still are allied with Popular Unity, who treat me with fondness and affection.

After a while, Don Fernando Léniz—a splendid finance minister —arrived and began to work on transferring economic control to the private sector. Everything was becoming normalized, and it was no longer necessary to have military personnel in the ministry. We were all leaving, and General Benavides, the minister of the interior, called me in to tell me I was to be appointed mayor of Quinta Normal.

I was still in uniform, and a military mayor seemed odd to me . . . but there had been others, and I thought I should give it a try. Besides, I must confess that I am a man with a great feel for social work, for helping others. Actually, soldiers are the biggest communists and socialists in the world, in the basic sense of those concepts. As members of the military, we spend our lives worrying about our people, about our conscripted soldiers, about our leader, our sergeant, our lieutenant . . . about solving things. In this sense, we make splendid communists.

But Marxist communism is a different story! What they have in Russia is something that doesn't fit with our Western ways. It's another way of being, of living, that doesn't give man the freedom he needs to think, to do things, or organize his life. There is always someone up above guiding you by the hand. And that's no good!

When I arrived in Quinta Normal, in 1975, the town was still a little chaotic and only beginning to recover from the coup. They had eliminated the aldermen and installed a mayor to govern the community.

There were a lot of people with leftist ideas, people left over from the old regime, and I didn't expel anyone. No one! Even today, July 10, 1984, I have people with leftist ideas in my township and I've never touched them, because they work for me honorably. As long as I don't discover they're activists, I'm not going to tell them they should change their ideas; people can think whatever they like, so long as they fulfill their duties. One day a member of the Movement of the Revolutionary Left (MIR) even approached me:

"Colonel," he said, "I'm a Mirista, I've been in jail, and I need your help. I'm dying of hunger, I have seven children, and I need a house."

I gave him a house. I gave him and his wife work, and I placed their children in schools.

"My dear friend," I said to him, "as long as you don't do anything to hurt me, stay calm. But if I catch you fooling around, I'll crucify you!"

I don't think this has been the general rule; in other places they've taken more drastic and severe measures against this kind of people. I don't agree with that approach. Soon we'll be in the twenty-first century, and I don't think punches, slaps, and kicks are going to get us anywhere. I don't think that I'm an exception either; the majority of people feel the same way. But there are also some extremists. We have people here whose hair stands on end at the mention of Christian Democrats. I think the path that allows us all to work together peacefully is the one we ought to follow.

That's what I told the PEM people last year when they demonstrated and made demands. Eight thousand people got together in Santa Anita Stadium and shouted that they wanted to speak with the mayor, alone. I arrived by myself in a private truck. They even had a microphone . . . They wanted better wages, social welfare, food allowances, money for transportation, a series of things it was impossible to grant at that time.

"My dear friends," I addressed them, "let's get one thing straight: I don't give a damn if you're Communist, Socialist, Christian Democrat, nationalist, radical, or whatever you like. What matters to me is that we work together peacefully, that we be concerned about our homes, that we're sure of having work."

That got the first applause, and from there we sorted things out.

We don't have any special security forces here. I only have the police forces—that's it. And there haven't been any acts of terrorism with the exception of one bomb that was planted in the municipal building and blew up the second floor. That was barbaric, but I think those things are inevitable. At that time people kept asking me what kind of controls we have, and we have very few because we have too many people coming here to the mayor's office, the local courts, the Treasury, the Transit Department, or the Office of Public Works. We can't possibly control all those hundreds of people—it would mean terrible delays and people would complain, because their time is money. We have some city employees who are trained to watch, to see, to report back, but that's it.

A MAYOR'S JOB

When I was put in charge of the town, there was a lot to be done. One of the reorganization efforts after the eleventh of September was the extraordinary push for regionalization. The country was divided into regions, provinces, and towns to make things easier.

The volunteer corps was newly founded, and it has been truly marvelous. It's made up of extraordinary women who are ready to do all sorts of work—sweeping and cleaning. My wife, Julia Oportot de Deichler, is the president of the Joint Foundation for Community Aid, and she's responsible for all the volunteer organizations dealing with children, the elderly, the disabled, all the community centers. The volunteer corps is a worthy calling and requires great devotion.

I took charge of a town that had fourteen shantytowns, and now, thank God, I have none. That's an important achievement. We've done away with over 5,000 slum dwellings, and since these were homes with large families, multiply by seven, and there are between 35,000 and 40,000 individuals who now live under a roof, out of the rain. That's very nice! The eradication of the slum areas was one of my first objectives when I took office, and even though it took seven, eight, or nine years, we did it.

All of this was financed by the Ministry of Housing and now the residents have to pay a fee of 610 pesos, which is within the means of any family. With a job through the PEM or the POJH * job-creation programs, or in a factory industry, they have more than enough to pay, and everyone pays the same amount.

It was awful to see families living on the riverbank. Now, instead, they all have their little houses. One day a very old woman wanted to kiss my hands . . . not something a military man is accustomed to. "Colonel," she said to me, "look! There's running water in my house! For forty years I walked four blocks to a standpipe in order to make breakfast for my family. Running water in the house is a miracle from God."

And with the eradication of the shantytowns came something else very important. All the people that I had in the Nueva Matucana slum had criminal records, were bad people. Yet the moment we got rid of the slum, they all "got good," as we say here. As soon as they stopped living in that horrible netherworld of cardboard and tin, they stopped being bad and have conducted themselves splendidly. So families need a roof over them to be able to live peacefully. Now they have their neat little homes, and it's a pleasure to see how they take care of them. I'm sure that if we gave all delinquents a house and the opportunity to work in order to live peacefully, the problem of delinquency would disappear . . . with the inevitable few exceptions.

The new government modernizations involve the mayor in all aspects of life: sports, education, health . . . Quinta Normal was the

---

* Created by the government in 1982, POJH had about 228,500 people enrolled by November 1983. The average salary was around $25 a month when a pound of bread cost about 25 cents.

first community in Chile to turn education over to the municipal government. The results have been excellent. My thirty primary schools and my two high schools hadn't seen a drop of paint in twenty years; now they're all freshly painted, with clean, sanitary bathrooms.

When they made the changes, I thought I would get one teacher for every forty to forty-five students, but I ended up with a surplus of teachers. I didn't fire any of them. We worked out their hours in such a way that our children's teachers are happy, and I've even tried to raise their salaries.

The Community Council on Social Development operates effectively on the funds it gets from the Ministry of Education. The town only has to help a little with feeding the children, because there were some children fainting for lack of breakfast. Now everyone has breakfast, and we give many of the children lunch. That's a positive step as well.

As for health, in my town they haven't made any changes yet, because, according to what the ministry tells me, Quinta Normal offers relatively good health care. I have the San Juan de Dios Hospital here, the Félix Bulnes Hospital, and the Santa Anita, Andes, and Lo Franco clinics. Also, in many neighborhood councils there are doctors and nurses to help people.

Today, a mayor's got to be involved in everything. And we have to recount what we do for the press and for our constituents. At first, as a military man, I didn't like dealing with television or the press, but I recognize how important it is to report the enormous social changes this government has brought about. That's a *sine qua non.*

And in all of this we have the assistance of the Committees on Community Development, which include some of the most important people in the community who want to help. There are business leaders, professors, bankers . . . unfortunately, my priests have not really gotten involved. I would have liked to integrate them into the committees so they could help me, but that hasn't happened.

A few years ago I had some minor clashes with Monsignor Enrique Alvear, who has since died. He was second in command, after His Eminence Cardinal Silva Henríquez; he was a very good, very capable man, but he had some very strange ideas. Once, when we were demolishing Nueva Matucana, he actually asked, in front of me, how it was possible that we could deceive these people, moving them to an even worse pigsty. That's where we clashed! And we exchanged some words in front of my superior, General Rolando Garay.

The Church welcomes many people with leftist leanings. But in spite of this, relations with the clergy in my community are excellent. Without a doubt, my best friends are the evangelicals. They've supported me most avidly, been the most helpful, and haven't created any problems. Since they don't drink—they're very virtuous people —they're the most honest.

THE PROBLEM OF WORK

Another concern I've had as mayor has been the business situation. This is a community of 1,200 businesses. There are large companies like Lever-Chile and Hoechst Chemical, and smaller artisans' workshops that also count as industries and are treated as such. You'd think I would be rich with all of this. But that isn't the case because of the Common Municipal Fund, to which each community must contribute a percentage of its income, which is then divided by the Interior Ministry among those communities that have nothing.

I know something about those communities too, because for one year I was a double mayor and, in addition to Quinta Normal, was in charge of Pudahuel. Then, if the ministry gave my town one peso twenty, it meant that it had to give Pudahuel eighteen pesos eighty to even out the inequities and allow the mayor to proceed with his plans. That was a wonderful system!

While I got Quinta Normal with fourteen shantytowns, in Pudahuel I had forty! There were also a few more destitute citizens there, poor people living in subhuman conditions. As a result, there were also a lot of people with different kinds of politics churning up the waters.

After the eleventh, everyone was happy, but there began to be some rumblings over the lack of work. People complained to me about it. Thank God, there were no acts of violence while I was there, but there were petitions, strikes, and big meetings. "Mister Mayor," they said to me, "how long will we be out of work?" They told me about schools closing down, about industries failing and dismissing fifteen hundred employees.

I always met with them calmly, speaking honestly, without promising them work, or money, or new schools, only the truth, and that way we understood each other.

In Pudahuel, the police have little control because of the many agitators. They belong to the Communist Party, or the Socialist Party, and since they're upset over the change in government and the loss of their president, they've dedicated themselves to political agitation, staging strikes, disrupting traffic, burning buses, mugging, holding up supermarkets, and causing shortages. Unfortunately, there's fertile soil for this, because the problems are real, and the people are somewhat needy and are suffering. But if everyone would make an effort to work, to produce things, to care for their children, it would be a different story.

In Quinta Normal the situation has been very different. In '73, businesses had been taken over and we had to get them going again little by little. Some shut down and others kept fighting and working to get ahead. So when I began to realize that many of my industries were going bankrupt, it came as an enormous emotional shock.

The economic policies being applied didn't strike me as good. I didn't like the idea of free imports when there were plenty of businesses right here to supply our country. In Fanaloza, for example, they were manufacturing a switch for streetlights that cost seventeen pesos. Of course, without duty, it gets brought in from Taiwan and goes for five pesos. That was one flaw in the Chicago Boys' economic policy: the free importation of everything, instead of stimulating our own industries.

I don't know why the Chicago Boys managed economic policy for all those years. It certainly wasn't my decision. As mayors, we were involved in the daily life of the community, and we weren't in charge of those things. We didn't have access to those spheres of government—and we didn't have any means of getting it—where we could make an opinion known. With our superiors, we were permitted only to focus on what was happening with the people of our community, no more.

And the truth is that during the economic boom years, we were all right. We had money, and we were able to do plenty of things: we got rid of a lot of slums, we paved the roads, we improved services, we provided light for everybody . . .

In the era of the economic boom, from '78 to '81, the standard of living rose greatly. It was evident in education, in clothing styles, in the number of people who joined volunteer organizations, and in sports. Even in the slums that we got rid of, people had their television, their blender, their little lamp, and their radio.

Still, jobs were always a problem, and as a result we implemented the PEM. But before the recession, it was a problem that affected primarily Santiago, and it wasn't that serious. In the provinces, they had almost no one on the dole, and here there were families with two or three members in PEM, and together they had an income that allowed them to eat perfectly well.

That was precisely the idea: that people who didn't have jobs wouldn't die of hunger. So they came up with some projects to give these people something to work at and let them earn their pesos. I used them to paint my schools, for instance, and to clean all the sewage drains. But the work yield was very low. With the 2,000 pesos they get paid now, there's no denying the low yield; the people are weak, and since many of them are old, hand them a trowel or a pick and ten minutes later they're tired. They're exhausted, because they haven't eaten breakfast. They must be treated with great care, much deference, good judgment, and humanity.

I realize that they're paid very little; there are people who refuse to work, I don't dispute it, but this is an effort the government has made to give them something. Furthermore, to give an even larger salary to those who were heads of households, the POJH was created in 1983, and they oversee slightly more ambitious projects, such as the creation of greenbelts or the paving of certain streets.

In this new program, workers make 4,000 pesos, foremen 8,000, supervisors 15,000, and professionals 30,000, because there are unemployed engineers, architects, and builders as well. At one point I had 28,000 people in the PEM and POJH together. But that was because of the recession, which is a global problem that affected everyone. Copper has gone from a dollar to fifty-eight cents a pound! That's when you've got to get innovative, to diversify so that copper isn't everything. Some people understood this and have started exporting everything under the sun.

FAITHFUL PATRIOTS

In 1977 I retired from the military, but fortunately, with my activities as mayor, I didn't feel it. Of course, military men don't like to retire, because we'd all like to become generals, but only one in a hundred makes it.

A strange thing happened to the men of my class. In '73 we completed thirty years of service and we should have retired; then came the military intervention, and we continued on active service, which began to cause problems with seniority. Finally, as we began to retire, several became generals: General Orozco, General Ortíz, General Ewing, and General Patricio Torres.

Today I receive my soldier's pension and my mayor's salary, but according to the law, because I have both, the mayor's salary was reduced by 65 percent.

As a colonel in the army, I clear about 65,000 pesos, because I am still paying for my house. It's very interesting: we soldiers, with only a few exceptions, have never worried about having our own houses, because throughout our careers we've been provided with accommodations. Recently, when I retired at over fifty, I realized that I didn't have a house.

I get another 65,000 pesos from the city, and I'm very content with and grateful for this. If I'm careful, I'm able to live perfectly well.

The economic situation of the army has not improved the way some people think. It's gotten a little better, but it's not prosperous. When people say that the military is rich, they lie. The fact is that before, things were truly awful. As a commander, I was only recently able to buy a small secondhand car. Now things are a little better, and it seems there are more opportunities for young officers. My other son, who is a captain, lives very modestly, but he does have his little car.

We soldiers are decent people. We're all very patriotic, and the only thing we want for Chile is peace and tranquillity. So much so that during the thirties, the Ministry of War was renamed the Ministry of Defense. Our aim, in terms of the general population, especially the young people, is to teach them about patriotic and moral values. We're outstanding at that! We're also outstanding at doing things as mayors.

An authoritarian government simply means there are chains of command and rules of conduct. We're accustomed to command in our units, and so the transfer from our units to the community is natural: one must observe rules, laws, and orders. For us it seems very simple. At times it's harder for civilians because they're not used to it, but when they are told they must comply with these arrangements, things become easier.

I would say that politicians are more superficial and a little more selfish, because everything is done according to party. Although there are, of course, some splendid politicians.

But even if they're great politicians, we're different. And we're reluctant to get involved in political matters because we don't understand them. We find the different factions confusing. For example, I don't understand what the MAN, the UDI,* or this, that, and the other are. One faction is a little farther this way, the other a hair more that way, and another farther out still. There are a lot of different groups, and they all want different things.

General Pinochet, by contrast, has no desire for power. He sees things differently, and when the country is paid up and secure, he will go home.

When I was a cadet, he was my lieutenant instructor. I've known him for over forty years. He's a man with an extraordinarily big heart, a great teacher and writer, a very capable man who, at times, because of his military upbringing, doesn't externalize things or let himself be known to others, but he is still an excellent man. He has an extremely clear plan for the political progress and administration of the country. He is a man of extraordinary energy and a vitality

* The National Action Movement and the Independent Democratic Union, civil movements supporting General Pinochet.

more extraordinary still. He is deeply concerned about children and the disabled, and when he sees a problem in one of the shantytowns it affects him greatly. At times, I believe, he wishes: If only we had more so that we could help more! He is an excellent man. The mayors once had lunch with him, and he was happy to be singing boleros and other songs with Señora Lucía, some secretaries, and the governors. He's a very cordial person and a most upright leader.

Señora Lucía is also an extraordinary woman, vital and very charismatic, who has created a volunteer corps in Chile that should be an example for the world. She's like a diligent little ant who works in different areas and also collaborates well with her husband. She has tremendous capabilities; I remember that I was most impressed to see her on her own, facing the mayors, speaking and conversing perfectly well and with very clear goals in mind.

The present government is an honest government, a government that wants to accomplish things, that aspires to better the country so that Chile can be as it should be.

Certainly some questionable things may have occurred with respect to human rights, and some midlevel officers may have overstepped the limits, but in any case, those excesses don't go to any higher levels of command. People who have some axe to grind are always the ones who are prone to get arrested and, as human beings naturally do when they are imprisoned, most of these people react violently and then are the object of the kind of behavior that is resisted by the general populace. I don't in any way justify it, but it can happen that some people overstep their authority.

Undoubtedly this is happening less, because the CNI* is only an information agency. At worst, it has a detention facility to help clarify things, but it's not a repressive apparatus. I understand that when one of those kids gets out of line and is detained, the family has the right to make claims against the government. But that doesn't mean that the CNI is a repressive instrument; it's an information agency under the control of a general.

* National Information Center.

As for the DINA,* speaking as a colonel in the army and as a mayor, I think at first it was good. When this regime was just beginning there was a veritable war against the pests who were running around doing stupid things. During that time a lot of people were killed, on both sides: a lot of policemen were shot and killed. And the minute we're dealing with war, everyone assumes responsibility and . . . whoever dies, dies. For that reason, I don't blame anyone for those who disappeared. I think that it was ridiculous, like the dirty war in Argentina. But there, more than 35,000 disappeared, and in Chile, did we have even 600? I also think that all those disappeared people were like mad dogs—dogs with rabies! And rabies has to be eliminated, although I don't justify this. Not in the army nor in any of the National Defense institutions are the disappeared justified.

On the other hand, are they all disappeared? A neighbor of mine was mourning a disappeared who came back from Argentina two weeks later. There's a lot of myth in this business of the disappeared! Many of them are in Argentina, Cuba, Venezuela, and elsewhere. It's true there are some disappeared, but not as many as they say. During my travels I've come across a lot of Popular Unity friends who were "disappeared," and they were doing fine—I even had a few drinks with some of them. In Mexico, Guatemala, Panama, Colombia. I don't remember their names, but there were a lot of them, so not all those people are disappeared.

In terms of maintaining order, General Contreras was the strictest, but he was never evil. I know him well; we were together in military school. I was a year or two ahead of him; he was always first brigadier, first rank, first place at the War Academy. He's very capable, very energetic, very military, and a good man. I've always considered him a friend.

He had nothing to do with the assassination of Letelier or the attempt on Leighton.† Nothing! I'll put my head in a guillotine and

---

* National Intelligence Agency. It was replaced by the CNI, or National Information Center, beginning August 6, 1977.

† Orlando Letelier, secretary of state during Salvador Allende's governnment, was assassinated in Washington on September 21, 1976. Bernardo Leighton was

my hands, not in fire, but in boiling oil if he had. Other people, maybe . . . But he didn't give the orders for those things. He didn't cause them or encourage anything like that. He may have let them happen . . . maybe . . . If he let them happen . . . the one in charge is responsible for what happens and what is allowed to happen. It's possible he had something to do with it. But that he's inhuman, that he's a tyrant, or a murderer, no way! He's a general in the army.

ALL SWORN TO THE TASK

The first of the protests disturbed me. Where I live, in La Reina, the crowds were much more violent and vocal than here in Quinta Normal. In La Reina, a terrible mob showed up from Lo Hermida, from the big shantytowns in Ñuñoa. And cars drove along with little kids banging pot lids together like cymbals, adding to the noise from the houses. All of this had me very worried.

I had the sudden thought that the government wasn't doing its job. But then I realized that wasn't so. This mob wasn't there because of a shortage of provisions or a lack of transportation; it was there— maybe—because of a lack of work. That had me thinking for several days, but steps were taken quickly. The economic team was changed —the Chicago Boys were out—and the POJH was created for a few more pesos.

Fortunately, Quinta Normal hasn't been affected by the protests; it's a quiet community. Elsewhere, there was destruction, traffic lights were destroyed, supermarkets were held up, buses were burned . . . But that didn't happen here. People say to me, "Colonel, it's because you have a good image in the community and the people like you." I don't know, I don't think it's that . . .

In any case, I don't think the protests mean a rejection of the military. Perhaps a certain resistance to government agencies, but not to the army. Nor to the navy either. Maybe a little to the *carabineros,* who are the most visible, because the people don't like to be

vice-president of the republic during Eduardo Frei's government. He and his wife survived an assassination attempt on October 6, 1975, in Rome.

controlled by them. And that's exactly what's good about democracy. Western democracy.

What I'm adamant about is that communism should be against the law, forever! Forever, because the Communists have committed such atrocities! To begin with, they're atheists, they don't believe in anything. And furthermore, they do things that don't fit in with the way we Westerners do things. The Communists are responsible for many bad things that have been done and that are being done in this country. So I would not in any way allow the Communist Party to rule my country. It would mean pure chaos and problems.

I would like full democracy, in which our middle class, which is splendid, would participate in everything. That's what we're aiming for! But we must be patient. We're going to stick to our timetable. Until 1989. That's what has been determined, and that's what must be done. To my mind, everything must comply with this plan and must be in strict accordance with the Constitution.* I'm sure that the only thing my general wants is to be on a firm footing in this and to reach full democracy. If it were up to him, if everything had gone along more normally, he would probably have speeded up the transition. But not now.

I've never thought that the government would fail to go all the way. Never! Because the armed forces are sworn to the task and this will continue *sine qua non*. In the army everyone thinks the same way —everyone! Between civilians there may be discrepancies, but in the army, in the navy, in the air force and the police force, we all think the best, and the best is what is happening. This must continue and everything will be fine: the mayors working and everyone at their posts, laboring for the good of the country.

* I.e., Pinochet's 1980 Constitution.

THE DECLINE AND FRUSTRATION OF A BANKER

SERGIO ASTRAÍN TORRES

A SOLID MEMBER OF THE MIDDLE CLASS, HE HAS MADE *every effort to improve his status, but all in vain. He started two decades ago, and since then his aspirations have been repeatedly frustrated, so that now, at forty, he feels the only thing left is to wait passively for retirement.*

His job as head of foreign commerce at a bank did not challenge him, and in the hope of a promotion he got a degree in technical finance. When he finished the course, they congratulated him, threw him a party, and gave him a pen set, but his status and salary remained the same.

He's part of the generation of people who, during the last decade, believed they could do anything they chose. He tried to become an entrepreneur, and the results were so disastrous that, while the economy was thriving, he and his wife were unemployed, on the brink of total poverty.

He takes pride in being rational, and though he can't seem to help radiating tension and frustration, he discusses lucidly why he rejoiced at the military takeover, how he became disenchanted, how many people's rights have been violated, and why the country's current state of crisis is the result of purely economic factors.

Eighty-three has been an evil year. I've come to see what this government stands for, what suffering means. I see many things now. Until last year I was so concerned with helping myself that I had no time to think. I worked all day, then studied, and on weekends I studied even more. I had no time for anything that wasn't related to improving myself. My salary wasn't bad, but I thought I could do even better.

I hadn't stopped studying since the sixties; I was in my fifth year of administrative studies, I had two years of law, and in between I studied accounting and a variety of other subjects. Now, for the first time, I have a whole year in which I am doing nothing outside of work, and I have time to think.

I've just begun to realize things about the behavior of the DINA and the CNI over the years . . . I recognize the social injustice that exists right now and the catastrophic level of deterioration. What's happening to the poor is incredible! I've never seen a crisis as severe as this, and to my mind, the root of the crisis is economic.

I was truly happy when the armed forces took over. I'd been a Christian Democrat since I was a kid; I joined the youth movement when I was fifteen and took part in the Frei campaign in '58. I was very active until about '67 or '68, but then I became disillusioned with being active. There were certain things about Frei's government that I didn't like . . . maybe I was too romantic and idealistic at the time; in your twenties you have that luxury. But ultimately you realize how things are, that everything is a bureaucratic mess and things are done or undone according to the interests of the same old groups.

So by '73 I found myself against the Allende government. I lived across from the Technical University, in a lower-middle-class neighborhood, and most of the people there were against Popular Unity. I don't think we opposed it in principle, but we objected to all the foolishness: the supervisors, the land takeovers, the JAP, the food lines, all the stupidities. I think most people were pleased when the army came. Besides, everyone thought they were going to intervene and then call for free elections, clean and honest, within six months or a year. Two years at the outside!

I thought they would institute a truly good and, above all, just government, because they had the advantage of being unopposed and of not having to deal with a congress making useless laws. Because they were the army and would have to stay in Chile in order to practice their profession, I thought they would form a nationalistic government, something good, not the ridiculous thing they came up with. A small, mangy country like ours with practically no assets can't declare itself a free-trade zone. If it doesn't protect its own industry, what is happening now starts to happen, all national production is replaced by importation, and we're all doomed.

By the middle of '74 I began to wake up because I saw they weren't providing any protection. The politics of confrontation set in—layoffs, salary cuts, unfairness, and arbitrariness. Everything, indiscriminately, became privately owned, which caused greater and greater inequities. Many people, even friends of mine, were barely surviving because they had been supporters of Popular Unity. And you began to suffer yourself, because it was harder and harder to get things.

TO HAVE MY OWN FIRM!

I was working at that time in the Bureau of Planning as the head of employee salaries. Since I got the job through a relative of mine who is a mayor, and since my grandfather is a member of the political right, it looked like I was affiliated with that kind of people. After a while, it got out that I had been a Christian Democrat, and a woman who worked as a spy said that I had been part of the Christian left. In fact it was my brother, but four or five days after this woman appeared in the office, they moved me to a different area. It was very clear—although I don't remember the exact details, I'm quite sure it was that woman.

Although I was never politically persecuted, I began to see how they were making things difficult for me. I had a chance to get a promotion, and, despite my getting the best score on the qualifying test, they didn't give me the job. They said it was for reasons of "better service," and they transferred me. After a few months they moved me again.

They had completely blocked my progress, and since '75 was the most severe "shock" year, my salary was cut several times. I was put on a very low level on the Escala Única* and there was no possibility at all of doing any better.

In '76 I had the opportunity to go to Bolivia. I was about to finish my studies at the university, and since there were no prospects in my field, I left the country. I went alone, because my wife—who had also studied political science—had a job in a textile factory. In Bolivia I thought I would get my degree and that it would serve as a jumping-off point for going to the United States and getting a master's or a doctorate.

But I never got used to being there, and so I came back. I didn't know what I would do here. At the beginning I worked in a consulting firm that put out a newsletter and organized meetings. I had a large list of clients, and since I've always been good with people, I made friends with a lot of people in the firms in the productive sector that were still staying afloat. In the middle of '77, I decided to quit because I had a chance to use some of my contacts and start a business of my own with some friends.

My friends knew some people who imported television sets, and we began to sell them to institutions, offering monthly discounts. I was very enthusiastic about this whole setup, because at that time we had free trade.

I had always wanted to manage a firm. You operate alone, not dependent on anyone. Managing means both helping yourself and helping others, if possible. I have always had businesses going apart from my full-time job, like selling Easter cakes or working at a Christmas fair.

We knew that the craze for televisions had to pass, but the idea was to take advantage of the climate to put together the capital for

* The salary scale of the Chilean Public Administration.

another business. My idea was to set up a take-out sandwich place, for instance. A small concern that wouldn't make us millionaires, but would give us an excellent living—a middle-class existence, quiet, carefree, to be spent reading and taking trips.

The first two months we sold televisions like crazy. In the third month, things began to slow down; the fourth month was a disaster, and by the fifth it was all over. The importers were doing their own business, and we could no longer be competitive. That year we came closest to actual poverty. One of us was always out of work. We simply subsisted, paying the rent and eating, that's it. We had no money for clothing or anything else.

I have always had certain bourgeois tendencies, so I took all this particularly hard. The economy was in full swing, and we were denied everything! A nice apartment, a car, a color TV, everything. We were at rock bottom, unable to take part in cultural and educational events, or any of the finer things in life.

My daughter, thank God, was not severely affected by these problems because my mother and my sister had always helped us. But never before have we been that close to absolute poverty. Maybe I'm exaggerating a little, but I find being poor horrifying. I have a primal fear of everything about poverty: the monotony, the inequality and everything it implies.

When the television business fell through, my wife was also unemployed. The first days of '78 we didn't have a cent. With her last change my wife bought a ticket to Talca where her family lives, and I stayed here with only a hundred pesos to my name. My wife was there for about ten days, and on January 18 the O'Higgins Bank called me with a job. The next day I began work.

SURVIVING AND LANGUISHING

I started at rock bottom, as the lowliest peon in the foreign commerce department. It was sad and frustrating; I was on the same level as a novice of eighteen or twenty, and I was already thirty-five. Nothing motivated me or appealed to me, but I had no choice. A bank is a thoroughly success-oriented, elite, consumerist organization. If I was relieved for the moment—because I had money for food and rent—I also realized that my prospects were nonexistent.

I didn't realize how a bank worked and I had to build up my credit. But I was moving up the ranks quickly, because most bank workers were mediocre employees. In four years I became the head of foreign commerce, which was a big step up. I've always made good progress in the things I've done.

With the correct background and preparation, it's relatively easy to keep moving up. I spent four years taking a course at the Bank Studies Institute; I went to work at eight-thirty in the morning and was busy until ten at night, until I got my technical finance degree. It's the only title I have, despite all the different things I've studied.

I got the degree in December of '82, but nothing happened. I thought that when I'd finished the course I would move up to the commercial section, which is what really interests me. But I finished, and that was it—which is to say they congratulated me, threw me a party, and gave me a pen set. But in terms of money, of a promotion, of status, nothing happened.

The world of finance is horrible! It's incredibly competitive. Everyone is duplicitous and a person's qualities or merits are of no value —only his ability to trip up everyone else. Being friends with a boss or being a good soccer player is much more important than being bright.

The soccer thing sounds funny, but it's true. I didn't believe it at first, but I learned. A lot of competitive sports are played between the banks, so a good athlete or soccer player is highly rated, because he represents the company among its peers. Actually, banks are becoming more efficient and hiring more professionals, but traditionally that was how they operated.

Bank workers are ridiculous. They have absurd aspirations that bear no relation to their actual salaries. They spend all their time in a world full of money, they're in constant contact with millionaires, and this creates all kinds of illusions. You begin to think that it's possible to reach these same levels, you start to dream about it, and you end up in a world full of credit and loans to affect a look that has nothing to do with how much you really make.

Fortunately, I haven't gotten involved in this, because my own business disaster left me too wary. Also, you can't live on a grand scale on 65,000 pesos per month, especially when you don't know how long you'll have your job—today you're at work, but tomorrow morning at nine it may all be over.

You live in a permanent state of anxiety. I'm even being treated for stress and a possible nervous breakdown. They gave me Calcibronat and Neurobionta because I have such a case of nerves . . . too much work, too much responsibility, the fact that you can make a mistake at any moment, and a mistake means dismissal and no more money.

My wife has also been unemployed for two years now. It was very difficult to get her career started, and she has had very little professional satisfaction. She had to study extremely hard; while I'm a natural student, she isn't. She had to go back to school in '78 for a degree, and that was very difficult for her. I would keep after her to stay up late at night and study for her tests; the whole thing strained our relationship, and now she's not able to use the degree anyway. She worked for a year and a half at the Department of Education, and she's been out of work since then. She sent out eighty résumés and had fifty interviews during a year that was full of illusions and delusions, and ultimately nothing happened.

This year our lives have declined enormously. You suddenly realize you're forty years old and that you are limited, that you can't just go back to school and take up another course of study, because the maximum age is forty. You realize you're no longer growing, that the only thing left is to continue existing—quietly languishing— you've become a bureaucratic being, simply passing the time until retirement.

I think that at any moment there will be an enormous explosion in this country. Things are going to explode from all the tension, the injustices, the repression, the frustrations, all the bad and negative things we are enduring. It's like something under pressure, over a slow flame, that ultimately has to explode.

. . . . .

A COUNCIL OF ELDERS

The explosion will be the direct result of economic forces, not political or moral ones. If the army, when they took power in '73, had given the CORFO* more power, they could have promoted national production and exports; if there had been full employment—the logical goal of any society—everyone would have been happy. No one would have cared that the army was in control, because the majority of people—70 or 80 percent of the population of Chile—don't give a damn about politics.

The truth is that the issue of human rights does not affect the majority of people. How many people were really politically active in '73? How many were truly persecuted? Suppose it was 50,000 to 80,000 people; taking into account their relatives, about 300,000 in all would be affected, and in a country of 10 million, that's practically nothing—it's 3 percent of the population.

It's not something to be happy about. We can't brag about a repressive police force that tortures people or commits whatever other atrocities. I'm a Christian and a humanist, and I think forcibly imposed suffering is despicable; to take someone's life—left, right, good, bad, black, or white—is an atrocity. But I also recognize that if only 300,000 people had been affected in this way and the rest of the population had had a real windfall, we wouldn't have this crisis. Chileans wouldn't have given a damn about anything else.

But this government's economic policies have about 700,000 people working for the PEM and the POJH, and including the other unemployed people that makes over a million people with employment problems. Add in their family members, and practically half the population has reason to be against the government.

I've seen the most terrible repression through the cashier's window at the bank. I work at the window that faces onto the first block of the Calle Estado, and I've seen the military put down protesters, clearing them away with their clubs. I've seen them remove peddlers, hitting the ones at the entrance to the bank, striking out at anyone who gets in their way.

* Organization to Encourage Production.

I'm amazed to see how civil agents respond to this, since being an informer goes against all human nature. It's scary that there are people who make a living by informing on others or abusing them. The fact that the police attack pedestrians who walk through the center of town protesting is incredible. It frightens me the same way I'm frightened when the leftists attack someone from the political right, or the police.

In the bank we don't talk much about politics, but when we do, it becomes clear that fewer and fewer people sympathize with the government. The Christian Democrats have a lot of followers in the banks. I was surprised by the number of opposition members who showed up in O'Higgins Park* last November. I went with about thirty people from the bank who had never done anything like that before, and it was good to see that people were not so afraid any more.

Still, I was horribly afraid! I think we went in such a large group because we were all so scared. We were worried that they would arrest us or beat us, and also of course that if they pressed charges, we would be fired from the bank. It was a big decision to go; I didn't feel safe until the meeting was over and we were several blocks away from O'Higgins Park.

I went to show my discontent, and I felt I had to overcome my fear. Taking a stance against the regime was the only way I could maintain moral integrity; if I hadn't gone to the meeting, it would mean that I was allowing cowardice to impede my principles and prevent me from criticizing the government. Being critical among a group of friends is very different from going out into the streets to protest, and in those entire ten years I had never done that.

In my opinion, the gaps between Chileans have deepened in the past years, and in many cases hate has sprung up. The day Chile explodes, it will be with the accumulated hatred of three years of Popular Unity and more than ten years of this government. Chile has become increasingly divided in these thirteen years between those who have more and those who have very little, between those

* Site of a meeting staged by the opposition on November 18, 1983, the first authorized by the Pinochet government.

of the left and those not of the left, between the government and the antimilitary forces. Everyone is "anti" something, and the result is, for example, hatred of a policeman simply because he is a policeman. It's very grim.

The way things are becoming polarized, the only solution is going to be through violence. And that means death, destruction, hunger, and even more misery than we have now. It's terrible.

In spite of this, I think that Chileans have moral values that would allow them to take the country forward and forget their hatred. But to achieve this we would need a truly conciliatory government to take us through the transitional period, one that would represent all the different segments of the population and be composed of good people of proven morality.

If, in spite of everything, Chile is able to become unified, it will mean that the country has the moral integrity and human qualities necessary to move forward together.

A YOUNG
APOSTLE'S REBELLION

CARLOS

HE'S BEEN TRAUMATIZED BY SIRENS EVER SINCE HE WAS
seven and watched from a window as a young neighbor was shot.

*It's hard to believe that he's one of the leaders of the student protests
and that he leads a double life. He seems more tender than angry, and
more naive than smart, when he painfully describes the murders of
various friends, fighting the regime with eggs and tomatoes, teaching comrades to make Molotov cocktails, or the enormous pleasure he derives from
beating up a cop.*

*In spite of everything, he says, he has been happy. He is proud of having
joined "the great family of communism," and he has no doubt that this was
the best thing he has ever done. It was not easy to make the decision, because
for as long as he can remember, Communists have been arrested, tortured,
and killed. But if other people can do it, why not he?*

*"You can't let fear get the better of you." This is perhaps the most important
lesson he has learned since he first drew a hammer and sickle on the playing
field at school, knowing only that it signified something terrible, a lesson that*

allowed him to be one of the student leaders at the Pedagógico, a university center whose history of activism led the army to change the school's name and dissociate it from the University of Chile, the oldest and most powerful university in the country before 1973.

In '85 fear began to get the better of him, and he was about to abandon everything, but his comrades came to his rescue and made him see that he didn't have to leave the party. He knows that only a small number of students are politically active, because academic requirements are designed to impede participation and any activity whatsoever results in brutal repression—which carries the clear moral that violence has become necessary in return.

He would like to spend all his time on his studies, but he must keep fighting "until there is a truly democratic, popular government."

It's not easy. When he's about to participate in something dangerous, he prefers not to think. Fear might get the better of him.

"**Y**ou could see it coming," my father said when we heard about the coup on the radio. My mother had died a couple of months earlier. We didn't go to school, and my father stayed home from work and went out into the street to take pictures. How naive! He came back about twenty minutes later, sweating because a jeep full of soldiers had chased him and shot at him.

We listened to the announcements and put our mattresses under the windows because there was so much shooting. We lived in the center of town near the headquarters of various political parties, including one of the leftist MIR, where the activitists put up a lot of resistance. They brought in a tank and blew up part of the building. My father made us get down on the floor when the explosions began, but we were still able to see through the window.

That night they shot the brother of a friend of mine against the wall of a bar across the street. I don't remember if it was a police or an army car, but the siren was awful. They got out, threw the kids against the wall, asked to see their papers, and shot them with machine guns . . . then they got in their car and left. Since the curfew was in force, the two bodies just stayed where they'd been flung. I don't know if it was one or two days, but I know that one morning I looked and they were still there. When they let us go out again, the owners of the shop had cleaned up.

I was afraid they were going to kill us all. My friend's brother had been super-nice to us, and I didn't know why they had killed him—he was always playing with us kids. When the police came to the house to inspect, I thought they'd come to kill us. But they just asked how many people lived there, looked around the dining room, drank a glass of water, and left. They did the same thing in all the districts. They patrolled the streets and shot their guns in the air.

An aunt of mine who worked in the Contraloría* told us that some of the workers there had been shot also. My grandmother was pro-Allende and cried and cried because two of her sons had to go into exile. My father was upset about the bloodshed, but otherwise pleased. He's a Christian Democrat and said that there was no other way to end the problems of Popular Unity.

All day long on the TV they talked about "Plan Z," † and we had a housekeeper who was dating a soldier and told us that terrorists had taken over the sewer system and were still putting up resistance there. We thought the soldier was a hero; he showed us photos of the confrontation and sometimes he showed us his pistol.

I was about seven, and I don't really remember the Allende government. I know we had to wait on lines when we went shopping and that we had a closet full of sugar, milk, oil, toilet paper, and other things that were hard to get. Sometimes my father went out with his gun to defend the building against the Marxists. Nothing ever happened, but we always expected something, and the neighborhood organized guard groups. When we went back to school after the coup, they had a mass to celebrate the salvation of the country.

* The State Finance Office.

† A fictional plot to overthrow the head of the armed forces, attributed by the military to Allende's government. It was one of the chief justifications for the military coup.

. . . . .

AGAINST FASCISM

Everything was getting supermilitarized. They taught us a new verse for the national anthem that talked about the brave soldiers, and we celebrated the eleventh of September by dressing up as soldiers. Someone was Arturo Prat, someone else was O'Higgins, and I was once Mendoza.* They played marches as we walked in and out of the classroom, and in music class they taught us the songs of the four branches of the armed forces. We were always celebrating military anniversaries, the heroes of some battle, or the day of the *carabinero*. We had to draw pictures and write compositions on these themes to get good grades. In high school, they showed us films that talked up the advantages of going to military school.

During the early years we liked those things; soldiers were our heroes, and we really thought Pinochet was our savior. I had a friend who went into exile—I think to Moscow—and we often used to get into fistfights over what was happening. He had a sister who was a teacher and who had to go into exile because they had killed other teachers at the school where she worked, but I still thought the military had done the right thing.

One thing that began to change me was belonging to the scouts. People think it's a military organization, but we even have elections, and that was where I read the Declaration of Human Rights for the first time. That made me think, and when we had the plebiscite in '80,† we began to realize how much power Pinochet had. My father no longer supported the regime, but he was obliged to vote for the government or he would have lost his job. A friend who worked in the ministry said that the ballot boxes were transparent.

---

* General César Mendoza Durán, police chief at the time of the military coup in 1973, was one of the four members of the Military Junta who took power along with Augusto Pinochet. He resigned on August 2, 1985, after twelve police officers were accused of the murder of three Communists. Arturo Prat and Bernardo O'Higgins are two leading Chilean heroes.

† A referendum on September 11, 1980, in which Pinochet legalized his constitution.

At the same time, things began to happen at school, and as a result of the plebiscite, there was a tremendous leafleting campaign. The police and the CNI came and searched all our bags. We came out of our classroom and saw civil guards with machine guns and riot gear on the school grounds. I was terrified, especially since I had seen a friend handing out leaflets. I saw him by chance as we were going from one room to another. He realized that I had seen him, and since he was bigger, at the next recess he told me to keep quiet about it. After the initial shock I felt fine, and I was pleased about what he had done.

From then on many of us became active, and in '81 we really began to do things. One day while they were inaugurating a room named after a former minister, the older students went up to the second floor. We blocked the stairs with furniture and, shouting and passing out leaflets, we inaugurated two other rooms: the Salvador Allende and the Fidel Castro. They were the two most provocative names we could come up with.

They threatened to expel us, but they couldn't find the culprits, and they couldn't kick us all out. Some of the teachers with whom we had become friendly thought the whole thing was funny. They were the ones who spoke to us in the hallways and who dared to speak of democracy in their classes, and to respond to the jokes that we made. The history teacher even explained the meaning of Marxism to us.

We were all very uneasy. In the afternoons, a group of kids would get together at the Plaza in the middle of Santiago. A handful of girls and boys from all the different schools would get together and flirt and talk, but everything we talked about touched on the subject of democracy. It was a lot of fun, but it never lasted long because the cops would come to the Plaza. I don't know why, but they always made us leave.

About that time a girl told us that at her school they had formed a CODE, a democratic committee. She told us it was against the fascist dictatorship. She couldn't explain any further, but it seemed like a good idea to us, so we organized our own CODE. It was anti-Pinochet and specifically against our principal, who represented the government at the school. It was also against the repressive investigators such as those from the CNI. We heard that some of them were from the police school and others were detectives.

The CODE was a secret organization. We told a few of the friendly teachers, and we began to make up leaflets and to scrawl "CODE" on the walls. We also wrote "Allende," because he seemed like a good person who would agree with what we were attacking. On TV they kept saying how awful Allende's government was, that he wanted to take everything away from the rich, that he would kill us all, that he would ruin the country and make it into a new Russia. At first you believed it all, but later you saw that Allende had just tried to make things a little fairer.

We never studied that period in history at school, but when we talked about capitalist economies, I saw the differences between Allende's government and the current one. I kept thinking about this idea of fascist dictatorships; none of my friends knew too much, and I decided to ask the history teacher. He was a little surprised and didn't dare answer me. But he found out who I was, and at the next class he gave me a book where it said that it was a government of the middle class that ruled through fear inspired by the armed forces.

THANKS, COMRADES

We continued to organize activities to combat this fascist dictatorship. Every Monday during the raising of the flag something would happen. Sometimes the flag would appear backwards, other times the cord would break as it was about to reach the top. Once the police band came, and when they started to play we began to suck lemons right in front of them—they all went out of tune!

At that time none of us was affiliated with a political party. The folk bars were very important and I was sorry that I hadn't ever been inside one. They were cozy places where you could drink a little hot wine and sing meaningful songs, like those of Quilapayún or Víctor Jara, which made the rounds on illicit tapes.

The folk bars also let you get to know other democratic people and begin to get organized. One day they invited us to a meeting with the CODEs from other schools. A lot of people came, and we formed the Middle-School Students' Group. Then things got complicated.

Suddenly we were spending hours discussing whether or not we were allies of the proletariat. My friends and I didn't understand those discussions. We realized there were many concepts that we couldn't grasp. We wrote down the difficult words and later looked them up in books we got hold of so that we could learn a little. Our group concluded that we were indeed allies of the working class and that we should go out into the towns and the factories.

We chose a factory that was near the home of one of our comrades. He had noted the time at which the workers left, and he prepared a map that showed us where to place ourselves and which walls we could poster or paint slogans on. We made up about 250 flyers that said "No to Pinochet" and about a hundred copies of a letter that described our grievances and our solidarity with the workers. We took a bus with our paint cans, brushes, and pamphlets hidden under our clothes. There were eight of us. We were very quiet, sweating, scared to death.

The plan was for one of us to read the letter out loud, but when the workers began to leave, none of us had the courage. It didn't even occur to us to cover our faces with handkerchiefs! We were paralyzed. We watched as the workers left and we weren't able to do anything. Then suddenly we went at it: three guys began to paint on the wall, two others threw leaflets, and the three girls who had come with us took turns reading the letter.

It was a big factory and tons of people came out. Some of them were scared and kept walking, others stopped to look at what was happening. They were surprised, and they were smiling. A few said, "Thanks, comrades."

A factory guard realized we were marking up the wall and came to throw us out; the people began to whistle and shout. We were scared as shit and got out of there. For the first time I felt my legs quake.

We went to a friend's house and celebrated. Everyone described what they had felt. At last, we had actually *done* something more than just talk. Our next goal was to do something big at the school. Until then we had only done a little painting on the walls of the bathrooms and made a few bomb threats—they would empty out the classrooms and bring in some experts to search the school.

Afterwards we did some things that had a little more impact. In the courtyard we put up a Chilean flag with the resistance "R" on it, and on the ground we drew an enormous hammer and sickle with chalk. We knew it was the Communist sign, but more important, it was something terrible to the authorities.

Although there were only a few of us in CODE, a feeling of protest was growing throughout the school. On Mondays no one sang the soldier's verse of the national anthem any more, and more and more frequently some group was passing out leaflets and flyers with the opposition stamp on them. The school inspectors always had some stuck to their backs.

I remember a meeting the workers organized at the Plaza Artesanos. We got together downtown and bought some eggs and half-rotten tomatoes to throw at the cops. But we didn't have a chance to use them because behind the cops came the gurkhas* and civilian members of the CNI who were beating people up. It was awful. A lot of people were hurt, but we managed to get out.

At home no one knew that I was involved in these things. My brother was much more like my father, opposed to the government, but not showing it. But I didn't miss any opportunity to show it.

When there were protests, we went downtown. There were a lot of groups that were openly involved, the way we were. They staged rallies on street corners, they shouted slogans, and a lot of people who were going home from work joined in, until all the cops in the country were there—at least, that's how it felt. Then there would be clashes with stone-throwing.

The repression was brutal. They got hold of a couple of guys and beat them up in front of everyone as an example. The cops got me once, but some people came and rescued me. They didn't know me, they just helped because we were all in this thing together.

---

* Gurkhas were Nepalese soldiers known for their ferocity and dexterity with the kukri knife. Young Chileans have given this name to secret agents.

That was in '83, when we began to overcome our fear. Fear is like a little dictator inside you that prevents you from doing things. We had all been scared to death during the first protest, but after that we got more and more indignant about what was going on, and also began feeling that we could win.

THE BIG COMMUNIST FAMILY

The next year I entered the Pedagógico* to study Spanish, and I discovered a whole new world. It was a world where people spoke openly about national politics, where you could see walls with slogans on them everywhere. We had a freshman party where the older students explained the problems of the university clearly and invited us to take part in the student movement. They spoke of the glorious Pedagógico—it was like the heart of the battle. This is where the first slightly more violent meetings took place, and even the Christian Democratic students, who didn't do anything in high school, were active. Lots of students were expelled and even killed.

The other thing that surprised me, but in a different way, was the faculty. At first I didn't come across any professors that I could be friends with. I had to be careful around them, because they thought that everything was subversive. In the years following the coup, they denounced Marxist students, many of whom had been expelled— some had even disappeared. But recently the more democratic professors had formed an association. Their attitude toward their more politically active students began to change, and they started inviting them to their offices after class, where they would speak in hushed tones.

The university was tightly controlled. There was a repressive group of security agents contracted and paid for by the university. For the first few years they looked like any other students, but

* Teachers' College of the University of Chile, reorganized several times after the coup until it became, in 1985, the Metropolitan University Teachers' College.

when I got there, they were already wearing the blue uniforms of the guards who had been posted throughout Chile. They said that their presence was justified because students stole books or because trespassers came onto university property, but we were the only people they ever beat up. Whenever one of us showed up somewhere alone, they would get him; they even beat us up in the bathrooms.

We had a newspaper that was called *El Rapidito;* * it was only one sheet that was put up on the wall quickly, and read quickly, because the security guards would take it down quickly. Once they caught three students putting the paper up; they gave them a terrific thrashing, and then carried them to a basement room where they beat them some more and took their photographs. This got everyone scared. And the truth is, very few people were actually taking part in these things. When we started the protests in '83 and '84, most people stayed home, or went to class but ignored the teacher—that was as rebellious as they got.

I already felt a part of the political left, and just after I arrived I joined the National Union of Democratic Students. First of all, I was interested in Allende. During his government everyone had the chance to better themselves, and he himself is a symbol of unity, a person who ended his days as an example of morality, defending La Moneda palace † and combatting dictatorship. Later, through the magazines and other documents that were passed around, I began to get interested in "La Jota" ‡ because I like the Communist Party's policy of popular rebellion. They recognize a community's right to self-defense, and at the university we saw that as essential.

I had several friends who were part of La Jota, but I put off joining for a while because I was afraid. It wasn't easy deciding to become a Communist; a lot of people sympathized with the party, but to be a member is different. The Communists have been the most perse-

* "The Quickie."

† The government house, bombed by the air force on September 11, 1973.

‡ The popular name for the Chilean Communist Youth Organization.

cuted group of people, and the war waged against them by Pinochet has been very harsh.

But I came to like the leaders of La Jota more and more—they had the clearest positions, and they represented the greatest number of people, which became clear when they held democratic elections, and they all became their class presidents. I wanted to join the party, but I couldn't get over my fear. I realized that it simply meant I would continue to do what I was already doing independently. But to be a certified Communist—to be a Communist!—was something else. It's not the same to be arrested as an independent agent and to be arrested as a Communist. We all knew what had happened to them after the coup and what continued to happen. I was afraid of being tortured or of appearing in a headline in the paper: "Communist Killed." It was hard to get over this, especially when from the very day you're born they tell you that the Communists are just out to use you. I finally decided that if my friends could do it, why not me?

I spoke with a friend who told me all about La Jota, and after a while she invited me to a meeting. I was very proud. I was going to be a part of the Communist Youth. Many people that I admired, like Neruda and Picasso, had been Communists. I also remembered the example of Víctor Jara in the Chile Stadium, and I knew that Communists fight for their principles to the end. It was very significant for me to be a part of this great family.

I was very surprised when I got to the meeting—I knew so many people there! It meant a lot to see friends that I hadn't known were part of La Jota. I thought that very few people were members. I realized then what "clandestine" really meant and how important this moment of "confession" was. Because no matter how proud you are, you can't walk around saying that you're a Communist. You can't tell who else knows and who doesn't. In high school we had classmates who sang the "Internationale" in assemblies and then turned out to be in the CNI. There were always people around trying to get you to slip up. To admit to being a Communist is like putting your head in the guillotine, and it hurts the whole organization.

On the surface I continued as I had been in the student movement. But as a party member I was better oriented politically and had better information with which to analyze the situation, which allowed me to handle myself better in my mass organization.

After that, I never had any doubt about what we were doing.

FAIR AND UNFAIR VIOLENCE

At the university they still don't know that I'm a Communist. It hasn't been easy to be a student leader. There is so much course work that it's hard to do anything beyond academics. This is one of the ways they limit student activism. I often stay up through the night so I can do both my political work and enough of the academic work that they won't throw me out of school.

It's very difficult to get people to be active. Whatever we do ends in repression. A march we organized ended with a rally in the cafeteria. There were five hundred students listening to one of our leaders speak. Suddenly the guards came running in in a triangular formation, shouting. They knocked over everything they found, broke all the glass in the dining room, and hit two girls with chains. They chased one philosophy student up to the second floor, beat him up, and threw him off the balcony. They were like gangsters. At first everyone was terrified, but then there was a reaction, and when later protests were organized, more and more people came.

At first the encounters with the cops were just in the streets. We would stage a march, run through the campus, and go out into the street and stop traffic. We would put up enormous barricades, sometimes burn tires, and steal the fences they had used to try to trap us in the campus. This was all highly symbolic, because for a long time they insisted the fences were electrified.

During the first demonstrations, a number of students disagreed with those of us putting up the barricades, calling us violent and saying that this kind of behavior was unacceptable. But that didn't last long, and everyone agreed that the violence was started by the cops when they threw tear gas and fired buckshot at us. The self-defense committees were in charge of giving out masks, salt, lemon juice, and vinegar to treat the effects of the tear gas. When someone fainted or was hurt, they were there to help, and since they were helping, everyone else saw that we weren't violent and they began to see that we were simply defending ourselves.

Gradually people began to participate more and more. No one ever questioned the need for barricades after that, and the Christian Democrats participated right alongside the leftists. Everyone agreed that the barricades were fundamental to stopping the repression and to demonstrating the lack of government, not only within the university but in the streets as well, because we were trying to show how out of control things were.

Sometimes the cops had orders not to be so aggressive, and then we were able to move in and fight man to man, them with their clubs and us with our feet and fists. That's when they weren't firing at us. It was scary, but it was also very gratifying to lay into a cop, even if it was just a kick! We would fight and then run back to the campus, while our comrades defended us with a shower of rocks. The self-defense committees went out onto the roofs and other high places with slingshots so that the cops couldn't get near them. It was important to keep the cops out of the campus.

They got in on October 30, 1984. The National Workers Committee was meeting about unemployment, and it turned into one of the most violent days at the university. There were seven hundred very active people; they had organized defense groups on all the different routes, they had prepared first-aid teams, they had gathered materials to counteract the tear gas, they had some slingshots, and, for the first time, they had Molotov cocktails. It was my job to make these along with the people from my area; we used benzine, cooking oil, and a little sawdust to make it burn awhile.

There were a lot of people in class that day. There were about 150 of us in the street when the armored police van arrived. We had taken down the fences and put them in the middle of the street. The police van drove right up to the campus and came partway inside, spraying water at us. Some comrades put rocks behind the wheels and then it couldn't go back. We beat the shit out of it. It was great because the only thing that it was able to do was shoot water at us, and we were already drenched. There were a lot of women—there were always more women than men at these things, some of them very elegant, with pretty polka-dotted handkerchiefs over their faces. It was incredible! A guy got up on the top of the van and turned the nozzle until it stopped spraying water. The other cops couldn't get near enough to help because we were still throwing rocks at them from all sides. Finally, they started throwing tear gas and firing buckshot. They got onto the campus, and beat up everyone they found. They took the van out with a crane.

That was the first time they got in, and we noticed that they were scared too. They fired some shots, ran around pointing their guns at everyone, arrested a few people, and promptly left. People had spoken so badly of us that I'm sure they thought we would be waiting for them with machine guns and cannons.

As more people began to be active, the repression got more intense. In '85 we mobilized between one thousand and two thousand students, and the cops routinely came to the university. To celebrate one of Allende's anniversaries—I don't remember if it was his birth or his death—an enormous action was organized. In the street a small number of people put up a barricade as a large number of cops surrounded the campus. In response, all of us who were demonstrating peacefully inside began to march toward the street.

About thirty plainclothes cops got out of a police van and, along with thirty university guards, entered the campus via a playground for staff children. They took shelter and barraged us with buckshot and rocks. When we responded, they took pictures and film footage of us that later showed up on TV to show how students had destroyed the playground. Then suddenly all sixty of them began to run toward us, striking out right and left. We got out as best we could and took refuge in the dining hall. Everyone was outraged.

"The time has come for a confrontation," said some of the comrades who had stopped to confer. "We have to get the gurkhas out of the college."

Everyone, including the Christian Democrats, took clubs from wherever they could get them—some broke up the tables, others took chairs—and we gave it to the gurkhas! They took a tremendous beating. I broke a stick over the head of one of them who was beating a comrade with a chain. A lot of people were hurt. There were so many people that they couldn't deal with us, and they had to hide in the guard quarters in the basement.

We had some tear gas that they themselves had tried to throw at us and that hadn't gone off, so we threw it into the basement. We sealed off all the exits and made bonfires around the edges so they would fill with smoke. There were about two thousand students around the building, and they all wanted to lynch them, show them who was boss. We knew they were from the CNI, and they deserved it.

They sent more than thirty vans full of cops to surround the college. The chairman had to come out and calm everyone down. Everyone was very worked up, and they wouldn't calm down until an agreement was reached to get rid of the guards.

They gave us two weeks of vacation, because whenever things get agitated, they close the university. But the important thing is that we won. We won with sticks and clubs. This is one of the experiences we use to show that, suddenly, violence *is* necessary, and that our policy of self-defense is fundamental. We had to use clubs to get rid of the guards.

We can't wait for them to kill us the way they killed Patricio Manzano. They killed him in the volunteer corps. It was at the beginning of '85, in the first volunteer forces that the Federation of Students organized after the coup. The government hadn't given authorization, and everyone was scared, but about two hundred people showed up anyway and were sent to various places about two hours outside of Santiago, near Los Andes.

We went out to the country, to an area where they grow fruit for export and exploit the peasants, who work from sunup to sundown for a miserable little salary. The idea was to form social organizations for the area, to help them start unions, cultural centers, and sports clubs. In three days we managed to get seventy people who had lost interest reinvolved in the unions. We explained how much exporting fruit meant to the regime, and how it would be affected by a national strike. We started reading courses and set up a social headquarters. Nothing we undertook was paternalistic, and we worked solely in conjunction with the peasants.

At the beginning, no one came near us. A few cops, who weren't from around there, had come by saying that we were setting up a guerrilla school. People looked at us from a distance, but on the second day we organized a soccer game and the whole place showed up.

We had just arrived, and we presented ourselves to a public official, who was like their mayor, and we asked his help for our volunteer work. He told us that such work was prohibited but ended up by lending us shovels and carts. He also offered us coffee, and advice: "I recommend that you concentrate less on politics and more on other, more serious problems, such as alcoholism and juvenile prostitution. People here have very few resources, and on payday young girls go out to meet the workers. Of course, I didn't breathe a word of this to you!"

There were two cops in the police station. They lent us a typewriter every day, so we invited them to a cultural event we had organized. We put on a play showing all the different stages in the process of growing grapes, from the time they were planted to the time the gringos receive them in the United States. The cops came, and by the end they were sitting with us, drinking wine.

The next morning we were awakened by a van full of cops driving at top speed right onto the field where we had pitched our tents. They were cops from different cities and, we later learned, had been quartered there the day before and been shown maps with guerrilla camps marked on them. We froze when we saw them getting out of the van and handing out ammunition. They arrested us, searched for guns, and found a box that made a noise when they shook it. They thought it was full of bullets and turned it over. Out came pencils, notebooks, and drawings the children had made. The cops looked very uncomfortable.

When they were taking us away, people came out of their houses to say good-bye, calling the cops murderers and waving to us with their handkerchiefs. Some cried, especially the kids, who used to show up at nine in the morning and stay with us through the day.

They took us to the School of Special Forces at Los Andes, and other vans had already arrived with comrades from other towns. They had missed only the two groups who were staying in the church lodgings.

They separated the men and women, and a guy, who acted more

like Rambo than a doctor, examined us. Then they made us cross a field full of cops, who kicked us as we walked past. Then they made us run six laps, then another two squatting with our hands behind our necks, and then crawling. Anyone who fell, they got back up by kicking them and beating them with sticks. Finally they made us lie down, and they ran over us. We kept shouting things because we didn't want to give up. We were in the sun for about four hours, getting very dehydrated, and I think that's how the problem with Pato began, because he was diabetic. In addition to keeping him in the sun that day, they wouldn't let him have his insulin shot.

They took us to drink water with our hands in the air and machine guns in our backs. Some of the cops asked us to excuse them—they were just following orders.

That night they took us to Santiago. The convoy stopped near the Mapocho River at about one in the morning. We didn't know what they planned to do with us, and it suddenly occurred to us that, in effect, they were going to treat us as if we'd been running a guerrilla school. Some people were worried that they were going to kill us and throw us in the river. It seemed possible after what they had done to us that day. But the convoy kept going; men to one police station, women to another.

Pato Manzano was very sick. Every so often the cops would come, make noise, turn on the lights, make us get up, count us, and then let us lie down again. Pato was worse every time they came, and the medical students tried to help him. They took him out of the cell where they had us, and told the captain of the guard that they had to take him to the clinic because he was seriously ill. They said they would take care of him there. But since he kept getting worse, they decided to take him to the hospital in a police vehicle. They wouldn't allow anyone to go along, although Pato kept fainting. He died in the truck.

We found out in the morning. We had managed to smuggle in two radios with tiny batteries, and that's how we heard. It was very sad— we had a minute of silence, we sang the national anthem, and various comrades spoke of what had happened. The cops came into the cell and made a circle around us with their clubs in their hands, but they didn't do anything.

After Pato's death our treatment changed radically; the food got better and a captain came to speak to us, but we wouldn't let him. We decided that we would cry for Pato when we were let out, but in the meantime we would dedicate ourselves to talking to the cops. We never let them alone; as soon as they came in, two or three of us would approach them. We knew there was a difference between the officers and the others, and we tried to play on it. It was like a continuation of our volunteer work, but with cops. That went on for three days until they let us go.

In truth, that year began very badly. In addition to Pato's death, three Communist professionals were found dead, with their throats cut, and so were the Vergara brothers. One of them had been the school director and the other was an old high school friend of mine. They ambushed them as they were going home and riddled them with bullets . . . they say that they brought them in half-dead, and then they finished them off.

Everyone was outraged. These were very key moments; so much repression occurs at once and you suddenly realize what they are capable of doing. The first actions of '85 were funerals. For me it was a year full of fear.

In addition to what had happened, I had started to date a friend who had had awful experiences with repression. When she was twelve she had been raped by cops. They detained her in a taxi, but she shouted so much that people came out to see what was happening, so they let her go. That left a mark on her.

The sense of internal repression began to surge up, and every day I felt more panicked. I dreamed that they arrested and tortured me. I would have liked to give it all up—I even thought about leaving the party for a while, because at that point I had party responsibilities. I wanted to call a halt, but the comrades supported me and made me see that it wasn't necessary to leave the party.

I was even afraid to go to meetings at the headquarters. It was real bullshit! I had ridiculous fears that I put behind me as I realized they were just personal problems. I was predisposed to be afraid. I think that repression is most successful when it succeeds in imposing such internal repression in each individual, against which one is constantly fighting.

There are people who are more active than I am. During another protest I was at my girlfriend's home in Pudahuel, a poor neighbor-hood. There, massive protests, with people banging pots and pans in the streets, can last until seven at night. Then there are confronta-tions between the MIR together with the Manuel Rodríguez Patriotic Front* and the police.

The first time that I saw the Rodriguistas I was very impressed. Boys of thirteen and fourteen were marching by, armed with pistols and submachine guns. They all wore knapsacks and handkerchiefs over their faces, printed with "Manuel Rodríguez Patriotic Front."

I had never seen them before. I was scared, on the one hand, and then I felt a great sense of security in knowing that these comrades were there, capable of protecting people and keeping out repressive forces. Out in the neighborhoods it isn't like the campus, where they arrest us and, in general, let us go a few days later. In the neighbor-hoods, they come in shooting.

They marched by, handing out tools of self-defense—Molotov cocktails and hand grenades that they showed us how to use. People cheered them on, and some of the people who had come for the cultural action joined the march, to take part in the confrontation.

I didn't participate. It wasn't my front and I didn't know the com-munity well. The people went home, and a tremendous burst of gunfire began. You could hear the bullets and the shouts of the militia and the soldiers. The militia were using megaphones to tell the soldiers to stop defending the Pinochet regime and shooting the citizens.

Having seen this, how can you oppose stockpiling arms for the people? † Neither I nor my party are in favor of armed struggle, but we are in favor of all forms of fighting that will lead to Pinochet's rapid fall, and we are for a democratic uprising of the masses.

Most of all, I'd like to dedicate myself to my studies and become a professional who works to better the country. But I know that can't

---

* A paramilitary organization, related to the Communist Party, that led a failed attempt to assassinate Pinochet on September 7, 1986.

† He is referring to a large quantity of arms brought into the country illegally by the Communist Party in 1986.

happen in a society like this. Sometimes I think of those people who live happily, playing pinball, smoking marijuana, but I realize that I couldn't be one of them. Since I was a boy in the scouts, I've felt a great social commitment. That has allowed me to be happy despite everything. And since I joined the Communists, this social commitment has strengthened along with a political commitment.

Being a Communist means much more than fighting for communism. There are very few authentic Communists, like Lenin or Che Guevara, because being a Communist means being an apostle of a just society, of a society without classes, the way Saint Peter or Saint Paul was. You have to be consistent with their original plan, which is hard because we all have vices and we can't all of a sudden stop enjoying ourselves. But there are people who can transcend those things. Allende, for example, as a member of the middle class, was able to leave aside everything and die in La Moneda palace.

I think the best thing I have done in my life is become a Communist.

A MODEL MILITANT
PARTY MEMBER

RAQUEL

*N THE CHILE OF 1984 IT WAS STILL RISKY TO ADMIT TO BEING
an active Communist, so we will call her simply Raquel.*

*Her story seems exaggerated—as if the author of a novel had concen-
trated the experiences of two or three people into one. She's seen it all: the
"war" of '73, persecution, torture, exile and return, unemployment, marital
problems, separation from her children, hunger, and loneliness. And she's still
intact.*

*We had very long sessions in which she was constantly catching me off
guard with some new horror story. If I hadn't seen her start to shake and cry
as she recalled her horror and suffering, I wouldn't have believed her story.*

At six in the morning, I dressed my daughters and dropped them
off with my mother. The night of the tenth, my husband didn't
come home, and since he never stayed out at night, I knew that

something must have happened. Besides, I worked at the Technical University, and there we had known since the previous day that the coup was coming.

I spent a little time with my mother and the girls, and then I left for work. I was a cashier at the university, and when I got there, people were outside listening to Allende on the radio. That's when it hit me, because until then I hadn't understood the gravity of what was going on.

The party orders were to stay at the university. I was a Communist —at fourteen I became active in the youth movement, and at twenty-two I joined the party—so I stayed at the university along with three hundred women and a lot of men. I later learned that the leftist organizations had given a counterorder telling everyone to go home, but the person in charge of our university failed to convey this, and we all stayed where we were. We were empty-handed, and all those stories about our having been armed are just lies!

At about three in the afternoon, when the soldiers put a stop to all movement, they shut the women into the School of Arts and Trades, and the men, led by the chairman Enrique Kirkberg, stayed at the central office building. At six, the bombardment began.

It was horrible! I've never lived through such hell, never heard such bullets. We had prepared some food and were in the dining room when the first bombardment began—bombs and machine guns that made the building shake. The lights went out, and every-one got down on the floor. The only thing I could think of was to feel for my legs. I didn't know if I had been hit by a bullet or not. It was terrible! And it went on throughout the night.

A lot of women became hysterical, and we had to go around calm-ing the ones who were screaming and crying. I don't know why I didn't get hysterical. On the contrary, I became resolute and went around slapping everyone because it was the only way to calm them down.

They attacked with tanks, and we had absolutely nothing to de-fend ourselves with. If we had had a single weapon, it would have been fantastic! But we didn't have anything. A lot of people died pointlessly . . . people who went outside, who wanted to know what was going on, to see where the soldiers were shooting from . . . I saw a lot of wounded people bleeding heavily, and I'm sure many of them died.

At seven in the morning, they entered the university. At first they ransacked the central building and took the people away; then they continued moving in. They arrived at our area at about nine and began to bombard the building with us inside it. I remember I found myself on the floor leaning against the wall; a lot of people were trying to protect themselves under the tables, but I realized that nothing could protect us. I remained seated, and suddenly I saw a soldier come flying in through a glass partition. He came right through the glass and fell into the room. Then the place was full of machine guns, and they were hitting us where we lay, while other soldiers came in firing into the air. We had very few men with us, and the soldiers shouted at us the most disgusting things I had ever heard in my life.

They took the pregnant women out and brought them home. That was their noble gesture! I was expecting my third daughter, but since I was only a month and a half pregnant I didn't show, and I didn't want to say anything. They separated those of us who remained into different rooms and made us face the walls with our hands behind our heads. They had us that way for about two hours until a soldier came and said he was in charge of the women.

They put us in vans and took us to the Ministry of Defense, where they held us for over an hour and a half as an enormous shoot-out went on outside. We were all piled up one on top of the other so that the bullets couldn't get to us. Finally, instead of unloading us, the soldier in charge said he had received an order to take us to Chile Stadium. We were the first people to arrive there.

Anyone who knew anything about politics could see they were prepared for a massacre, and when they put us in the bleachers I thought the end had come. After a few hours, they started calling us one by one to interrogate us.

The interrogaters were civilians, who asked you what party you belonged to, and since everyone answered that they didn't belong to any, they began to insult us and to shout at us. You'd have to be an idiot to admit something like that!

When they finished with the group of women, a new soldier was put in charge and told us, "As a personal favor, I'm going to let you go free. Group yourselves with people who live in your neighborhood, and we'll take you home in the vans."

I didn't believe it. I didn't say where I lived, and I didn't group myself with anyone. Most people thought as I did. But in fact, they began to take us out of the stadium. As we left, we saw the men from the Technical University arriving. They looked terrible! Among them I saw Víctor Jara,* whose face was completely black-and-blue.

They really did let us go. It was about four in the afternoon. There were several vans, and I got into one that was going to my neighborhood. When we got near my house, I got out quickly and continued on foot. Since it was after curfew I was the only person in the street, and I saw people looking at me from their windows.

At my mother's house they already knew what had happened at the university, and they thought I was dead. When they saw me, it was as if a ghost had walked in! But just as I entered, a phone call came telling us that Jorge, my husband, had just been taken into custody.

They had taken him from his union, SIDARTE, the actors' union, and accused him of having weapons. What kind of weapons would a union have? He didn't have anything. But they took him down to the police station and then to Chile Stadium.

I looked for him everywhere. I even went to Chile Stadium because I knew they had detained people there, but they denied he was there. There were people everywhere looking for members of their families. There were some terrible moments; I've never felt more impotent in my life. Finally, on the seventeenth, he came home alone.

On that day, I believe they moved everyone to the National Stadium, and—who knows why?—they let Jorge and a teacher go free. I think it was because my husband looked middle-class. The people they had detained were students and workers, and since Jorge looked like he had some money, they let him go.

* A famous popular singer who was killed there after his hands were cut off.

FOR A MISERABLE SALARY

When the coup came, Jorge was automatically unemployed because he had had an administrative position at the daily *Puro Chile,* which was shut down. But fortunately he adapted well, and he went right out and got work as a wine seller. I was able to keep my job at the university, although my salary was cut. I was one of the first people to go back to work. I showed up to count the money, and since not a nickel was missing, they couldn't fault me for anything.

I had always worked at the Technical University: I started by taking the exam in '60, and because I was efficient, I kept moving up until I got to the treasurer's office. I never left work to go to a rally, never! Work came first, then everything else. That's why they had to keep me on.

Since there were very few people, and they had to be paid, I was sent to work in the salary department . . . that was a very difficult time. There was a guard permanently installed at my desk who looked over the lists and asked me to identify such and such a person when he arrived for his money. I thought, "What am I doing sitting here for so little money?" I never pointed them out to anyone; I would say that those people worked in different parts of the university and were paid at different times.

Beyond that, you would go to the bathroom and run into guys beating up a student . . . the only thing you could do was take a deep breath and go back to work. At lunchtime, the guards would follow people to question them and get them to inform on others. I always refused, and they watched me very closely.

I never denounced anyone, and furthermore, I arranged to pay a lot of people that they wanted to arrest, without their knowing. The university departments were full of people waiting to be paid, and I would take their checks and manage to give them out. That made me feel a little better—as if I wasn't there simply for the miserable salary they were paying me. Those were horrible times. Even for people of the right; they didn't have any idea of what we were in for either. They never thought that they would walk through the park and see people they had worked with for years being beaten up; they

· · · · ·

thought it would be a simple change of government, and they never dreamed of such terrible things.

In '74 I took a pregnancy leave, and after my baby was born they wouldn't let me come back. It didn't really bother me that they kicked me out because it had been an awful place to work.

A friend of mine and I began to work at a newspaper stand downtown, selling imported cigarettes. At first it went very well, but after six months the police began to bother us. They would make us give them cigarettes, and if we didn't they'd threaten to shut us down, because all our merchandise was contraband. We finally gave up, and I went to be a secretary at a cosmetics firm, where I stayed until our situation became unbearable. Because even if we were able to stay employed, the military continued to hound us on other fronts.

CONSTANT HARASSMENT

After the eleventh we stayed with my mother until the end of October. We lived in San Bernardo, in a military neighborhood, and within five days of our return home soldiers came to the house. At about eleven at night five vans came, circled the block, and set up machine guns.

The girls and my mother-in-law were with us. I went to open the door, and a group of soldiers came into the house. They took Jorge out of bed, sat him in the living room, and three of the soldiers pointed their machine guns at him. They took the girls from their room and put them in with my mother-in-law. They wrecked everything, searched the attic, pulled up the floorboards, slit open the mattresses—it was incredible! And they didn't find a single thing except a postcard with Lenin on it that a friend had sent me from the Soviet Union.

They accused Jorge of having had military training in Cuba and they arrested him. The accusation made me laugh, because he's never been to Cuba.

The girls cried, and my mother-in-law went crazy. I took the girls to bed with me, managed to calm them down, and at the break of dawn we left for the Infantry Regiment of San Bernardo where I thought they must have taken him. He wasn't there; and the official I talked to told me he didn't know anything about it.

I went home again and told my mother-in-law we would have to get some friends active in helping us find him. Jorge's family is very prominent. His father is German and his sisters are all married to Germans. We called one of the brothers-in-law, and in half an hour he called back to say that Jorge was in the Chena hills.

Evidently there was nothing in those hills. The concentration camp was high up, and there was only a guardhouse lower down. I went there, and it turned out that the boy on watch came from our neighborhood and recognized me. He confirmed that Jorge was there, and he was very helpful throughout. Every day I would give him a package for my husband, and he would bring back news. Jorge was held there twenty days . . . and he was a mess by the time he got out.

He arrived one evening, and when I saw him I almost died. My husband is a very strong man, but at that point he had been completely broken. He was thin, unshaven, and a wreck. My oldest daughter was also very upset by the sight of him—she began to cry and to ask what had happened to her daddy—the poor thing didn't understand.

To be in that condition Jorge must have gone through some horrible things. He saw them kill people right in front of him; he saw people tortured—it was frightful. They didn't treat him too badly— his brother-in-law was important, so they gave him special treatment. After twenty days they let him go: they put him in a van, drove him to the highway, and told him to get out.

About eight days after he got back they came again. At about six in the evening a van of soldiers pulled up, and one got out—I think he was a colonel—to tell us we had to move to a different house immediately. After a short discussion, he pointed out that we lived in a military zone, and he gave us one week to move, warning that before leaving San Bernardo we had to give him our new address.

We decided to go immediately, and the friend who had sent me the postcard of Lenin lent us an apartment he had in downtown Santiago. It was tiny, because he lived alone, and we had to divide our furniture among several different places and take only what was absolutely necessary. I was about three months pregnant, and I felt very bad, but at least we would have a little peace.

The calm lasted only about a month, because in January of '74 they visited us again. The girls were playing outside, and a man came up to them and asked if Jorge lived there. After saying yes, the oldest ran to tell us what had happened:

"Mama, Mama, a man came looking for Papa, and I told him that he lived here."

"That's fine," I told her. "He does live here and you have nothing to hide about your father."

The next day, they came again. There were eight guys in civilian clothes who wanted to confirm that we lived there and simply wanted us to know they were in charge.

After that, the harassment became unbearable. It was a daily occurrence. They kept on walking around the neighborhood or coming up to the apartment asking for Jorge, to the point where we decided he should live somewhere else. At first I kept the girls with me. But when I was ready to give birth, I left them with my mother and stayed on in the apartment alone.

Since I had been only a month and a half pregnant when the coup took place, I didn't have anything with me that I would need for the baby. But the people from my party organized themselves and offered moral and economic support. In May, when Paulina was born, I had a hundred diapers, two cribs, and two carriages!

On September 11 the party was disbanded, but it reorganized quickly, and by December it was functioning again. I hooked up again while I was still working at the university, without even making an effort. At first, our work was simply to reorganize; you would meet with your contact for ten minutes to find out who had been taken in, who had left the country, who needed help. Above all, we were concerned about the many single women party members who were not versed in politics. It was like a support group—exactly the way I had been helped with having my baby.

Around the middle of '74 we began more organized political work. They asked me to protect people who were wanted by the police and who would certainly be killed if caught. My work was to save lives.

Whole weeks passed in which I didn't hear from Jorge, in which I had no idea where or how he was! Sometimes I would run into a friend who would tell me he had seen him and that he was okay. Even though I'm not a model housewife, it was very upsetting not to know if he had food to eat, clean clothing, or anyone taking care of him.

I was so distressed that the baby wouldn't come out, and I had to have a Caesarean. I never had a drop of milk. I had hardly arrived home after the delivery when they came again looking for Jorge.

Every two or three weeks someone would say to me: At such-and-such time, in such-and-such place. I would go, and there would be Jorge waiting for me. We would spend half an hour together and then each go off in a different direction. Sometimes they would tell me to take the girls, and I would. We had no choice because all of our lives were at risk.

The girls were completely disturbed. From the outside, they were normal children, but inside they weren't. The oldest developed an emotional dyslexia that affected her writing and made her unable to complete her normal studies. I know the girls didn't lack anything material, but emotionally things were terrible. I sat up through many nights because I hadn't heard from Jorge and because I could feel the tragedy my daughters were experiencing. My biggest fear was that Jorge would be caught, because if he was, they would kill him. Sometimes I would hear it raining and wonder if he was outside . . . I had no peace, night or day! But I began to take refuge in the new baby.

At the beginning of '75, I rented a house on the other side of the Mapocho River to live in with my daughters. I put them in a nearby school, and I thought we would have a little peace. After about six months it was decided that Jorge could move there as well, but a month and a half after he returned, the harassment began again. Every time the girls went out to play, someone would ask them in a friendly way about their father.

In September a brother-in-law lent us his beach house and we left. Jorge visited on weekends, and we managed to live more or less peacefully until November. I kept up my ties with the party, and continued to hide people at the beach. My contact was my friend

Mario, of the postcard and the apartment. One day in November, at about nine at night, he came to the beach, in lousy spirits.

"There are problems again," he told me, "and this time it's going to be much worse than before."

Mario had married a friend of mine, and they had just had a baby. That night he asked me, above all else, to take care of his wife, because she was very weak. I promised him I would have the presence of mind to face whatever happened. He didn't explain further, and he left at dawn.

It turned out that the Central Committee of the party had been arrested, dragging down with it many people . . . and some people were denounced. Mario and my husband were identified by various people.

Jorge showed up several days later, also to tell me that terrible things were about to happen. He stayed with us overnight, and then I didn't hear from him for several weeks.

In the middle of December, Mario and his wife, Cecilia, arrived with their baby and Jorge. They brought meat for a barbecue and and were in a very good mood, ready to spend the day with us. They looked so good that I naively thought things were getting better. We went to the beach, laughed, and had fun until it was night and Mario came to say good-bye.

"I'm going," he told me, "and I'm leaving you Cecilia and the baby." He handed me a large sum of money, asked me to look after it, and insisted that I take care of his wife and son. I didn't understand what was going on, and I asked Jorge to explain.

"Things have gone very badly, and we have to go into hiding."

"But why were you in such good spirits all day today?"

"It's the last thing we were able to give you," he answered.

I took Mario to the bus, and I've never seen him since. Cecilia is still a close friend . . . she had no idea what was going on . . . she's very good, very noble, but very frail.

Since Mario had told her to stay at the beach, on Monday she decided to go to Santiago to ask for a leave from work. She took the baby, because she was breast-feeding, and I gave her instructions about what to do.

"If you have to take a bus," I explained to her, "keep your eyes open. Get off after a few blocks and take another one. Watch people's faces very carefully, especially their noses, because you can change everything else."

I gave her enough money so that she wouldn't have to worry about economizing, and I stayed with Jorge, who was scheduled to leave for the south the next day. Unfortunately, she got to Santiago and she didn't pay attention to anything. She went directly to her house, and upon entering discovered four DINA guys who were there waiting for her. They let her leave the baby with a cousin, and then they arrested her. They tortured her, committed enormous atrocities, gave her an injection that made her forget where she was, and . . . my friend couldn't resist, and she turned us in.

A GOOD ONE AND A BAD ONE

At four in the morning we awoke to find our bed surrounded by strangers. They told us we were under arrest and made us get up. We got dressed, gave all of the money we had to my mother-in-law, who was staying with us, and said good-bye to the children, who were crying uncontrollably.

They put us into a Citroën, and we left. There were two men with us, one in a poncho and cap, the other in a more elegant parka. Behind us, in another Citroën, were three men who seemed much rougher. The questions began immediately, and they told us that Cecilia had been arrested, that things were very bad for her, and that Mario and Jorge were accused of being KGB spies.

When we got to Santiago, they blindfolded us and we had to pretend to be asleep. Judging from the amount of time that passed and the kind of road we were on, we thought they had taken us to Colina. When we got there, they put each of us in a separate cell.

Mine was a small room with a cement floor, a small window that let in a little light, and an iron door. There was a thin mattress, and I covered myself with some blankets I had taken from home. I could tell that Jorge was two cells down from me, because he has a problem with his nose and he breathes in a certain way that I was able to hear. I breathed deeply and thought I would be able to resist whatever lay ahead.

They gave me lunch, and in the afternoon one of the men who

had arrested us showed up—the more refined one who seemed to be the leader of the group. "Take off your blindfold," he said to me amiably, because we weren't allowed to have it off even when we were alone, in case one of them came in and didn't want us to see him. "I've brought you paper and a pencil," he explained, "and I want you to write down the story of your whole life. The important thing is that it be true, because your life depends on it."

He left me alone, and I heard him go into Jorge's cell. The stories that we each wrote coincided completely. One part was true, and the other was believable, thanks to Mario's teaching . . . he never left me alone, he always did everything he could to prepare me. "Be aware," he said, "if they take you, there will be a good guy and a bad one. They'll take turns. The good one will treat you fine, and the other will do everything under the sun to you."

The good one was the one who had arrested us, who let me take off my blindfold. When he came back for my history, he brought me two cigarettes, recommended a cure for a tooth that was hurting me, and patted my head. "Stay calm," he told me. "As long as you tell the truth there's no problem. I went back to the beach—the girls and your mother-in-law are fine, so stay calm and tell the truth."

Of course, it was a lie that he had gone back to the beach.

When he left me alone, I slept heavily. I woke up to enormous shouting and someone kicking the door like a crazy man. It was a lunatic who was cursing and who, suddenly, flew through the door and flung himself on top of me. He was shouting and accusing me of being a Communist and a spy. I stayed completely calm, and the only thing I did was to say, "I am not a Communist." To admit to being a party member at that moment would have been suicidal.

I had very long hair, which I wore in a braid that reached below my waist. He grabbed me by the braid and began to drag me around the cell while he continued to shout at me. Finally he let me go and told me to sign a declaration admitting that both I and my husband were Communists. I insisted this was a lie and that I wouldn't sign. He got furious, and I could hear him continuing to shout as he went away.

After a while I began to hear them torturing other people. I heard their moans and plenty of threats: "You jerk, I'll hang you by your head until you tell the truth."

Night came, and suddenly I began to hear that they were torturing Jorge just outside my cell. There was a stone courtyard, they had him running naked, and they wouldn't let him stop.

"Run, you son of a bitch, the fascists are coming!" they shouted at him. I heard them beat him, and then make him run again. He ran and ran, and I could feel his exhaustion. I suffered enormously . . . but I sat with my back against the wall and thought, "They will not defeat me. I must be strong, and I will be!"

They tortured him that way for three or four hours. Then everything was quiet. I didn't hear Jorge any more, and I thought they had killed him.

Early the next morning the good one appeared, knocking on the door before coming in. Once again he told me I could take off the blindfold. He was friendly. He assured me he believed everything I had said, but the problem was he couldn't convince the colonel. Since it was sunny, he suggested going out onto the stone patio. I replaced the blindfold and he took my arm and led me to a chair. He ordered them to bring me breakfast and clean my cell. Then he left me alone. I tried to explore my surroundings and reached out to see if there was anyone near me, but I didn't feel anyone until suddenly someone asked, "What is your name?" I gave my name, and he left. A little while later he came back and asked the same thing. He went and came back, went and came back. He asked me about twenty times until the good guy came and took me back to my cell as if nothing had happened.

I think the whole day went by. In the afternoon the shouting monster reappeared to ask me to sign the paper. In the middle of his shouts and insults, he told me they had a photo of me, and that they had followed me one day when I left my house with a suitcase and went to the Forestal Park, and then they had lost me downtown.

"Where did you go with that suitcase, what was in it, and who did you give it to?"

I acknowledged that the incident was true and explained that, before going to the beach, we had wanted to sell some educational games for the holidays. I told him that the suitcase contained some samples, and that after they had lost track of me downtown, I had met my husband and delivered them to him.

He threatened me, saying that they had pictures of everything we had done, and then he left. A little later the good one came and congratulated me for having acknowledged the incident with the suitcase, but at the same time he tried to get me to admit that I had had papers with me, not toys. He gave me two more cigarettes, patted me, and left.

I don't know how much time went by, because when you're blindfolded you lose your sense of time and other things. The door opened and the good one came in, but this time he told me I couldn't take off the blindfold and that I had to go with him.

"I didn't want this to happen to you," he said. He took my arm and hurried me down several passageways until we arrived somewhere where he put me in a chair.

I was wearing a purple sweater, and below the blindfold I could see from the smudges that he had chalk on his hands. I realized that he was the torturer, because the chalk was to prevent him from being shocked.

I was seated and I didn't hear anything. Then suddenly I felt a bucket of water being dropped in front of me. At first I didn't understand, but I had the sudden thought that they were torturing Jorge and that he had lost consciousness. And that's what had happened. They threw water on him to wake him up, and a minute later I heard him breathing.

He had barely regained consciousness when they began to ask him about the suitcase, and I realized that he had been denying everything. I still had the blindfold on so I wouldn't recognize the torturers, but I could tell that it was the good one and the colonel. They applied the electric prod to Jorge's penis, to his anus, to his eyes . . . it was terrible. I knew what was happening from his awful screams and the way he was moving . . . every scream went straight to my soul. But I didn't move or express anything. I was suffering enormously, as if they had my heart and they were squeezing and squeezing it. His screams were horrible.

The only prayer I had was that they wouldn't go too far with the torture. That he wouldn't die. But I would be lying if I said that I had for one second thought about saying something to save him. It never crossed my mind. The only thing I longed for was that he continue to resist . . . I couldn't be an informer; I couldn't betray the cause that I had loved my entire life, the cause I had been defending since I was fourteen years old. For me, betrayal is the ultimate sin. If I had talked, I would have been like a piece of trash, and moreover, I would have felt Jorge's contempt.

They kept on about the suitcase, and he wouldn't admit anything. Suddenly they told him that I was there too and that I had already confessed, but he kept denying it. They got me up, took me out of there, and threw me back in my cell. I cried a lot. Only when I was back in my cell did I let go, not knowing if Jorge was still alive or not. I listened for his breathing but couldn't hear it, and once again I thought they had killed him.

It was morning again when they came back. They had me sit in the room while they tortured Jorge, but at least I knew he was still alive. He was in a bad way, but alive. They wouldn't get off the subject of the suitcase. I thought about it, figured they might kill me, but decided to risk it, and stood and shouted to Jorge, "Remember when I delivered the black suitcase!"

The colonel gave me a push in the chest and I fell back into the chair.

"Do you really think, you fucking bitch, that you and this shit are going to work your story out right in front of us?"

When he heard me, Jorge responded by saying that the suitcase was white, not black.

"That's right," I said, "the white one, the only one we have."

They began to smack me something awful. They hit me in the face and took me back to my cell threatening that they would torture me next.

I sat down to wait, and I heard them bring Jorge to the bathroom. They told him not to drink water since they had been using the electric prod and he could get a shock—they didn't want to kill him, just to get some information. I calmed down a little after I heard them put him back in his cell.

I think a whole day passed before they took me back to the torture chamber, not to torture me but Jorge once again. They kept going on about the suitcase, and I made the same comments I had in the previous session. They hit me again and threw me back into my cell. I slept well that night because I knew Jorge was alive. Very early the next morning the good one came to tell me they were going to let us both go free.

"The colonel is convinced," he told me."But if your husband is still alive, it's thanks to you, because it was your strength and persistence that convinced them."

I didn't believe they would let us go, but after taking me to the bathroom so I could wash up, they did indeed take me to a car. I got in, and when I put my hand on the seat I felt Jorge's hand. We held hands and the car left . . . he squeezed my hand . . . he was thanking me! That made me very proud, because I didn't want to seem like a coward in front of him, someone who would let others go to protect herself.

After a while we realized that we were in the city. They told us to take off our blindfolds, but to keep our eyes shut and pretend to be asleep until, suddenly, the car stopped.

"Get out right now, and don't look back because we'll kill you without a second thought."

When we opened our eyes, I saw him, he saw me, and we didn't see anything else. We embraced and stayed that way for I don't know how long, without having any idea where we were. It was near Mapocho Station.

PUNTA DE TRALCA

After rejoining our families and children, we decided that the girls would go with my mother and that we would have to look for a safe place because they weren't going to leave us alone. We left after a few days for Viña del Mar, where an aunt of Jorge's lived. We felt completely safe there because they were very well-connected government supporters. We told them what had happened, and they were totally shocked.

At the same time our comrades were trying to find a place for us, and when we returned to Santiago a priest took us to Punta de Tralca. We were introduced to the religious order that lived there, and they gave us a pretty, well-furnished room to recuperate in.

It was very difficult not having anything to do, being able to think all day. We were most worried about the children—we thought about them constantly. We became so depressed that we decided to ask the mother superior for work before we went crazy. She insisted we continue to rest, but we couldn't. The next day I began to work in the kitchen, and Jorge went out to help with a construction project they were working on. This provided some relief because at least we were busy all day.

We made friends with everyone, and the mother superior was so kind to us that in April we brought Paulina to live in Punta de Tralca. And every time the mother went to Santiago she would stop by to see the older children and bring back some news. She was wonderful to us, and we can't thank her enough.

We stayed there until November, and despite the length of our stay, I remember it was very pleasant. We made such good friends that nuns and priests would come to see us on Saturdays bringing news from Santiago. Through them we discovered that our house had been broken into and everything taken. They stripped it bare and left the door wide open.

Even in Punta de Tralca the DINA didn't leave us alone. They came to look for Jorge, and the mother superior went to greet them with Paulina in her arms. She told them they were not permitted to enter because the house belonged to the cardinal and it was a house of God. Another time we were at mass and they came into the chapel. We are atheists, but the mother superior always told us when mass was taking place, and we understood this to mean that she wanted us to attend. That time Father Cristián Precht* was leading the service, and when they came in he stopped the mass and made them leave the chapel immediately while at the same time he moved Jorge to the front of the chapel. They made other attempts later, but they never got into the grounds.

After a few months at Punta de Tralca we realized that we couldn't continue to live in Chile, and the Vicariate of Solidarity and the International Actors' Federation began a process that would allow us

* The Catholic priest who was head of the Vicariate of Solidarity from 1976 to 1979.

to leave. I didn't want to go. In spite of everything that had happened and all that we had suffered, I thought everything could work itself out, and that at any moment we would be left to live in peace. Jorge told me it was crazy to believe that, but the mother offered to let me live there with my whole family as long as it was necessary.

Then one day the government told us that the girls and I could leave, but that they wouldn't let Jorge go. I realized that he would have to go secretly and that he couldn't do it while we were still in Chile. So I decided to leave with the children, although I was completely aware I might never see him again.

A LITTLE HAPPINESS

We went to Sweden, a country covered with snow, where we didn't know anyone. In the airport the girls looked at me and I looked at them, not knowing what to do, until the directors of the Actors' Federation appeared and took us to a small town in the south.

The first few months we lived in a hotel. I studied Swedish, Paulina went to a play group, and the older girls began school immediately, with the help of a teacher who spoke Spanish. I had a struggle with that frightful language, but I studied like crazy, because the only thing I wanted was to be able to work and not have to depend on anyone. After three months I could manage to speak, and Peter, the director of the federation, was incredibly proud.

After this initial stage we moved to a larger city, but not to Stockholm, because that would have been too difficult alone with the children. There are a lot of problems with alcoholism, drugs, delinquency, and impoverished foreigners begging for money.

When I finished my course in Swedish, I went out to look for work and got a job cleaning the floors at the university, which is the only thing they have for foreigners—for "black heads." Peter was indignant and wanted to find me a job as a secretary, but I turned him down.

That's how we were putting together our lives, the four of us alone, when I got news that Jorge was in Sweden and that he would arrive by bus the following day. The news was surprising, since we had gone for a whole year without hearing from him at all.

My oldest daughter didn't want to come wait for him. That made me realize how much pain she had endured and how badly things had come unstuck between her and her father. Still, when we came back with Papa, she had prepared a lovely meal complete with a bottle of wine.

Jorge was totally changed: he had a big thick beard, and the littlest girl didn't recognize him. She ran around saying that that old man wasn't her father, until Jorge went into the bathroom and cut off the beard.

That day the five of us ate together, happily! We went to bed very late. Our life was in total chaos that week. I didn't go to work, the girls didn't go to school, we just walked around, and Jorge met the directors of the Actors' Federation, who had not forgotten us during this entire time.

From then on our life changed.

When I left Chile, Jorge had stayed in Punta de Tralca several weeks, and then they had moved him to a place from where he would be able to leave the country. I do know that he was never authorized to leave, and I don't know how he got out. He only told me he had spent seven days in Buenos Aires and from there he had come to Sweden. I don't know any more because we are both very respectful of the secrecy of everyone's relationship with the organization, and I have no reason to know what he does, just as he has no reason to know what I do.

What he did tell me was that he had missed me very much. I laughed and told him I didn't believe it. Jorge is a man of many attributes—one of a kind: he is direct, honest, warm, and tremendously understanding.

"When I married you," he told me after he arrived in Sweden, "I thought that I wasn't sufficiently in love with you. I married you because I thought you had many important qualities, but not because I loved you. But there is no doubt that now I am completely and totally in love with you."

I didn't know what to do or say . . . after everything that had happened. After almost a year of being apart, I had never hoped for anything like that! I'd always been realistic, and I'd often thought that I had the support of my daughters and didn't need a man. He, on the other hand, was alone. I'd prepared myself for his arriving and telling me that he had found another woman and it was all over between us, but exactly the opposite was true.

I felt wonderful. I was happier than I had been in years, and it completely changed me. Jorge was extremely attentive: if I coughed, he worried; if I breathed heavily, he worried; if I didn't feel well, he worried—he made it very clear how important I was to him, and we became very close.

He began to study Swedish as I had. Although it was harder for him, after three months we moved to Stockholm because Peter had enrolled him to study theater make-up at the university. We continued in that stage of our lives, until the persecution came to Sweden as well.

KGB SPY

At the invitation of the Actors' Union, Jorge took a boat trip to East Germany. On the way back, he was on the deck of the ship, and the next thing he knew, he was in the offices of the Swedish police.

I was waiting for him in Stockholm, and when he didn't show up I decided to call Peter, who lived right by the port where Jorge was supposed to come in. He found him, and the police explained that this was part of a security operation, because they had been tipped off that Jorge was a spy for the KGB.

The next day I was fired. I was doing cleaning work at a nursery school, and the director let me go without giving any reason. At the same time, Jorge was informed that he could no longer attend the Dramatic Arts School. The DINA had followed us to Sweden and were still insisting on this KGB business!

In the middle of all this, we received an invitation for the whole family to spend the summer in the German Democratic Republic. We accepted so we could try to get some rest and forget about these problems, which we hoped would resolve themselves while we were gone.

They treated us like royalty. It was a marvelous experience for me, because I had never been to a socialist country before. They took us everywhere; if I wanted to go to the mountains for a few days, there we went. Those were two fantastic months. They took us to the best hotels and showed us the German way of life.

DISCOTHEQUES AND SWEDISH FRIENDS

Evidently our return to Sweden convinced the police that their accusations had been false. Jorge was able to return to school, and I found cleaning work at the same university. We started again from the beginning, but soon we faced the hardest test yet: the girls were beginning to feel at home in Sweden.

We realized how uprooted they had been, how they were growing away from us, and sensed in them a deep rejection of our lives. Pia was already fourteen, and Lorena was twelve. The older one would get furious every time we tried to tell her something about her country. We would reminisce, and she would get angry. "How long are you going to keep harping on that dump of a country?" she would say. "Stop talking such nonsense!"

I saw that my daughter was moving away from me. For her, Chile was a nightmare . . . The only dark-haired person she could deal with was me; other dark people made her hysterical.

She began to bring her friends home, but we refused to speak to them in Swedish. We never stopped speaking Spanish at home so that Paulina, who had been very young when we left, wouldn't forget it. They accepted that, but then there was the horrible discotheque incident.

In the Stockholm discotheques, drugs flow as freely as Coca-cola. So when Pia asked to go, Jorge offered to accompany her and her friends to find out what kind of place it was. She went crazy, flatly refused, and said she preferred not to go out. Every Friday we had the same conversation, and she would end up crying and stamping her feet. The only thing that interested her in the world was going to the discotheque with her Swedish friends.

On top of all that, she started dating a Turkish boy, which exasperated us. He was a young boy who did menial factory work so that he could buy the biggest car, the best jacket, and the nicest pants.

Completely false values! When we tried to point this out to her, she complained about us to the school nurse. The nurse sent for me and told me the school was going to look for an apartment for Pia because we had alienated her and wouldn't let her go out with boys.

"What's happening," she added, "is that you won't let her have sexual relations, and Pia is at an age when she is ready to have them. I'm going to give her a prescription for contraceptives."

I was furious. "I won't allow it!" I shouted at her. "I have my customs and my culture, and if the problem were contraceptives, I would have bought them for her myself!"

That night Pia didn't get home until about twelve. We went to bed without waiting up for her, and the next day we got her up at six in the morning. We talked until about ten that night, and Jorge proposed that she go to Chile to study there for a while. If she didn't like it after she had tried it, she could come back to Sweden, and we ourselves would rent her an apartment, and we wouldn't interfere any more.

Two weeks later she was at my mother's home in Santiago. She quickly began to write to us how much she liked Chile, but in all of her letters she asked me to come back.

We had barely begun to get over all this when Lorena began to have the same problem. This, together with Pia's letters, made us decide that I should go back to Chile with the girls.

Jorge stayed in Sweden alone, and we had no idea how long it would last, since he didn't even have a Chilean passport. I thought I might never see him again, because in Sweden women are very easy to come by, and he had contact with a lot of very cultured women. The truth is that throughout those ten years nothing I did had been by choice. In one way or another, everything had been imposed on me and involved a certain risk.

HUNGER AND LONELINESS

As soon as we got off the airplane I knew I was in my own country. It was as if I had never left.

We arrived in '81. I was very eager to see my family, to be with my mother and my two sisters, and to spend time with them. A few days later, however, one of my sisters, the one who lived with my mother, proposed that we come to live with them, but that I should also abandon all my political ideas. I thought it was terrible! I hadn't stopped being who I was in Sweden, and I certainly wouldn't here. This produced a very deep rupture between us that has not healed to this day.

My mother lent me a house that she had vacant, and I went to live there with my three daughters. With the little money I had brought with me I began a small business selling groceries—vegetables, fruit, and chicken. But since I had very little capital and the recession had begun, we ended up eating the stock we had. After a little while, we decided to close the shop and keep the merchandise—which lasted us about six months—and I invested what I had left in imported stockings and socks, which I sold door-to-door.

During the first months, Jorge sent us some money, but then he went to Nicaragua and was not able to send money out of the country.

We had had a deal with him: he would only leave Sweden once we were economically secure in Chile. He broke this promise and left without even letting me know. Once he had arrived in Nicaragua, he sent us a tape to tell us. It was terrible, and I'll never forget it, because that wasn't our deal, and I told the girls about it. It was a personal decision of Jorge's. If it had been a political decision I would have understood, but it wasn't, and Jorge let me down.

In all of '82 we didn't receive a single word from him or about him. The girls asked what had happened, and I told them I didn't understand, because it's one thing not to want to be in touch with me and another to forget your own daughters.

One day we received a few lines with a telephone number in Nicaragua. In May of '83 I called to tell him to come get the girls because I couldn't feed them any more. I gave up. I saw that everything had gone from bad to worse, and I didn't want the girls to suffer any more.

Jorge wanted me to come too, and he assured me that things would be the same between us, but I refused. The girls left in June of 1983, and I remained alone. I was incredibly lonely—I couldn't escape it. I became so acutely depressed that I ended up going to a psychiatrist, who, fortunately, was able to help me.

I also met a man . . . Since I was so lonely, I began to live with him. He was a very good man, very worthy, and he helped me to get over my depression. When I was with the girls I had never looked for anyone else. After they left, I began to work a little in the neighborhood organizing people for protests, although in fact I don't think this country has any options besides armed struggle, because I don't think we can escape through democratic means.

So that's how I was trying to reorganize my life when Jorge appeared on one of the lists of exiles that the government had authorized to return.

My new friend understood that I would try to repair my marriage, but Jorge reacted very badly to him. He arrived in December, and I received him in my house. I told him about everything that had happened to me. I told him that I was deeply hurt by his attitude at our last parting, and that I could never forget it. He gave me a thousand reasons for it, but none of them seemed valid to me, and a lot of damage was done between us. He told me he'd had various women during these years, but none of them had meant what I meant. Still, he couldn't understand the relationship I had with my new friend, and our marriage broke up completely. Jorge is convinced that it's because of my new relationship, but it's not. On that point he's mistaken, because I never intended to keep on living with that man.

What I do want is to have my daughters back! And since Paulina came back a little while after her father did, she's fulfilling all my needs. I'm very happy with her.

Pia and Lorena stayed in Nicaragua to finish their studies. From the letters they write, it's clear they've matured a lot. Along with her regular studies, Pia is studying computers, and Lorena is doing languages. The two of them are dating excellent Nicaraguan boys, one of whom is a commander in the Sandinista army—he was already a guerrilla by the time he was ten. Maybe the girls will stay there, because their happiness comes from those boys and not from me. I have not had a single truly happy day in the last ten years.

A PINOCHET DIEHARD

ELENA TESSER DE VILLASECA

NO FACT OR ARGUMENT WILL SHAKE HER FAITH IN THE *goodness of the regime. Not even the fact that her daughter and three grandchildren are currently living in her home because her son-in-law is unemployed. For her, these last ten years have been "fabulous."*

She fondly recalls the eleventh of September, 1973, and the day she gave her jewels for National Reconstruction, in exchange for a symbolic copper ring that she will wear "as long as Pinochet lasts." Nervously making excuses lest she insult me—since she knows I don't agree with her—she tells me of her unquenchable faith in the government of the armed forces. Afraid of Marxism, she helped establish this government, working through groups such as Female Power, a women's organization created in response to Allende's government. She tells me of the humbleness and sensitivity of the president and Señora Lucía (whom she does not know personally), of the need for security forces to maintain order, and of the return of the politicians who have come to "urge the people on."

She gets up daily at six-thirty to prepare a lunch and goes off to one of her many activities, such as volunteer work at the Women's Council. She has set up training courses in the community, helps undernourished children, works to eradicate the shantytowns, and participates in all types of events designed to show Pinochet what broad support he has.

Neither I nor my husband are political. We have never belonged to a party, but I did join Female Power to fight against Marxism. We were all married women, who didn't want our children and husbands to suffer communism, which is really horrible. In a Marxist government you can't educate your children the way you want, only the way the party decides. Children don't belong to their parents any more; at a certain age the party enrolls them, and that's it.

We worked ourselves to death with all the things there were to be done. When Allende won, Female Power discovered that the election results had been completely fraudulent. Then, during the stoppages, we brought food to the people on strike. We fought against the ENU* and others, supporting everything that was democratic and anti-Marxist. In fact, on the eleventh I was getting ready to leave for the Female Power office when we heard on the radio that Allende had fallen. This made a big impression on me—I began to cry for joy! That's the truth.

The day before, my daughter had given birth in the Alemana Clinic, and we were worried that something would happen to her because there was shooting and bombing in the streets. We got the doctor to discharge her and we brought her back home, because bombs could have fallen on the clinic. It was very scary walking outside, but at the same time, we were very happy.

Everyone from the block got together in a neighbor's house to celebrate, because we all felt the same way—democratic and anti-Marxist. Everyone brought something and it was a very joyous occasion, but it couldn't last long because we were all scared to death of the new curfew, and worried that they would shoot us in the street.

* National Unified School, the educational reform proposed by Allende's government. It was one of the main focuses of the opposition's struggle.

Then there were a few days when we weren't allowed out in the street at all; you could hear a lot of shooting, and we were very scared, but at the same time we were very happy about Allende's fall.

A STRONG AND HEALTHY PEOPLE

When we were able to go out again, we got together in Female Power and discussed things. If we had thrown out the government, if we had worked so hard for its overthrow, if we had asked the military to intervene for us, now we had to support the armed forces. But we couldn't keep on as Female Power because the power had to come from above—from the government. So we became the Women's Council.

When they said that anyone who wanted to could give their jewels and other valuables to National Reconstruction, I went crazy! I asked my husband for his ring, put it together with mine, got out everything that was worth anything, wrapped it in a handkerchief, and delivered it to the Central Bank. They gave me two copper rings, this one and my husband's . . . I find it all very moving . . . I felt wonderfully happy to have contributed in some way to moving our country forward. This ring is all that I have; I haven't taken it off since I gave up my things, and I won't take it off as long as Pinochet is here. I adore Pinochet. I adore him because he is a superhuman person who is also sensible and worthy. If he could, he would have us all living in wonderful circumstances, but unfortunately he can't.

To help the government of the armed forces, they were organizing different volunteer groups, and people were being divided up according to what they wanted to do. First I joined Women in Pink, who were working with undernourished children in the Calvo Mackenna Hospital. Then about forty of us formed another group to work with Dr. Fernando Monckeberg in CONIN * and on the Health Council, which had started the famous open clinics in the barrios for children under two.

In the clinics, the children come in at nine in the morning. We

* The Infant Nutrition Council.

bathe them, give them their bottles, play with them, and feed them lunch. The main thing is to be affectionate. In the afternoons, other volunteers come who take care of them until six, when they are returned home.

CONIN now has these clinics throughout the country, but we started with just eighteen beds where we put seriously ill children while they recuperated. The clinics now have a staff and certain amenities, but at that time we had to wash and wax the floors, wash the children's clothing, iron, bathe the children, feed them . . . we were like worker ants.

We felt that we were doing important work for the government, raising the standard of living of the people. When I first saw these children, they had been thrown into beds to stare at the ceiling. They would just lie there. But at the end of one or two play sessions, they began to smile, they gave us hugs, priceless things. It was very moving and the work fascinated me. We wanted to make the Chileans a sound race again, to make the country healthy.

Once the children are better, we don't just abandon them. They have to come back periodically, and we also visit them in their homes. We try to educate the mothers, especially in hygiene, showing them how to prepare bottles, telling them how important it is to wash their hands and use clean utensils. What these people need most is to be taught. Poverty certainly exists, and there's no denying it. But there is a great lack of education, which of course leads to a lack of hygiene, which produces dreadful diarrhea, dehydration, and finally malnutrition.

At the same time, the Women's Council holds courses to train us, because you can't just start working haphazardly in all the different fields we are involved in. They have classes in reading, current affairs, consumer education, a series of courses on different topics. Then you go out into the community to share what you have learned.

I am the consumer-education instructor, and I have given the classes in many different neighborhoods, in schools, in maternity centers . . . I try to teach the best ways to use the resources available to us, because these people squander their resources in the most appalling ways. They leave the water running all day, waste light and gas unnecessarily, and above all, they have no idea of how to make simple meals that are cheap and nutritious.

We teach them to plant, and to take advantage of every little corner of their garden. These people, for example, are addicted to pasta because it's quick and simple, when in fact there are many less expensive, more nutritious things that they don't know about, like certain vegetables. Beets, for instance, are delicious, but few people know that the leaves are more nutritious and that instead of boiling them, you can put them in a salad or an omelette, which is also good. I always do that in my home.

I find the community women remarkable—even more valuable than the men, who are irresponsible. Women pay more attention to their families. They're more concerned with order, liberty, and peace, because they want their children to study quietly and to become people who matter. They are always very receptive to us because they understand what we are doing. They're very warm, and they know we never go into the communities for political reasons. Our role is to help and to educate. If we were politically active, we'd have problems, but we never have been.

PEACE AND QUIET

There is an economic crisis that came here from Europe and the United States, and that has affected all of us. But maybe the big mistake was to have been wasteful when we were doing all right. People went crazy buying things: they have washing machines, refrigerators, televisions, everything! They went so far overboard that now, with so much unemployment, they have terrible problems because they can't keep up the payments. Still, they're not doing badly, because somehow or other they get by.

Unemployment has affected us the most, and it would be a lie to deny it. I myself have a daughter with three children living with us while they work things out. Her husband worked at a job making leather wall-hangings, and the company folded. They went to the south and things got a little better, but the truth is it wasn't a good situation for my daughter and her three little girls, so they came to stay with us. Everyone has had problems, some more, some less, but that's not unique to Chile—it's a world crisis.

I also think this business of political prisoners and political exiles is terrible, but that's what happens if you do something bad, and if we didn't take these steps, we'd have a mess on our hands! I would prefer, for example, that there were no CNI, but I think that right now it's necessary.

The issue of the disappeared is also scary, but we do know that some of them have showed up in other countries—that they're in self-exile. I wouldn't want this to happen among my friends; the disappeared and the exiles are terrible things. But we had to expel them because they revolt and provoke terrible upheavals with bombs and riots, while the government wants peace and order. That's why we had to exile them, and in reality, I don't think there are many like that; the majority are self-exiled.

Now those same people are coming back; they've gone for training in Cuba and other places, and no one knows how they get into the country. They're people paid by the Marxists to provoke trouble, because Marxism can't get over the fact that Chile has remained afloat. The politicians want to go back to the same state we were in before, the same horrifying politics.

That meeting in O'Higgins Park I thought was pretty overrated. Maybe I'm optimistic, but I don't think it was that big. Furthermore, they brought in a ton of people from outside. I have taken part in all the government marches, and they never forced us to go. In fact, there are volunteers who have never gone because they're tired and they don't like marches. To my knowledge they've never bused anyone in; the council has never pressured us, but we are so excited by the whole thing that we always just get together and go.

I love to participate, to show the president how many people are behind him. I'm happy when the president sees all this support because I think he must be hurt by all the ingratitude he sometimes endures from the poor—people he has helped and who haven't responded.

In spite of the problems, I have never doubted, and I never will as long as Pinochet is in charge. He's an honest and well-intentioned man. You won't see him at parties like other presidents. He never travels abroad, either; he just travels through the country learning about our problems.

He and his wife are the plainest people in the world. The first time

I met him was among poor people. Women just adored him—they kissed his hands, full of joy. I've never actually met them personally, but I've watched them very closely. Señora Lucía has dedicated so much of her life during all these years. I don't know where she gets that much energy. They're both very sensitive to poverty and unemployment. The president suffers with the poor, but unfortunately he can't solve everything.

I have never doubted him. If I had, I wouldn't be wearing my copper ring any more! With the latest economic problems, I can see lots of ingratitude toward him. I'm sure the day the president leaves, those same people will ask him to come back. He is the one who gives us peace, order, and tranquillity.

COPPER: BOOM, STRIKE, AND UNEMPLOYMENT

VÍCTOR LÓPEZ RIVERA

PIGEONHOLING DOESN'T WORK WITH HIM. I HAD TO *change my labels for him several times during the course of our conversation until I realized that Víctor López has a very personal set of experiences and opinions that make him both the same as and different from everyone else.*

My first shock came when the president of the Potrerillos workers' union appeared with the Bible in his hands. Potrerillos is where the refinery of the El Salvador copper mine is located, a place where men don't happen to be especially spiritual. I was also surprised to hear that he was the son of peasants, taught to defer to the boss, that he had studied music at the university, had been a student leader after the coup, and had then been brought by hunger to Santiago, where he discovered that he couldn't even work as a salesman because he didn't have a jacket.

One minute he seems like the fiercest of militant leftists, the next he becomes a self-searching, spiritual young man—and he's convinced that the two are not contradictory.

He is part of a new generation of leaders in the copper industry, in a country where copper represents the main source of national income—"the Chilean salary," as it was called in Allende's time.

The Copper Union, currently with more than 20,000 members, is certainly the largest in the country. Its actions have frequently helped define the social and political life of Chileans. Thus, for instance, in 1972 and 1973 the strikes and protests of an important group of copper miners contributed significantly to Allende's fall. A decade later, in 1983, it was that union again which promoted the first national work stoppage. Ultimately there was no stoppage, but we did have a huge national protest, which started a whole movement of political and social action to reestablish democracy. The military government wasn't able to stop it.

López is one of those leaders, one of those who dared to speak about strikes after ten years of dictatorship, one of those who encouraged the first protests. That's why, at thirty-two, married and with a child, he is an unemployed miner.

At first I didn't appreciate what was going on. When we left our lodgings to go to the university, we found the streets full of soldiers, who told us about the coup. It didn't affect me as it should have—it didn't really penetrate.

I remember that I left for Valle del Elqui to see my parents. Even though I studied to be a chemical laboratory technician in La Serena, I'm the son of peasants. Today that would be practically impossible, but then, if you had the ability, you could get an education because there were loans and university scholarships.

At home, nothing had happened, but after a few days they arrested my father and kept him in jail until Christmas of that year. He was a peasant union leader during Frei's presidency, and they accused him of organizing meetings in Pisco Elqui and other areas. As they often do, they invented things that he had done, at times when he wasn't even a union leader and on days when he had been in some other place.

They took him off to the police station . . . I think that I was pretty shocked by all this, because I didn't even follow them . . . I wasn't able to do anything. I don't know if I began to cry that day or later, but I cried a lot.

From '70 to '73 the media kept talking about the chaos, the shortages, the food lines, and all that. They blamed Popular Unity for everything, in circumstances where there were a lot of different forces at work and where everyone was using the means at their disposal for their own ends. The opposition defended its property and its system, while the Popular Unity government tried to reaffirm President Allende's program.

I remember this all very clearly, because, as a member of Popular Unity, I participated in the opening of warehouses that were stocked to the rafters with wheat, oil, all the things that were supposedly in short supply. Huge stockpiles of sugar, wheat, everything! That allowed me to see clearly—not as an activist for Popular Unity, but as a person—that these problems had been intentionally caused, and I was hurt by the injustice that followed.

I remember that during Popular Unity there was money around —I don't know if it was hard money or if there was nothing behind it, but people had money. My mother would go to Vicuña, a slightly larger city, with sacks to bring back provisions for the next month. After '73 things got dismal; I know what hunger is, what it means to eat stale bread, and what it means not to eat. All of this made me sad.

I saw the injustices that befell my friends who had fought for their ideals. They believed what they were doing was good: they weren't looking for high-ranking positions or personal gain; they believed the country's wealth could be better shared, and as a result most of them were put in jail, where they stayed for several years, and came out greatly affected.

Two or three years after the coup a woman friend of mine, who had been a local official, asked me not to come near her because I didn't know the condition she was in after coming out of jail. "You don't know, Víctor," she said to me, "what I went through inside. For all you know, I might even be a stool pigeon. So please, don't come see me or try to talk to me."

I didn't belong to any party, but at the university I worked for the

MAPU.* I was always very active, although toward the end, in '73 itself, I didn't participate much. I explained to people that I wasn't in a position to participate, because I was involved in something else that interested me very much—a personal inner search. I thought that if I put politics to one side for a while, I could concentrate on my inner search, on finding God. I was disturbed by many things.

I've never been able to prove it, but I think that this withdrawal from activism caused them not to be too hard on me at the university. Thankfully nothing happened to me, and the next year I was able to continue my studies.

HUNGER AT THE UNIVERSITY

In '73 I continued to work in the country. I am the oldest of eight children, and I had to help out. I was also a little unsure of my future, and I took the Academic Aptitude Test again to try a different field. This was related to my soul-searching and my desire to do something artistic, so that in '74 I began to study music education.

When I arrived at the university, my friends seemed happy to see me alive—they didn't know what had happened to me. There had even been a rumor that I was in training at a guerrilla camp, although I had never fired a gun in my life. The course coordinator at the chemistry lab called to congratulate me because I had been absolved of all the charges against me at the public prosecutor's office, and I had no idea what he was talking about. He explained that there was an accusation lodged against me, but that it had lapsed, and as a result I was free to continue for my second year in the chemistry program. But I preferred to study music, because since 1970 I had been singing with a chorus in La Serena.

I stayed in music until '76, and I think those years increased my need to look inside myself. I was walking around lost, and I wanted to find myself, in the broadest sense of the word. A friend who came

* Part of the Christian Democratic Party that joined Popular Unity in 1969, just before Salvador Allende's election.

from Santiago to study medical technology taught me to look in the pages of the Bible . . . this was a very rich time for me. At the same time, I was active in the Student Music Center, and I ultimately became its president.

I began to see how manipulated the student centers were, and I realized they allowed them to exist only to show that there was freedom within the university. There was a lot of fear on the part of young people in music, because a great man, Jorge Peña Hen, who was the director of the children's orchestra, was executed. He was a Socialist, but above all he was a musician and an artist. What happened to him had a great impact on everyone, and no one wanted to take part in anything that had any whiff of politics about it. Furthermore, students were already beginning to be brainwashed by the regime.

There were very few activists, and those of us who did take risks were very much on display. I saw the university DINA begin to appear. A friend would come up to you and tell you not to get involved in certain things; you began to realize he was an informer, a rat. Once they even insinuated that I could become a collaborator. I refused because my political ideas were very clear-cut, but I was afraid. Still, I rebelled and tried to change things, to rescue the fearful. Even if we weren't able to take specific concrete action, those of us on the left could at least stand out as the best students.

Despite everything, these were good times for me. I liked teaching and music, the two things I was studying. All of this was tied in with my spiritual search. I spent a lot of time in my father's home in Valle del Elqui, which has a special tranquillity. It was the time when I was most moved by music. I learned the classics, the greatest works for oboe and flute. Unfortunately, the life we lead now, this savage fight, doesn't allow us to appreciate those things. Man also has a right to be emotionally thrilled. He shouldn't always be enraged, fighting for a crust of bread.

That whole period may seem very contradictory, but I don't think politics and spiritual things are contradictory. If I'm more spiritual, I'm a better social being working for the cause. I'm going to relate to people as a human being, not just as the carrier of an ideological message—I think it's an effort we must make. To me, that period wasn't contradictory, but very well-rounded.

I did well at the university. I became an assistant teacher and gave classes at the school where I had studied. But unfortunately my finances began to decline. I had studied on a university loan, but it wasn't enough, and I couldn't put together the money I needed. I made very little from my teaching, and by '76 I couldn't support myself, and I got tired of being hungry. University students in the provinces are often hungry; even the ones from better families are hungry, and of course, being the son of poor peasants, I was too. I finished the six semesters of music, started on the fourth year, and then dropped out. It was a very painful decision, because my dream was to be a professor of music. But I didn't have just a physical hunger, which is hard enough to bear; I had a hunger for justice and for liberty. I saw that I wasn't the only one, that there were a lot of others who, like me, had left the university.

A SECURE SALARY

I went north to the El Salvador mine. I asked for work but was refused. Finally I had to sell my guitar to buy a ticket to Santiago. I arrived without knowing anyone and learned what it means to be at the mercy of a large city.

I lived in lodgings and became a salesman, the most frequently advertised job. I was selling fabrics door-to-door, but in reality I sold very little. I would walk around all day thinking about the rent I would have to pay at the end of the month. I also sold pickles to supermarkets. Then I got a job promoting a tourist magazine that was scheduled to appear. I would have to wear a suit and tie to be able to go into certain offices with plush carpets where pretty women would wait on me. This scared me, not because I was worried about what to say, but because I realized I didn't even have the clothes to be a salesman. I had to get a jacket because all I had was a tie and a couple of shirts.

Some smarter people began to show me how things really were. You were hired on a trial basis, and you had to show that you could sell in order to get a permanent contract with a salary. During the trial period you would get a series of clients, but afterwards they would tell you that you weren't good enough to continue. They would take on new people, and the coveted salary would never appear. They took advantage of all kinds of unemployed people this way, rotating them in and out.

I also sang in some choruses and gave some private music lessons, but I never had a permanent job, and ultimately I began to fall apart from anguish and fear; I wanted to leave. I had arrived full of illusions, and I returned to the country quite downcast. But work was scarce; I couldn't find anything steady there either, and after a year I decided to move again.

A WORKER AT LAST

My brother had gone to Potrerillos in '77, and I went in '79. I went to live with him in a single room that they gave him. The foundry and refinery were being modernized, and they were refurbishing some houses, so for a while I was doing some construction.

It was quite a change for me from working in my valley, full of greenery and trees, to working in the north, which is so incredibly dry. It's nothing but desert, and it was very depressing at first.

Since I always liked to sing, I asked for an audition and joined the Potrerillos chorus, where I met some of the executives who later helped me to get work at the plant. It was difficult to do because there was a lot of specialized work, and the contractors would bring in people from outside. I was lucky enough to be hired as a refinery worker, and I think that man must now regret having given me the job.

I worked in the refinery . . . if there was ever hard, killing work, that is it. My job was what is called wet ironing; you have to walk around with a trestle that weighs about twenty kilos, lift up the copper plates, align them on the trestle, and stick them together with an aluminum iron. You begin at eight in the morning, and by noon you've had to bend over more than two thousand times. The air is about 150 degrees, and what is coming out on top is 110 to 130 degrees. You're breathing the acids the whole time; you have to wear goggles to keep them out of your eyes, but they still get in; you wear acid-proof clothing, but it gets through and burns anyway. The acid burns are terrible; it's painful to work there. The old workers say the devil is there. They also push you and push you, and if you're too slow, they say you're sabotaging the plant. It's terrible; it's an inhuman job. The boss throws his weight around and justifies everything by saying he's just following orders. Someday I'd like to speak with whoever's giving the orders, because everyone says they're following orders from above. You have to follow the chain back to see who is giving these orders. And I'd like to destroy the myth that the copper worker is a privileged person. I don't know if they're supposed to be privileged because they get old sooner or because they become useless sooner. In the camps, men sign contracts for eight hours, but the plant rules their lives. In the refinery, for instance, if there is emergency work, wherever you are they come looking for you. If you don't want to work for some reason, you are marked forever. It's not like other places where you work for eight hours and then go do what you want.

Being there outraged me. With apologies to my friends in Potrerillos, I found the people there to be very servile. I was angry to see that there were certain neighborhoods for workers, some for middle-level employees and supervisors, and some for the big bosses. Dublé is the workers' neighborhood, Central is for workers and some white-collar employees, and then there is the "American Quarter." People who have lived in Potrerillos for a long time told me that when the North Americans were there they had guards, and Chileans weren't allowed in: it was a territory within a territory. Somehow the trend set by the gringos has continued, and the workers want to live in Central for status reasons. People who live in Dublé feel bad, although some of the houses there are much nicer than those in Central. All this infuriated me, because from the time I was a child I've had a certain rebelliousness . . .

The peasant has always been very submissive, and that's what they teach you. My grandmother taught me that I had to have respect for the boss, that I should always greet the boss's daughters respectfully. "Don Ramón's daughters are coming to visit us," she would say, and I would be on my best behavior to receive them. I was a clever little boy, so I always had to recite for them, which was a chore. Even as a boy I was aware of this, and once I started high school at La Serena and began to see a different world, I began to say no. Why did I have to respect the boss and his children if they didn't respect me, when they were people or children just as I was? As they got older, the boss's daughters became show-offs, and sometimes they would greet me, other times not; so I began to do the same and greet them only when I felt like it. This came as a shock to my grandmother, since I was bringing new ideas from La Serena. I saw how submissive people were, how much respect they paid to money and class, and I didn't do it.

This happened again in Potrerillos.

THE LIBERATION OF THE AUTOMOBILE

Maybe for this reason I never adopted a consumer mentality. At times I was tempted, but everything inside you makes you analyze and reject those things. I knew that I wouldn't be happier with a car, and furthermore, I got some good advice from a fellow worker.

"Look, Víctor," he said to me, "I came here the same as you, with some education and the idea that I would work here a few years, then go back and finish my career. Suddenly you buy a living-room suite. It lasts a year or two, and then they come out with a more modern one. You give yours away or you sell it, and you buy yourself another. Time goes by, and you've no way of saving."

It happens to a lot of people, and I understood that to go into debt means to tie yourself down and become a slave like everyone else. When I got married, my house continued to be very simple: I have some secondhand furniture, a huge table with chairs, a sideboard, a refrigerator, and a cassette player. I don't have a color television or even a black-and-white one. And I don't have a living-room suite either, because I don't think that's what happiness is about.

Still, consumerism is very marked among the people of Potrerillos. In '80 and '81 car dealers began to arrive. People were going around in expensive cars that they bought on credit! Terrible competition set in.

Many people said they were liberated by their car, that they could go to the beach whenever they wanted. Others didn't want to get drawn in, based on advice they got from friends, but their wives tipped the balance. They would say to their husbands, "What do you mean you're not buying a car, when our neighbor who makes less than you do can buy a Suzuki?"

I know this because later the men would secretly confess to their friends: "My wife made such a fuss I had to get a car!" That's when the tears would start, when they were up to their necks in debt because they owed so much and there wasn't enough money to get to the end of the month. Their buying power was diminishing and prices were shooting up. Some stopped making their payments, and their cars were taken away. Others sold the cars and continued to be in debt. People who guaranteed loans for friends also suffered and their property was seized because the debtor hadn't paid.

A teacher told me that one of the kids began to cry because he said that at night, when he asked for food, his father told him they didn't have any and took him out for a drive in the car to distract him . . . The poor kids are going hungry for a car. Free breakfasts for students help considerably, and people are sending their kids to eat these because they can't pay their bills. That's where you begin to see the crisis.

One day I spoke out in a meeting and people got a glimpse of my political ideas. Some of them began to talk with me, without mentioning parties or anything else, just acknowledging that we were against something we considered bad, people who spoke the same language.

I talked to people, and advised them not to get involved with the car business, but it was very hard. The same thing happened with the pension-fund administrators. We weren't able to have much contact with the other workers. We talked to them about the company plan a little at lunch break, brought them newspapers and magazines, and talked to them a little more before the work day began. But even though they realized we were right, they were very easily swayed. The bosses were very influential in this. They had everything they needed on hand: lawyers, policemen, promoters of the pension fund, everything. They have a lot of control over people. Many workers must have thought, "Why am I gonna believe that son of a bitch López when the boss is an engineer and knows what he's talking about?"

I began to be known because I spoke up and put my views forward at meetings. The older workers were afraid; a lot of them wouldn't even go to the meetings. Some people criticized them for not being interested, or for being lazy, but it was a physical fear. It might be because they had some relative who'd disappeared, somebody in their family who'd been beaten up or suffered from what's going on. And, above all, they might be intimidated by the biggest headache, which is unemployment, because they'd go home on vacation and see the tremendous poverty there.

"Keep your nose clean at work, pal," people would tell them. "Keep your head down and don't get involved in any shit."

As a result, there was a period when people would walk by and not even look at the union—they'd turn their heads the other way. Also, the workers were afraid of the union leaders because they were appointed by the government. When someone had a complaint, the union leaders would send them to talk it over with the bosses. The union leaders were in bed with the company.

That began to change with the arrival of people who asked questions, young people who began to stir up the waters; and then others who were not so young also began to participate. The old people would get all worked up when someone said something that expressed their own feelings: "That son of a bitch has balls," they'd say.

The revival of the unions came in '80, when they let us have free elections, with secret voting, in which everyone could express his preferences. At that time I didn't have the two years of seniority needed to be a union official, but I went to union meetings and was interested in what was going on. I talked with people, read things, and brought in articles to show the others.

I was most in touch with the leftists, but I didn't join any particular group. Some people tried to get me to join, saying that the parties were a useful base of support, but I said no, because I felt that my position gave me more independence. The parties can quickly become very top-down, especially the workers' parties, which at times send down orders from on high.

The two strongest parties there are the Christian Democrats and the Communist Party. I don't like either one. I don't think the CDs represent the workers, and the proof is that there are no Christian Democratic leaders in my union. I find the Communist Party very authoritarian. It's a political group that has a lot of popular support, but I don't agree with their methods. I continue to support MAPU, not because I'm a card-carrying member, but because of their style of doing things—there is discussion of the issues, and they don't impose their ideas.

The bosses began to censure me. They sent me two cautionary letters, and things got really screwed up. One of them was for not using safety devices. It's true I wasn't using them, but there were other people who weren't using them and nothing happened to them. The other was because I climbed up into a crane and changed its position. I used to do that all the time and the bosses would see me and not say anything, but at this point they were looking for things to accuse me of because they realized I was stirring things up.

I spoke for many people, for a majority who at that time were silent. So in November of '82, they elected me their leader and made me president of the workers' union.

We made contact with the Workers' Central Advisory Board, and lawyers and other professionals began to come and explain what was happening throughout the country in the copper industry so that the workers would be informed. We did this because we knew that collective negotiations were coming up in July. But in February the company staged a preemptive attempt to negotiate with us. They knew that, for the first time, the union would be a strong force; so they decided to stop it, and they brought out all their weapons to use against us.

They began a campaign to motivate workers to negotiate for themselves. They went from man to man, and the bosses, acting as lawyers and advisers, did their best to convince people that their offer was the best thing for them. They distributed pamphlets to discredit the union and to turn people against the leaders they had elected.

They said that the El Salvador division was running at a deficit, that we were the lackeys of CODELCO-Chile, and that workers had the inalienable right, granted them in the Workers' Plan, to negotiate individually—that they had to protect the source of their employment, that the union leaders would bring chaos, that they wanted a strike, that they were going to throw people out into the streets, and that they were on the verge of causing the plant to close.

People got scared, and they began to desert the union. The older workers couldn't see that they had to be here with us, not there with them—they didn't realize they were weakening the union. We went around trying to counter what the company said; because of our affiliation with the Workers' Advisory Board, we were actually able to quote figures and statistics, but the company had greater means at their disposal—they had a newspaper, the radio, and the bosses. All we had was our assemblies. It was a very tough fight, to talk and talk and talk, and finally to realize that if we kept on, people were going to defect from our side. We had no option but to negotiate a settlement.

THE STRIKE

The most important thing that happened during that period was the Copper Congress that took place in Punta de Tralca from April 19 through 21, 1983. There the union leaders finally came to see that the copper industry had to stop isolating itself, stop being an island, because it is part of the whole country, not a distinct entity. Because of the key role copper played in the national economy, we were the only people who could say certain things, take to a national level what was happening not only with respect to copper, but in the overall economic scheme that the government was using to screw all workers.

It was an excellent congress. From what we had heard, other similar congresses had been full of conflict, of personal attacks and fights with Medina,* and nothing like that happened this time. Many different directors participated and stated their points of view, and on April 21 we announced a work stoppage for May 11.

I think this was very exhilarating for the country. No one before then had dared to call a halt—it reverberated like a bullet in a church. It's not that we thought of ourselves as having reinvented the wheel, but Chile before Punta de Tralca and after Punta de

---

* Guillermo Medina, the official union leader, who supports the military government.

Tralca was two different countries. Later, the work stoppage was suspended, but it paved the way for the first national strike.

Of course, the only means the workers have to fight against the government is a strike, but if in effect it is going to turn into a massacre, everyone will be against it, especially a union leader who is responsible for the jobs and lives of his associates. And we had reason to expect bloodshed. Today I think the decision to call off the strike locally, at Potrerillos, was a good one, but at the time it seemed like a fraud, because while in Santiago there were tremendous demonstrations, with people banging saucepans in the streets, in Potrerillos absolutely nothing happened.

It was difficult for us to understand the importance of May 11, because we didn't experience it. It was a dark day for us. Potrerillos isn't Santiago; it's a town of five or six thousand inhabitants who depend on copper and who live isolated in the desert. Troops were stationed all around on the eleventh, making their presence known and intimidating people.

Later, by phone and radio, we found out how the protests had gone elsewhere, and we were satisfied. We began to plan a strike in June. And this time there was a strike, but not with the effect we had predicted.

The strike was on June 14, and it began at midday when people didn't go to the cafeteria. At lunchtime they went to the union office and stayed there. We hung a sign outside that explained about our protest against company pressure, but a policeman—the police are truly the bad guys in our part of town—came into the office one day and made us take it down. He was authoritarian and arrogant; he pushed one of the other union leaders around, took him out of the office and threatened to beat him up, said he didn't want to see any other signs at all and that he didn't want to hear another word out of the union.

We, who had started off being so combative, had watched with embarrassment as things were done in other places and nothing happened in Potrerillos. For the fourteenth we had prepared a march from the watch station to union headquarters, which was three or four blocks. As soon as we began to march, the police came.

They had on battle gear: boots, helmets, machine guns, tear-gas canisters. They attacked us and hit us, and we learned what police repression of the worker means. Our march was peaceful. They broke it up and we couldn't even form a line to walk to the office. But we kept going in smaller groups and we got there anyway. That night there were banging saucepans, blowing car horns, switched-off lights—all the things that the protest organizers had asked for.

In El Salvador, in response to the protest on the fourteenth, the workers agreed to arrive at work ten minutes late. The first shift did this, but when group B's turn came, they were told to start at the proper hour or not to start at all. The workers stuck to their agreement, and the plant shut its doors and didn't let anyone in. The workers stayed there their full eight hours, and so did group C, since the doors didn't open for them to enter.

The next day news came that they had fired twenty-three workers in El Salvador, and that was it for Potrerillos. We agreed to a full strike, and they immediately began to hand out termination notices in a very violent fashion. The postman went door to door with six or seven policemen and their machine guns. Their excuse was that they were protecting the postman, when in fact the postman is one of us, and what were we going to say when his job is to deliver the mail! They handed over the notices to the wives who were at home on their own, just to frighten them.

On the sixteenth troops arrived, posted themselves in various locations, went around in trucks, cleared out the union office, shut it up, and left two guards at the door.

I don't have the exact figures, but I think that at the beginning more than 70 percent of the workers went on strike. Later they started dropping out, scared by the pressure.

The foremen went from house to house trying to convince people they should go back to work. They would offer to reinstate their contracts, tell them that they could trust the company, that they shouldn't put their families in danger, that they were going to lose all their years of service, that otherwise all their belongings would be put in a truck and sent away, they would be kicked out, they would be arrested, they would be subjected to the internal security laws. In some cases they would wait until a wife was home alone to scare and intimidate her; when a worker got home he would find his wife crying, and she would tell him a horror story. Many people succumbed that way and began to break with the movement. Some foremen sent taxis to take their workers to the mines, paying for it out of their own pockets.

The foremen themselves had been presented with an ultimatum: "If this lasts one more day, you'll all be fired too." So they began to use all 200,000 to 300,000 pesos of their salaries as well as every means at their disposal to get people in: flattery, threats, fear, the soldiers . . . In a town as peaceful as Potrerillos, having soldiers in the streets changes things.

There was tremendous disillusionment, which was very difficult. The workers who hadn't been fired treated the strikers as if they had the plague. They avoided us, people didn't go out, and a mood of catastrophe prevailed.

I want to pay homage to the 130 workers of Potrerillos who stood firm, who believed in their leaders, who realized we were honest and spoke the truth. The others betrayed a cause, justly or not. Fear is human, but I can't understand treason, and there were people who weren't content just to drop out of the movement, but felt they had to seek out others and tell them about the torments of hell that awaited the strikers. They acted as recruiters for the plant, without being asked.

Those of us who stayed to the end are now very much alone. The people who were fired are now scattered throughout the country. They're unemployed, begging, living on the pittance of their severance pay for their years of service.

The company took the union leaders to court, and since the trial is still going on, they haven't kicked me out of Potrerillos. I'm still a union leader, but the police, who run the town, don't let me go anywhere near the union office. It's strictly prohibited.

Since we didn't sign our dismissal notices, they haven't paid us a cent. My wife and son and I are living off our little bit of savings.

In El Salvador, the unions met and agreed to set up a strike fund, but the three of us in Potrerillos haven't been offered anything by anyone. The directors appointed by the plant haven't even called a meeting, and they don't seem to realize that we're human and have families to feed. It's the only union in this division that isn't helping its prosecuted directors.

People are scared. They don't dare talk with us; they slink away and avoid us. No one has so much as come near our houses or left us a piece of bread. This seems strange to me. I think it's fear.

During these ten years of dictatorship, men have descended to such a low level that, to keep their jobs and their privileges, they have been capable of licking other people's shoes. Above all, licking boots, because the military have become a powerful social class, and therefore people respect them. But it's a cynical respect, full of fear and repudiation. People have to be educated so they can avoid being abused.

I never want to experience again the terrors of secrecy and silence, of not being able to speak out because someone will inform on me or accuse me of something. I don't want to see good projects go to waste because of blind sectarianism; I don't want to attack superiors simply out of opposition, to screw them. The only thing I want is for the people to participate by voting for their rulers. There must be much more active participation, not simply obedience to the orders given by the supermen at the top, who deserve respect but are not always right. Politicians have to get out into the residential areas, into the factories, into the homes of the poor.

I don't think the workers have unrealistic expectations. We want dignity, appropriate jobs, respect for our rights; we want to be heard, we want our children to continue to move forward, and we want the leisure time we have earned. We want the people of Chile to be happy, to be able to laugh as they please.

CORPORATISM: A PRODUCT OF REASON

ANDRÉS CHADWICK PIÑERA

THE COUP AFFECTED HIM SO STRONGLY THAT, IN BURNING *his books outside his house, he got rid of all his youthful leftist ideals. A member of an influential family that traditionally had ties with the Christian Democrats, the Church, and the judiciary, at seventeen he was one of the few members of Popular Unity enrolled at the Alemán del Verbo Divino High School.*

By a slow but dramatic process he was converted into an outstanding youth director for gremialismo, *the main political backbone of the Pinochet government. "My transformation," he said, "was a product of reason."*

It was also a product of his extended contact with Professor Jaime Guzmán, theorist and founder of the gremialista *movement—a rightist movement that grew in response to the Catholic University reforms of 1967. The* gremialistas, *however, are not traditional rightists. Closer to corporatism,* gremialismo *demands autonomy and independence of mediating bodies. It began by opposing the intervention of political parties in the university setting, and*

117

later rejected such intervention in society as a whole—an ideology that was adopted and enthusiastically promoted by General Pinochet.

Chadwick believed in the political project of the government, and after a decade—he is now married with four children—he goes on thinking that Pinochet is taking the country toward democracy. He knows the general personally and has never questioned his authority.

I found out about the coup from the radio like everyone else. I don't remember it very well, only that that morning I had gone to mass, and I learned about Allende's death there. I was sad.

I was confused because my friends were so pleased. My wife's family, neighbors, friends, the community . . . everyone was happy. It one big celebration, the opposite of what I was feeling; because the way I felt was pretty unusual in the circles I was part of.

I sympathized with Popular Unity, and it was a very violent occasion for me, mixed with sadness, frustration, and the feeling of being caught up in something strange and incomprehensible. My memories are of sadness, confusion, and fear. Fear, not for myself, but for my sister and José Antonio.* We didn't know what would happen to them. Those were very bleak days.

At home we were very much afraid, and we all tried to help José Antonio. I remember he actually thought that nothing would happen—that the coup had been predicted and that it wouldn't have any major consequences. My father insisted that he had to protect himself, and we all helped.

My sister came to my house with her two small daughters. It was frightening to be watching television and to hear José Antonio's name read off the lists. These were lists of people required to present themselves, to make statements. That, together with Allende's death and the bombing of La Moneda, was very disturbing, and we began to realize that all of this was going to have a much larger effect than

---

* Chadwick's brother-in-law, José Antonio Viera Gallo, director of MAPU and undersecretary of justice during the Popular Unity government.

we had thought. It was something bigger and unknown. A person as near to us as José Antonio, whom I saw every day, was wanted by the government, by the military, and had to hide and leave the country!

The rest of my family were almost all Christian Democrats and opposed to Popular Unity, but in my house we had always put family unity above political unity. Everyone was very concerned about my brother-in-law.

I was the only Allende supporter in the house, and I had to burn all of my things in the back yard. It was ridiculous! But a kind of fear had set in because no one knew the dimensions of what was happening. Since they were looking for José Antonio, they were permitted to search the house, and I had a lot of things in my room—typical leftist, adolescent stuff such as posters, books, and flyers that I had to get rid of. They made me burn everything! At first I resisted, but then I realized I was worrying my parents and that it was senseless.

From today's perspective I see that the moment I burned the books, I burned everything, and I erased an entire phase.

I can see now, also, that things got a bit out of hand.

I had been involved in something very idealistic, in an atmosphere totally contrary to my beliefs. I was in my last year of high school at Verbo Divino, and I was a supporter of MAPU. I was one of the very few government supporters at the school. But I wasn't active. During Popular Unity I was more of an observer.

I think that Popular Unity tried to unite a form of Christianity with the inspiration of a socialist society, and as a result, I was attracted to MAPU. It wasn't a purely political issue; I was greatly influenced by José Antonio because we were such close friends. Toward the end of Popular Unity I became disillusioned, but the coup was too abrupt an ending; it was as if I had been sparring with something and suddenly got knocked out.

I began a process of complete revision. I finished school totally disillusioned with idealism, thinking I would start college with a completely professional outlook, ready to explore, discuss, look for new ideas, and ready to keep quiet. I had the feeling of having gotten in over my head without really knowing why.

The worst part was that my friends thought I was a snob. "You have everything," they accused me. "Everything comes easy to you." It was like being the contrary-little-leftist. That was the worst because, before the coup, I was ready to take on anything—even to change my life-style or go to live somewhere completely different. I don't know if I was hurt because they didn't understand me or because I felt that they were right. Looking back, I think it was the latter.

CONVERSION TO GREMIALISMO

In '74 I began to study law at the Catholic University. I liked sociology and political science best, but after the eleventh of September becoming a lawyer seemed a way to find some kind of personal peace. I felt I had been doing too many unconventional things, and I wanted to find something more family-oriented, better suited to my girlfriend, Victoria . . . it was a way of finding room for both my political and job-related worries and my other concerns.

When I decided to study law, I chose the University of Chile. There was no way I would go to Catholic University with all the *gremialistas!* That was the last place you'd find me . . .

I enrolled at the University of Chile, with the idea of leaving my old environment behind and finding something that felt more appropriate. At the Catholic University I thought I would constantly be faced with a gap between my own thoughts and beliefs and those of the people I met. That's exhausting; it's hard work; it's much more natural to be around people who think the way you do. I saw that Chile University was a much bigger and broader university, with a different kind of tradition.

I enrolled one morning, and when I told Victoria and my family, they thought I was crazy, that I was doing it to hurt them, that I was doing it for some new political involvement. Victoria argued very strongly against it:

"Please," she begged me, "go to the Catholic University. Why do you keep on hurting us? You've managed to calm your life down, and Catholic will be much better for you."

By two in the afternon I was enrolled at Catholic University, thanks to an empty seat and some bending of the rules. I don't have a rational explanation for what I did; it was more an intuition that, as things turned out, marked a significant turning point in my life.

That was how I got to know Jaime Guzmán, who was a teacher of mine the first year. I was worried at first about being in a school that trained *gremialistas,* scared that they would make life impossible for me, even though I didn't speak up or do anything. But just the opposite happened: it was a very warm atmosphere. I was treated with great respect; no one said anything to me or tried to convert me or get me involved with anything outside the school. At the same time, no one from the other side approached me either, or implied that I should join a particular group of people: "Since you're one of us, why not join such-and-such a group?" There was nothing like that.

That kind of basic respect may be normal, but it meant a lot to me because I had been so worried.

The other thing I noticed was that, for the first time, I was hearing ideologies that were different from mine presented in a rational, coherent, and thoughtful way. For the first time I was able to discuss, analyze, and debate these ideas. In high school I had read a lot, because I was interested in politics, but I had not discussed things with anyone. In college it was different—there were people with positions that were clearly different from mine, but interesting, well thought out, not just slogans recited by rote or merely self-interested stances. These were people who all had a similar idealism and who brought it to bear on different causes. They had the same vocation, the same goals, they renounced the same things I renounced in a similar fashion. So little by little my political interests were awakened. Basically because of Jaime Guzmán.

Some people are embarrassed or afraid to name the people who have influenced them. But, just as in grade school José Antonio had had the greatest influence on me, in the university Jaime represented the same things from a different perspective. It was a very strong, very positive influence. After he was no longer my teacher, we continued to be friends, and when I ended my term as president of

FEUC* I went on to be his assistant for two classes. He is one of my best friends to this day. We became friends outside politics, where we thought completely differently. Over a period of time we had long discussions, which motivated me more and more.

I had an emotional understanding of Popular Unity, and now I was beginning to form a rational understanding that allowed me to perceive the bad as well as the good and to examine them from a different angle. I was studying Marxism, trying to understand exactly what it was, and becoming disillusioned as I found out. Although I had never been a Marxist, it had always held a certain attraction for me.

My first conversion, you could say, was to corporatism, was to the Movimiento Gremial Universitario. That was the first new thing that attracted me, once everything else had collapsed and my mind was free. At the same time I began to be able to justify the government and what it was doing. It is a very different approach from that of my friends, because they have an emotional relationship with the government, and for them September eleventh was a true liberation. My relationship, on the other hand, is rational; I came to my belief slowly, coming to understand the political project that was taking shape rather than feeling a gut identification with the government when it took power. My enthusiasm was for a project that was independent of the military and their coup. The political project struck me as interesting, novel, and attractive. I believed in certain things and thought they offered a good solution for the country.

TURNING OVER A NEW LEAF

I was always aware of what exactly was going on, of what was really happening, because a lot of changes are claimed that have never actually been proved. I believe there were three separate phases with respect to human rights. Initially there was a confrontational situation where excesses were committed as a result of the incredible

* A student organization at the Catholic University.

instability, because '73 was a year of great upheaval. In retrospect, it's clear how close we were to civil war; the armed forces had to take control to normalize and restore peace to the country, and that meant people were arrested, people went into exile, and people had to give up many things they were accustomed to doing. I think this was a classic example of life during a confrontational period. But then, once the government was installed, and it was assured of social tranquillity, I think there were excesses that were not justified or legitimate from any point of view. That includes the establishment and the actions of the DINA headed by Manuel Contreras. Later, thank God, when Contreras had left and there were more controls and greater accountability, the situation became more rational, more logical, more natural, and more peaceful in both the public and the political spheres.

When these kinds of abuses occur, I think the moral thing to do is to denounce them and try to prevent their ever recurring. The opposition limit themselves to publicly denouncing that kind of behavior; on the other hand, we supporters have inside routes for trying to head off mistakes, and the group I belong to has actually made all the accusations. For instance, we have been especially concerned with establishing strict controls over the security organizations, and we point out the evil that resulted from Contreras's behavior.

The Lonquén affair* had a very great, very powerful impact, but I think that those kinds of actions were clearly a part of that first phase, during the initial clash. In that sense, the amnesty that was granted in '78 or '79 has tended to clear things up—it was a very broad amnesty meant to put an end to a situation no one liked, but which did exist and for which we are all responsible. I'm not trying to make the guilty parties blameless, just to turn over a new leaf. I know there is a price for this and that it is very difficult for those who were affected to accept, but it is necessary for the mental health of the country, so that we may continue to exist as a country.

---

* Lonquén is a place near Santiago where, in November 1978, two abandoned lime-processing ovens were discovered containing the remains of the bodies of fifteen local laborers who had been missing since 1973.

IDEOLOGICAL WORK

Long before saying "I'm a *gremialista!*" I was absolutely convinced that I had been wrong, that I had been mistaken during Popular Unity. I was convinced of the value of what *gremialismo* had to offer in the university and of the interesting things that might result from the political project that had begun with the new institutional order. They weren't proposing a traditional military coup, but a very important political project. I was sure of that, and I began to enjoy political life, not ideologically as I had at seventeen, but vocationally. Nevertheless, despite having convinced myself intellectually, at first I had decided not to take any action.

I spent a long time thinking . . . "I don't want to appear a traitor, I'm going to look like a traitor, they're going to label me a traitor . . ." One creates a whole fantasy world. Probably what I did hadn't the slightest importance to anyone else, but these thoughts caused me to isolate myself for a long time.

One Sunday I was thinking the subject through. I remember distinctly that, in the middle of the night, I decided, and I called Jaime. "Look," I said, "I know I have a lot of shortcomings, but, if I can be useful in some way, count me in as a *gremialista* right now."

From then on I had a good relationship with the *gremialistas;* they invited me to their meetings, I began to participate in various ways, and in '77 they elected me head of the Catholic *gremialista* movement. It was a vote of confidence, of endorsement, solidarity, and loyalty to my ideas. Still, I don't like the public side; it makes me nervous. I know this is part of what has to be done, and I do it because it helps the cause, but it's more of an imposition than a pleasure.

In '78 I was the president of FEUC, and that was really a public post, with public responsibilities, because it entailed a very strong *gremialista* tradition. My job was to further student participation, and to have it approved by the student bodies and the university authorities, at a time when all talk of elections and related things was taboo.

Then I took a break, took my degree exams, and got married. I began to work as a lawyer and spent the rest of my time working for the Youth Front. The truth is that I worked the minimum required of me so that I would have plenty of free time, because I was more interested in politics. I began to develop my ideological work in several different areas, not just in the university, because the new Constitution project was beginning to establish itself.

As a youth leader, I felt that the Chacarillas rally* was the most important political event, because that was where the president took the first step toward an institutional order, and he chose young people as his audience. It was my job to participate actively in organizing that kind of event, and I found it very exciting because my political path began to be clear to me. Philosophical statements were replaced with a political project. Then came the Constitutional plebiscite of 1980.

TOWARD DEMOCRACY

I have no doubt that Pinochet will take us to democracy, not only because I believe in him but because—apart from him—we have a democratic constitution. I have no reason to think otherwise. Why should I, when General Pinochet himself has sworn his allegiance to the Constitution and has marked out a course toward democracy?

There may be a lot of different opinions on the subject, but they all agree that Pinochet accomplishes things. For whatever reason, he created a constitution; for whatever reasons, he established an agenda; and now he says that there will be a plebiscite, a parliament, and that we will continue to go forward. It's clear that we have a broader, more open political climate today than six months ago, at the beginning of '83.

Looking ahead, I'm worried about a polarization of the different sides and about irrationality on both sides, about closing ourselves off rather than searching for common goals. I'm worried because suddenly there are indications that such a situation could evolve, but at the same time, I have faith and confidence that sanity and responsibility will prevail.

It is important that everyone, no matter what difficulties they have

---

* The annual rally at Chacarillas, a section of Santiago, is where Pinochet meets with youthful supporters of the regime; it is also where, for the first time, in 1977, he put forth the idea of a transitional process that would limit the duration of the military government.

faced, realize that not only Pinochet is involved but the armed forces as well, and that they must come out of this with as much dignity as possible, as much respect as possible, because that will help everyone; it will help the country. To reach the stable democracy we seek, we will have to be sufficiently mature to face our political past, with all its flaws and all its strengths.

I think there are a lot of people trying to make the *gremialistas* into whipping boys. I'm not afraid. I would be afraid if I felt morally responsible for any wrongdoing or any political mistake, but I don't think that is the case. In politics, when you act morally, according to principle, you have to be prepared for both favorable and unfavorable circumstances. I personally have survived good times, and hope not to give in or be afraid in bad times. If we must assume responsibilities, no matter how difficult they may be, then assume them we must.

THE REBELLION OF AN OLD-FASHIONED PRIEST

DAMIÁN ACUÑA JARPA

BEING NAMED VICAR OF NORTH SANTIAGO IN 1981 SCARED him enormously. At sixty-four, after a decade as parish priest in the little village of Buin, he thought his mission was finally over. He didn't know that he still had lots to do as part of a church whose role in Chilean society has increased enormously during Pinochet's government.

The Catholic Church has been the only real counterbalance to the dictatorship. Since the very beginning it has defended the victims, and under its protection a wide range of social organizations, destroyed by the military coup, were rebuilt. Under these circumstances, Father Damián never imagined that Cardinal Raúl Silva Henríquez would send him to replace Monsignor Jorge Hourton, one of the most energetic defenders of human rights under Pinochet.

While he shuddered at the responsibility of leading a "politicized, leftist" vicariate, his new parishioners turned up their noses at the arrival of a village priest who knew little or nothing about their problems.

It's been almost three years now, and all of his worries seem to have disappeared. On the contrary, the fervor with which he defends his ideas and his

*outspoken analysis of what's happened in Chile show that he has wholeheart-
edly adopted the tradition of his vicariate. "I realized," he explains, "that the
reputation of this area stems from the fact that here, the Church is deeply
involved with the people." And that is precisely what he has tried to achieve
during his forty-four years of priesthood.*

*During the Allende government, he didn't like to see poor people waiting
in line for bread; he didn't celebrate the coup by ringing the bells of his parish;
he was horrified by the shootings and disappearances; and he is committed to
educating people so that "they will recognize their rights and not allow themselves to be defeated."*

*In the fifties he was an honorary chaplain in the army, and he acknowl-
edges that, as a man of order and authority, he sympathizes with his "military
brothers." Nevertheless, he was quickly disillusioned by their "uselessness"
and, in fact, considers the National Security Doctrine by which the country is
governed "horrifying."*

I avidly wanted a change of government. I am an orderly man who
appreciates authority, and I think that the Allende years were very
difficult for all of us.

It was a time of great disorder and violence. Allende may have
had good intentions, but his followers undermined order and peace,
instilled a lack of confidence, divided the family, and above all, made
the poor suffer. The scarcity of essential goods was horrifying—
people couldn't even get a loaf of bread, not to mention meat! The
situation was terrible, and I felt a tremendous inner rebellion against
a government that wasn't even able to provide its people with food.

I was the parish priest at Buin, and on the eleventh I had gone to
celebrate mass near Linderos. Suddenly, about eight-fifteen in the
morning, I heard the news on the radio . . . At first I was happy, but
a few minutes later it hit me and I realized that horror was to come.

Everyone had gone outside to celebrate, and a group came and
asked me to hang banners and ring the bells, but I had the sense to
realize immediately that I was a priest for everyone, without exception, and if I had a preference for one group, I couldn't humiliate
or ignore another. I told them I wouldn't do anything, because this

was a painful day. Since many of them were aware of my personal feelings—because without ever having been political, I had expressed my thoughts in church—they were surprised by my attitude.

I would have liked things to happen differently—for a different group of people to have surrounded Allende and exercised more control over those making all the trouble. But when change came that abruptly and violently, it had a tremendous effect on me—it was a shock. September 11, 1973, was like the day when the poor man with a gangrenous leg decided to cut it off to save his life. It was a day of liberation from something that could have been much more serious, but the price paid was too high.

I have always been a rebel, and I immediately rebelled against the violent situation that followed the coup. Even more so two or three days later when reports of all the victims began to come in. Along the highway to Santiago I saw three bodies next to the wall of the Metropolitan Cemetery. It was eight-thirty in the morning, and there was fresh blood on the ground! The next day there were two more bodies that stayed there unburied until the afternoon. We were in a regime of organized terror.

They installed permanent military patrols; girls were forbidden to wear pants, and boys were forbidden to have long hair. I saw all of this! Three or four air force cadets with their faces blackened would get out of a van, grab a boy on the street in the middle of the morning, and take him to the nearest barber shop. If the kid resisted, they would hit him with the butts of their guns. This all happened very early on, as if part of an effort to purify the atmosphere. Anyone with long hair was considered an extremist.

I also saw a jeep pull up in front of the government building in Buin and brake sharply to let out a whole lot of soldiers, who then spread out across the plaza, pointing their machine guns at everyone they met. And all because their commander was coming in the next car.

These people believe that to save the country we have to get rid of all the opposition and employ brutality and cruelty toward anyone who thinks differently—even if they think that way because they were taken in by false promises. Anyone with a gun has a right to judge everyone else, and what is worse, to make decisions about other people's lives. The result was a massacre of humble people who often had nothing to do with anything.

Friends of mine who knew me well began to worry about me because I was in such a rebellious mood. At mass on September 18, I read a text from the prophet Daniel that says: "We are a subdued people, a humiliated people, with no place to gather." And this astonished many people. I appeared to be against the regime.

Another time I asked God for good, clear-thinking people to govern, especially to help those who suffered and remained silent. Suspicious minds saw this as a way of speaking out against an authority that was not doing these things. They made crude accusations against me to the governor, who was the director of the infantry school in San Bernardo, and he ordered his police to follow this seditious priest of Buin. They even tried to have me moved to some honorific post so that I wouldn't feel the impact as strongly.

TERRORISM: ACTUAL CASES

Immediately after the eleventh people began to be afraid. Many didn't even dare to ask for help—they didn't want to know anything about anything, they just wanted to hide their pasts. Some of them came in to ask for advice or to turn in a weapon they had had hidden so that we could give it to the authorities. That was one of the Church's roles during the first few days.

I saw fear painted on everyone's face, including the faces of members of the regime, where I saw it even though it was concealed. Everyone was very careful about what he said, because during a trivial local dispute a neighbor could accuse you of being an extremist, which could lead to arrest. Out of fear, no one spoke and no one dared to discuss things that had happened to them. For example, some people who I'm sure were tortured would assure me they were fine when I met with them.

I remember in particular the case of a plumber working for the National Health Service who was also a member of the Communist Party. We had spoken, and I knew he was deeply committed to Marxism. One day he came to speak to me privately and asked me as a favor to direct him to a convent or other religious institution where he could work as a gardener and not have to leave or be in contact with anyone, because he wanted to live a life of solitude for a while.

"But what's happened to you?"

"Nothing. Nothing's happened."

That was his answer, even though I knew that he had recently been dismissed from the hospital where he worked, had been arrested, and had been tortured for the names of others. He was incredibly scared.

In another case I had to talk someone out of committing suicide. People who had been arrested at the very beginning were panicked by the thought of its happening again, and I knew several people who preferred suicide to going through that hell twice.

We were faced with some very difficult things in '73 . . .

The April 24 Settlement, where some twenty families lived, was invaded at four in the morning by a group in a panel truck. They found the people they wanted and made them get into the truck. They said they were going to take them to San Bernardo to get some information, and that they would bring them back afterwards. We never heard from them again.

The same thing happened in Viña Escorial. A brother of mine worked there as the right-hand man to the boss, and he had to leave in '71 when the farm was taken over by the workers. At the beginning of October of '73, the owner of the farm showed up to ask for my brother's address.

"Things have happened," I told him.

"Yes," he answered, "and a lot more's going to happen. I'm looking for your brother so that he can point out people who are making trouble, because those people must be punished."

The farm was at the foot of the mountains, and there was a small path leading up to it. At about five in the morning, the truck stopped at the first house, and people began to get in. By the time it was light, at about seven-thirty, the truck was on its way back down. The men were waving from the back of the truck, and the women and children looking at them were sure they would come back soon. They thought they were going to San Bernardo, but when it got to the gate, the truck turned the other way. At first people thought they were being held somewhere, and they ran around, abandoning everything, trying to get information, to see lists with their names on them, or to ask questions in the government offices. If someone so much as said, "You can find them at midnight on the bridge at the San Cristóbal pass," off they would go with their little bundle of clothing, their tortilla, and their little bit of meat to take to the poor soul who'd been arrested. But everywhere it was the same story: "He's not here." Even Bonilla* made inquiries, but no one knew anything about them. They had disappeared.

One day the women of Escorial heard from some people who had gone up into the hills hunting rabbits about a pile of human remains they had found. They went up and recognized the clothing of their husbands and their sons. In the middle of February '74 a judge from Buin ordered the police to bring down the bodies and examine them, even though four or five months had gone by and the bodies had been discovered by birds and dogs and rodents. The bones were still there and the people from Escorial knew they belonged to their relatives. Moreover, the number of skeletons coincided with the number who had disappeared from Escorial, because, confidentially, a *carabinero*—whose name I wouldn't reveal even under torture—told me how many skulls they had thrown away.

They named a special judge to investigate—he was a good man, respectful of the law of God and upright, but he was up against a stone wall. Some police who were not complete supporters of the regime told me that they had had to support their colleagues, attesting to their innocence when they knew the men hadn't acted correctly.

These are true stories! I saw the tremendous problems that arose for the women who were left alone and the moral dilemma they were faced with. They had to keep on farming, and in most cases they accepted the help of a male friend, and because they were living in the same house, they would become intimate. On the one hand, these women wanted to find their husbands, but on the other, they felt it

---

* General Oscar Bonilla, Pinochet's first minister of the interior.

might be better if their husbands didn't show up because they would be caught with another man and fights would ensue.

I don't endorse these attitudes, but I understand them. These women aren't able to opt for heroic or saintly virtue, remaining faithful to their disappeared; they need someone to help them with their farmwork so they can keep eating.

Knowing all these things fueled an enormous spirit of rebellion inside me. And it's something I still feel against a regime that has wrought terror in Chile, that has brought terrorism to the country. I don't know who's behind all of this, but it has been allowed to go on, and it has been tolerated in the name of national security and of peace—the peace of the graveyard.

I remember a poor Spanish priest I knew, Juan Alsina, who was found dead in the Mapocho River. We had very different ideas, and I never agreed with him. I thought his job in the National Health Service was inappropriate for him because I felt he had a much more important mission in life. He became staff manager at the San Juan de Dios Hospital.

The day of the coup, since his office was closed, he returned home to San Bernardo, where he lived with some other priests. When he went back to the hospital, some soldiers went to look for him and officially nothing has been known about him since. But a few days later, his body appeared under the Manuel Rodríguez Bridge totally naked . . . The friends who were looking for him went to the morgue and they recognized him. They were told that he had tried to steal a guard's weapon, which is false—absolutely false! Some captain simply decided to eliminate him, thinking perhaps that he was ridding the country of a serious threat.

Another priest was arrested in Cartagena along with two friends. He worked in a sanitation plant, and they accused him of wanting to poison the drinking water as an act of sabotage. They sent the priest into exile, but they killed his two friends. According to the military, they also had tried to steal weapons from a guard. Enormous lies!

The executions continued into '74. In Buin two men with a certain reputation in the neighborhood were arrested at dawn, and by ten o'clock in the morning they were corpses. Neither of them was a Christian, but one of them was president of the Rotary Club, and in

July I had attended a swearing-in ceremony at which he made a speech that I found very interesting. He told the story of the boy who goes into a church with his father and asks:

"Who are those men?"

"They're saints," responds his father.

"Why are they saints?"

"Because they let the light shine through."

I heard those words around July 15, and less than a month later, on August 13, that man was dead. He was a good doctor who was inclined to help everyone, and who wasn't interested in financial gain. People came to see him even on Sundays or in the middle of the night. He was a Socialist, and they arrested him along with a Communist leader.

They came to his house at dawn. His wife told him to take a blanket. But the person in charge of arresting him—an official or subofficial—explained:

"Don't take the blanket; where you're going, you won't need it. If you go to heaven, it won't be necessary, and if you go to hell, you won't need any protection against the cold."

His wife and family all heard this.

After they killed him, they spread lies about him in the community. They said that the two men had an understanding with three or four bakeries that on a predetermined day they would poison the bread. The families were not even permitted to have a funeral, and they had to take the body directly from the morgue to the cemetery. Rumors and lies spread everywhere, and people accepted them without further discussion. For the simple townspeople, the media have enormous power, and whatever comes out in the newspapers or on the radio is very difficult for them to discredit. I remembered that according to Nero, the Christians burned Rome.

FOR A MESS OF POTTAGE

For some twelve or thirteen years I was a military chaplain. I knew the military firsthand, and I sympathized with them. I was young at that time, and since I like order, I thought I could perform a valuable service. I was an honorary chaplain, and when they wanted to enroll me in the army, fortunately God liberated me. As time went by, I got to know my good military brothers, and I learned about their inefficiency. I could give you fifty examples. In '58, for instance, when the earthquake happened, I witnessed how it took the regiment several days to study the exact weight of the bread they needed to prepare for the injured.

They're ignorant and clumsy, because the best soldier is the one who does the least thinking. They are not allowed to think, and must carry out orders no matter what they are. It's the law! But I never would have imagined the things that I saw happen under the present regime. When I was there in the 1950s, there was a little more respect. There were certain punishments and sanctions within the military life, but it was different.

Now they have discovered the National Security Doctrine, a doctrine that uses the word "Fatherland" in capital letters and places Chile above all else. But anyone with even a little Christian spirit realizes that Chile means Chileans, that it is the human being who counts, that this other patriotic concept they use to exalt everything, this enormous worship of the country, is a fiction. It's a way of asking for and demanding a variety of things for the sake of a fictional entity. What really counts is the man, the person.

The famous National Security Doctrine is a true horror. It's even worse with those boys who thought they could save the economy, and who, in fact, have returned our country to what it was a century ago, to the most savage kind of libertarianism. He who can does, and he who can't gets crushed. The latter is not entitled to light, to gas, to anything. He's completely cut off. That's what has happened, and that is why I am rebellious.

Only in the last few years have people begun to open their eyes as they become unemployed or lack adequate medical care.

I'm a little older now, and I know that in the past our community didn't dress very well and didn't have all the conveniences, but we were well fed. There was milk in every house, and no matter how poor you were, you had something to eat. Obviously, this government didn't invent poverty, it has always existed, but I've never seen as much misery as this—though there is no question that for a few years our country was plagued by consumerism. I remember one Christmas that bicycles and televisions were everywhere when people didn't even have enough food. This whole business of importation seemed to me like the arrival of the Spaniards in Latin America. The Indians gave the conquistadors gold in exchange for a little bread or some other trifle; our community gave up its freedom for the promises of a man who said that one out of every five Chileans was going to have a car, that he didn't want proletarians but proprietors, and that he was going to build I don't know how many houses.

The same thing happened as in the book of Exodus when, in the desert, the people of Israel rebelled against Moses. They missed the onions and the garlic they'd had in Egypt, they missed the food they'd had as slaves, and they had no appreciation for freedom and the right of self-government. Our community has allowed itself to trade its birthright for a mess of pottage, and today has reached the highest point of its misery.

This situation reflects the poor education of our community. During the last few years in which I have assumed other responsibilities in Santiago, I have been very busy trying to get people to open their eyes, to recognize they have precious dignity, to know they are not owned by anyone. They must be able to control their destinies, to seek excellence. That's what I am trying to spread from the Northern Regional Vicariate. I repeat over and over that they must forget about the Mother Church, that they must free themselves of their ties to the Church and initiate their own actions.

I'm not a Marxist; I am completely the opposite. But I have to admit that certain Marxists or certain leftists have my sympathy because they accept responsibilities that Christians and people of the right don't want to assume. In San Antonio, for example, where there was terrible oppression because Señor Contreras* was director of the military school, they tried to find lawyers to defend people who had been arrested, and no professionals of the right or the center were willing to help. The people who took on these cases were Marxists, just as they were the ones who volunteered at the Vicariate

* Colonel Manuel Contreras, former head of the DINA.

of Solidarity and other organizations. That's why people say that the Church has been infiltrated. They go so far as to label us Marxists because we speak of the people's right to work or their right to health.

TERRIBLE RESIGNATION

If I was ever scared, it was when I came to Santiago to run the Northern Regional Vicariate. It had a reputation for being very politicized and very leftist . . . there had been long hunger strikes in the parishes of this zone.

Given my age—I'm sixty-seven now—I had thought that when I left Buin I would be posted somewhere with fewer responsibilities. But in '81 I was named vicar, and since I respect hierarchies and order, I didn't put up a fuss.

I knew barely five out of fifty priests in this area, and I was worried that I wouldn't know how to lead or direct all those people. From a distance, things seem enormous. I thought about changes in the Church and the fact that people don't follow blindly any more. In the past the word of the superior went without question; now, instead, true obedience involves dialogue. But I had learned obedience in an earlier era, and I was worried that I wouldn't be able to change my attitude.

Once I arrived, things were very different from what I had imagined. I met priests and other religious people who had completely adopted the life-style of the poor. I was struck by their humble, precarious lives lived at the same level as the people in the slums. These are truly worthy and generous people. I realized that this zone was so famous because the Church here was involved with the community. This is perhaps the zone of Santiago where poverty is most evenly distributed, because we have no rich people here and no middle class, only a few professionals who practice in this area but live elsewhere.

We are accused of promoting protests, but it isn't true. What we do promote is people. That's the Church's role, and promoting people means helping them and motivating them to achieve more. A famous adage says that if someone asks you for a fish, don't give him a fish, give him a fishing rod. That's what it means to motivate people. It's all summed up in a statement: Discover your dignity, your human rights; don't let them get you down, don't bow your head.

As a result of the protests, I've encountered a resignation that I consider terrible. There are people that I have begged to turn in a denunciation and pursue it through the courts, but they allow themselves to be browbeaten and don't follow through. People start to take legal action and then, evidently, they get thrown up against an impenetrable wall of bureaucracy and legalese, on top of which they are threatened and intimidated. That makes me despair.

I had a man come in whose wife had been killed. I think it was in August, when Pinochet sent his 18,000 troops out into the street, and they killed this poor woman from La Pincoya inside her house. It was about eleven at night, she was going from one room to another, they were shooting at the houses, and a bullet practically took her head off. Her husband filed a complaint, but later he wouldn't press charges, and he never took any legal steps. He was afraid. Afraid of the consequences, because he's a teacher and he depends on the state. He came to talk with me because he wanted to transfer one of his children to a different school, since he needed to have all three in one place to cut down on transportation costs. That's the only thing that concerned him.

In another protest, which took place near the Juan Antonio Ríos shantytown, a twenty-four-year-old man died. His family spoke with me, and I persuaded them to file a complaint, because if they didn't, I told them, these things would continue to happen and more people would die. They took the first steps, but a few days later a policeman guarding the house of a judge was killed, and this family was accused of participating in the attack.

The brother of the man who had died was in this vicariate when the police were looking for him, and we had to hide him so he wouldn't be taken, but they arrested his sister-in-law. They let her go since she wasn't guilty of anything, but after that no one dared to follow through on the report.

If we don't denounce and report all of this, things will go from bad to worse. We're looking not for vengeance but for correction. I don't think the police would act the same way if they were sanctioned when they overstepped their authority, if someone brought it to their attention, and if they were required to justify their use of weapons.

A policeman is a human being like anyone else; he has a wife, he loves his children and wants to educate them and worries about them. But when he is faced with *esprit de corps* and someone else is in control, he becomes a veritable puppet. He is made to live in a very different fashion, and that predisposes him psychologically to violence. A policeman should be a professional who isn't upset by slogans or stones. If a boy takes a shot at him with a slingshot, he cannot respond with gunfire.

There is hate and there is fear. This is an intimidated and humiliated country.

I think Pinochet should start to withdraw a little. He and his whole crew—everyone who is wielding power and enjoying it—should pull back and allow the people to decide things for themselves, so that the natural leaders may emerge and take responsibility for the advancement of the country.

The Church is not getting any stronger this way, because it is being asked to involve itself in affairs that don't concern it. It is being called on to resolve marital problems, and in those cases the only loser is the one who settles the dispute. Please, God, don't let the Church assume leadership in areas that don't concern it!

TO DISAPPEAR IS NOT TO DIE

ELSA ESQUIVEL ROJO

S
HE DOESN'T KNOW EXACTLY WHEN HER SON LUIS STOPPED
being "detained" and started being "disappeared." She doesn't know
because—although it's difficult to believe—after nine years she still
hopes to find him alive.

But together with this hope is the anguish of not knowing whether he
is hungry or cold, whether he has shelter from the rain, or if he has lost his
mind from so much suffering.

Hers is not an isolated case. There are too many mothers on this continent
who feel the same way. Their sons were arrested one day and taken who knows
where. Nobody heard from them again. For years the government denied the
facts. But of the 758 cases that have been presented to the Chilean courts by
the Catholic Church, 52 have been resolved. The corpses had been secretly
buried. The people who were responsible—policemen, soldiers, and civilians
—have since been set free under a general amnesty.

We spoke for many hours. She insisted on describing in detail everything
that has happened to her and everything she has done during all these years.

I tried to discover what it feels like to be the protagonist of a horor story of our time. It wasn't easy for her to unmask herself—the mask is the protection she needs to go on living with one son disappeared, another in exile, and her marriage about to fall apart because she can't stop searching.

They arrested Lucho a year after the coup—November 20, 1974.

Our other son, Carlos Antonio, was in high school and that day he had gone to borrow an English book from his brother. When he got to the apartment, the DINA were there. They had my daughter-in-law, and they said that if she didn't tell them everything she knew, they would get the girls. They took Carlos too and interrogated him about Lucho's activities, but neither of them knew anything.

Lucho was a member of the MIR, and during the Popular Unity government he had participated in the factory takeovers. He worked with concrete mixers at Ready Mix, and on September 11 they had planned to defend themselves. But when the soldiers arrived on the fourth day, they put down their arms; some people had already left the factory, and the rest climbed over the walls so they wouldn't be arrested. He came home shocked, and told us how there were plenty of corpses around.

Then we began to see corpses near the house, too. There were dead men clutching the lunch pails they had been taking to work with them. This coup business was incredible!

I remember that it was on Tuesday, because it was a market day. We had gone shopping, and when we heard the news we came back. In our community a lot of people were in favor of the coup, and as soon as they found out they hung flags and began to celebrate. But at night the gunfire was tremendous, because the people from Santa Adriana, the community across the street, confronted the soldiers. Since my house is on the corner, the bullets hit the wall and we had to stay inside.

Lucho said it would go on for a long time and that we had to prepare ourselves for what was to come, that it would be very difficult. He and his friends organized themselves and continued their political work. He couldn't go back to the factory because he had been fired, but he got by teaching English at a high school.

They didn't live with us, but sometimes my son got together with his friends at my house. I was very close to him, and he let me in on some of his secrets and told me about some of his activities. He treated me like a friend, mostly, so that people wouldn't realize I was his mother. A comrade found out once, though, when my daughter, who was young at the time, showed him a picture of Lucho with the rest of us.

I didn't take part in the meetings; they went into the bedroom and shut the door, and I brought them lunch. They brought a little bread or something else to eat, and I would make them a pot of beans and serve it to them.

My husband didn't know anything; he doesn't like politics—he's apolitical. He'd leave for work in the morning and wouldn't get back until night, so that there would be a few hours after they had left to clean up a little and get rid of the smoke. He began to pay attention when the MIR leader Miguel Enríquez died, because my son and a friend of his arrived very upset. I don't remember if they actually cried, but they were very upset.

My husband had always fought a lot with Lucho. He told him that he wouldn't get anything out of politics, that there were too many different parties, and that the workers had used the Popular Unity government as a free ride and stopped working. After the coup, he recommended that Lucho get out of politics, take his wife and daughters, and go to a different country. But Lucho never wanted to. He said that the bastards should be overcome, that the fight was here, and that he was going to stay. Even now my husband insists that he disappeared because he wouldn't listen.

My daughter-in-law didn't like what he was doing either. They fought a lot and almost got divorced. Lucho spent a lot of time away from home, out in the slums, until he had very little clothing left at the apartment. But the night before they took him he had slept there. He went out in the morning, and about half an hour later they arrested him on the street.

We found this out sometime later because people who knew him from the neighborhood told my daughter-in-law they had seen him taken away in a car. They said that he had tried to call attention to himself, to let someone know so they could pass the word along . . . But I don't even know exactly who saw him because they were scared and no one wanted to testify. Everyone was afraid to make a statement.

At about three that afternoon the DINA came to search the house. They told my daughter-in-law they had arrested Lucho, and they began to break things, looking for weapons. They lifted up boxes of books and papers and, according to them, they found maps and a bomb big enough to destroy the entire town. But no one else saw the bomb. Whenever they take someone in, they say they've found arms.

They kept Carlos until about eleven at night, and then they left him along the Pan-American Highway. They told him to run home, that if he didn't run they would kill him. He got here about to collapse from so much running.

He told us everything that had happened, and we got very upset. We were afraid they would come to search our house, but nothing happened. Lucho had warned me:

"Look, Mom," he said, "if anyone arrests me and they say they're going to kill me if you don't tell them who my friends are, let them kill me, but don't say a word; don't give them a single name. I know that the day they arrest me, I won't be seen again."

It was something he had inside . . . From all he did and everything I've learned since, I think he must have had an important position, because they certainly made him disappear!

The next day I went to Lucho's apartment very early to see what had happened and to try to find out where they had taken him. My daughter-in-law was very frightened and asked me not to do anything because they might hurt her, but I still found out about the existence of the Committee for Peace,* and I began to take the appropriate steps.

For a long time my daughter-in-law behaved badly. After two

---

* Cooperative Committee for Peace in Chile, an ecumenical organization involving the Catholic Church, the evangelical churches, the Orthodox Church, and the Jewish community.

months she had to leave the apartment because she couldn't pay the rent, and she went to live with her family. But they wouldn't take the children. I discussed it with my husband, and we took charge of the girls: the youngest was just eleven months. For years my daughter-in-law didn't concern herself with anything; she didn't know if the girls were alive or dead—nothing.

One day we ran into each other at the police department. They had called me in for information, and while I was waiting my daughter-in-law came out with a detective. They had called her too.

"Have you forgotten that you have children?"

"I don't come because you don't make me feel welcome," she answered.

"As their mother," I told her, "you should see them anyway."

That stage has passed, and now we are friends and she comes to see her daughters all the time. At first, it's true, there were a lot of hard feelings, because during her interrogation Carlos heard her give a lot of information about Lucho. Later, you could understand what she had been through. All the threats they made left her in a very bad state psychologically.

My son Eugenio was also upset by his brother's arrest. He was ten, and at Christmas they had to come get him with a stretcher because —from pure nerves—he became paralyzed from the waist down. He was very sick. He's in exile now because he decided to take up politics like his brother.

A very difficult stage of life began for me and for my marriage, starting with Lucho's arrest . . . I had to put housework aside to look for my son. I had to go out every day, and Eugenio and María Lina, the youngest, had to take care of everything. I never thought I would let my daughter do such work! She's the only girl, and while I had meant for her to have such an easy life, she ended up playing mother to everyone.

First we presented a writ of habeas corpus, and nothing happened. Then we presented another, and still nothing happened. To this day! They don't do anything with these writs except stick them away in a filing cabinet.

I went to all the detention centers and waited on enormous lines to get in and show my card. And everywhere it was the same thing:

"Who are you looking for?"

"Luis Omar Mahuida Esquivel."

"He's not here, señora," they would answer, and I would leave crying . . . He was twenty-six when they arrested him.

One day a teacher at the school where Lucho had taught came looking for me. She was the niece of Palestro, and they had taken her husband and were holding him at Tres Alamos.* During one of her visits he had told her that over the Christmas holidays they had moved a lot of people to Ritoque.† At about three in the morning, he told her, they had begun to read off names from a list, and he heard them say Mahuida.

On January 9 I went to Ritoque. Eugenio was convalescing by then and wanted to go with me so that he could see his brother. I took along a small package of clothing and some homemade bread for him. We thought we were going to find him! I prepared a thermos of milk and two hard-boiled eggs, and we left.

We took the train because my husband worked for the railroad and we had passes. I didn't know where Ritoque was, and at each station I would ask the conductor to let me know. I explained my situation to him and he was good enough to stop there, at a station in the middle of the desert. We figured out how to get to the camp, but when we got there they told me we needed a special permit from headquarters in Quintero in order to go in. I still didn't know if Lucho was there or not.

We started to walk toward Quintero. About halfway there a peasant came along in a cart and took us to the outskirts of the town. We kept walking until my son fainted from exhaustion. We had to get to the headquarters before two in order to get back to Ritoque. When we got there, it was closed. While we waited, my son fainted again, I took out the milk for him, and it had gone bad.

After hearing me out, they looked over some lists and told me I had no reason to go back to Ritoque since my son wasn't there.

---

* Mario Palestro was a former deputy of the Socialist Party. Tres Alamos was a prison camp in Santiago.

† A prison camp on the central coast.

I went to Puchuncaví, where there was another camp, but it was the same story. I practically lived at Tres Alamos in the hope that someone would have seen him and he'd turn up somewhere.

One day some girls came looking for me. They had been friends of my son and had been detained with him in a torture house over by Quilín. They had testified to the tribunals because, in that house, they were with three people who were among the disappeared. They said that one day Lucho was taken away, and he never came back. They also said that he was in terrible shape. These two friends went to France during the amnesty in '76, but while they were in Tres Alamos I clung to them because they were the last people to see my son.

"Mamita," they would say to me, "we're absolutely sure that you're not going to find him alive."

I kept looking. At night, when I would get home, everyone would be waiting in anguish to know how it had gone. But I always had the same news. No one knew anything. That was when my husband told me he couldn't take it any more. News was beginning to filter out about more and more disappearances, and he told me we would never learn anything about what happened to them. This made me incredibly angry.

"Of course," I said to him, "since he's not your son, it doesn't bother you."

He got furious and shouted at me that the only thing he hadn't done was literally to father him, because he had paid for his education, considered him a son, and treated him the same way he treated the others. I withdrew into myself and then we began to have some terrible arguments.

TO THE BITTER END

My childhood was very painful. I was the second of twenty-three children, and my mother was very intolerant. At eleven I began to work in a cigarette-lighter factory, and at seventeen I got married. My husband died nine months later, and I was seven months pregnant. He had told me that he had lung disease, but I thought he would get better, and I was so tired of my home that all I wanted was to leave.

When I became a widow, my mother didn't want to take me back because, according to her, I had lung disease too and I might give it to my brothers and sisters. Things were very bad. When Lucho was born I weighed less than ninety pounds, and when I left the hospital I didn't have a drop of milk. Since I had to work, I took an apartment where someone would take care of my baby during the day. That person was my current husband's mother.

One day he came to visit and we met. Lucho was already about a year old. We got married and, in truth, he did help me bring up Lucho. He paid for Lucho's education through high school. We couldn't afford the university because we had the others in school, but Lucho paid for it himself and studied English-language teaching.

My son was very special . . . not because he has disappeared . . . he was very conscientious even as a child. He started school when he was five, and by seven he was first in his class. He was very small— and a little fat—when he gave us that first satisfaction. He continued to be first every year, and he left grade school when he was eleven. We tried to enroll him in trade school, but they wouldn't take him because he was too small to use the big machines, so he entered high school, where he made very good grades and always stood out as a leader.

He was a happy, smiling boy, with a sense of humor, and my husband couldn't get mad at his jokes because they made him laugh. He was the best child I had. A pleasure for everyone. I have always been very proud of him.

He always wanted to be a well-educated person, and since he was smart we thought he could go farther there than we had. That was what my husband objected to the most: "What's the point of all that education," he would say, "if they're just going to get involved in politics?"

We were very close until these fights began. He is very bitter, but in spite of the arguments, I still go out every day to look for my son.

Five months after Lucho's arrest, my father died. He was Lucho's godfather. He had a blood clot and died suddenly. It was so awful for me that I gave up my search for six months.

I was very depressed; I shut myself in the house and didn't want to know about anything. I lost so much weight that I went down to ninety-five pounds. All I did was cry. It was a terrible year. In November I lost my son, in April my father died, a few months later my daughter-in-law's mother died—the one who lived with me—and in December my mother-in-law died. I thought I was the only person in the world having to endure these things.

One day I got a telegram from the Committee for Peace asking me to attend a meeting. I went hoping they would know something about my son, but it was a meeting to help the families of detained and disappeared people to get organized. I asked my husband's permission to go to their meetings on Saturdays, and, since I seemed in such a bad way, he thought it might do me good, so he told me to go.

At first it was a matter of telling our experiences; we drank tea, and everyone made their own contribution, and thus we passed the afternoon. For most people these get-togethers were very helpful— we got to know each other and to see that other people had problems as bad as or worse than our own. That's how we began to organize the Council of Families of Detained or Disappeared Persons, with about fifty people. Later the group got bigger, especially in '76, when a lot of people disappeared. There are two families with four disappeareds: Ana González, for example, has her husband, her sons, and her daughter-in-law. The pain of losing one person is enormous, but imagine losing everyone and being left alone!

As a group we have tried many methods of getting information. We've gone on hunger strikes, we've gone out into the streets, we've made declarations, written letters, spoken with judges . . . Someday they will have to respond.

Our first big act was a hunger strike in the ECLA* building. At the time I didn't know it was sponsored by a political party. They flew their own colors, as the saying goes, and only a handful of members participated. Later, at the end of the year, more than eighty people fasted for fifty hours in the Church of San Francisco.

---

* Economic Commission for Latin America, an organization of the United Nations, based in Santiago.

I didn't dare tell my husband. He didn't know all the things I was doing because he left for work early in the morning. I used to send his lunch to work by one of the children, and at night I would come back to serve him a late supper. The day of the fast I told the children what was happening, and I asked them to serve him his food when he got home and to give him a letter that I had left for him. The older ones didn't want me to go without telling Papa, and they were worried that fasting would make me sick. I explained to them that on many days I hadn't eaten, walking the streets without any response, and that maybe this would make them tell us something.

We left the church on December 31, and it was very moving because so many people were waiting for us outside. Some women friends brought me some milk and dropped me off at my home. The children had cleaned and polished everything for New Year's Eve. By the time my husband got home I was exhausted, because by the third day you really begin to feel the effects of not eating.

He got home, came inside, and didn't even look at me. I thought the whole thing would fade away, but when he saw I was fainting he got frightened and told me to lie down. We began to talk, he got over his anger, and I saw that I had won this round. But after a little while a friend came over to tell us that Carlos had gone to wait for me by the church entrance and they had arrested him. My husband got furious.

"That's what happens when you get children involved in this!"

I hadn't even known that Carlos had gone to look for me . . . Just as we were leaving for the police station, Carlos arrived—what a relief! They had let him off with a citation for disorderly conduct.

We didn't get any response to the fast, but the country began to wake up and to realize that people were disappearing. Until then we had been all alone with our problem, with no one else paying any attention.

A policeman who lives right next door to us insists that my son has not disappeared! Before, we were very friendly with his family, especially with his wife, but afterwards we had enormous arguments about the things he said. He repeated the same things the government did: that my son must be somewhere else, that he had surely left the country with another woman. I was so distraught that one day I became hysterical and began to shout at him, "Murderer!"

They went to report this to my other son, who worked as a driver for the police medical unit. He told them I couldn't stand to see anyone in uniform, no matter what good friends we were, and asked them to forgive my reacting that way.

With the hunger strikes, people began to get more active. In May of '78 we had the strike that lasted seventeen days in the Church of Don Bosco. That time I didn't want to go without asking permission, but I told my husband that it would be five days when, in fact, the strike was to go on indefinitely. In the end we were all cheated. We were ready to stick it out all the way, and the head of the group compromised with the church. The strike was suspended because they promised to exact a response from the government. They sent in the details in five hundred cases, but there was no response. We didn't accomplish anything. Everything was just as it had been.

They wanted to decree all the disappeareds dead and to compensate us. That meant the government recognized that there were detained and disappeared people, because they were willing to pay us for them. None of us agreed, and we continued to oppose such decrees because it would have been like killing members of our family. We would never accept any response except the truth about what had happened to them.

To protest against declaring them dead we sat down in front of La Moneda palace, and they arrested about eighty people. They kept us from ten in the morning until ten at night in a very small room, guarded by police dogs. We couldn't even sit down because we were crowded up against each other.

Many times they arrested us and let us go at night. My husband didn't even know, because I would go out in the morning and come back the same day. Until one day they began to apply the Internal State Security Law, and they kept us in jail for several days.

That was when we chained ourselves to the gates of Congress. Eugenio was there, handing out the group's declarations, and they took him too. At about two in the morning they went to verify his address, and my husband had to pick him up at the police station. They put him under house arrest and posted a guard at the house. He had to spend five days without so much as looking out the window, worrying that he was going to miss a year of school.

They took the rest of us to the police station, then to court, then to jail for five more days.

In '82 they took me in with my daughter because we were putting up posters in the Plaza de Armas. I was pretty sick, and at the police station my blood pressure shot up because the policemen were very nasty to me. The station has now become like a second home—we all know each other—but that time one of them began to jump up and down and shout:

"Nobody sleeps here! Everybody's got to do exercises, because why should you sleep if I can't!"

When we didn't react, he got madder, jumped harder, and made a lot of noise. My nerves weren't able to take it, and those same policemen had to take me to the clinic.

EXHAUSTION

By '80 I was already very sick. One day at a group meeting I began to feel ill, I couldn't hold my body up, and the women carried me home, totally dazed. They put me to bed, and I stayed there for three days until they took me to the hospital. I had what they call a nervous breakdown, and they had to take me to the hospital three more times.

By that time, my husband and I were getting along very well, but we had other problems, because our daughter was sick. At fifteen, María Lina was suffering from hypertension, something that, according to the doctors, affects people over forty. It had to do with her nerves. Everything in this house has to do with nerves!

She saw that her brother Eugenio was getting politically active, and that my husband was angry with me because, according to him, I was putting ideas into the boy's head. He was always blaming me, and I had nothing to do with it; when someone has ideas in his head, nothing gets them out.

Eugenio was the one who had gotten sick when they arrested Lucho; he kept waiting for his brother and never enjoyed his childhood. He matured very early, and at fifteen he already wanted to do the kinds of things his brother had been doing. Since he was politically active and there was so much repression, in '82 he had to go into exile.

When he left, my husband knew what had been going on, because since '80 he had been spending his days at home. They had made him retire in an effort to reduce personnel, and that made things much worse for us. He was very devoted to his children and cried a lot when Eugenio left, but, on the other hand, he was relieved. He is not in favor of the regime, but he thinks that all these activities are useless, that human lives are lost for nothing.

IF HE WERE DEAD . . .

We did so many things to try to get information! We asked for interviews with members of the government, but they never granted any. Still, we were able to speak in the courts. Some judges were very stern and said that they couldn't do anything. Supreme Court Justice Bórquez treated us very badly and told us that we had gone nuts over these disappeareds. Retamal was the most receptive, assuring us that he would try to do something.

In fact, the courts never clarified anything, and in the case of Lonquén, where they knew the truth, in the end they didn't even punish the guilty ones. And the same thing happened with Laja and Yumbel, where it was also proved that the bodies belonged to detained or disappeared people.

Lonquén was very important to us. There had always been stories of secret cemeteries in different locations, but in this case they were able to get the bodies, identify them, and discover the truth. We were horrified at the idea that all of them might turn up this way. We had never stopped thinking they were alive.

Our group organized a pilgrimage to the lime ovens of Lonquén to place a memorial plaque. It was very moving. There were some huts with bullet holes in them, and we saw the ovens where they were buried. As we walked, we felt as if we were making the journey the Virgin made when she learned that Jesus was to be crucified.

In the end, they didn't even hand over the remains from Lonquén, and threw them instead into a mass grave in the Isla de Maipo cemetery while people were waiting in the church to bury them. After everything else, they stole the bodies! I was already sick at the time, so I didn't have to endure that horror.

I never thought that my son could be among the dead at Lonquén. It never occurred to me . . . I always thought he was in some camp they had somewhere, on an island or in the Colonia Dignidad.* Who knows in what condition, crazy from being tortured and from so much suffering. I imagine him as very thin . . . old . . . I imagine him in a cell, not knowing who he is.

Our goal is to find out the truth. Either the government will tell us what happened or we will fight for the fall of the regime so that a new one can investigate the cases and punish those who are responsible.

Some people say that one day we will have to learn to forgive, but I don't agree. If I knew who had taken my son, I wouldn't pick up a weapon and kill them, because I don't believe in the death penalty, but I wouldn't pardon them. I would want them to experience what we have experienced, to have their son taken away for a while so they could know what suffering is.

Not everyone thinks the way I do; they call this vengeance, but I would want that even if it's wrong. I would give up my home to have some kind of an answer!

We have to have some kind of justice for criminals, but a justice without amnesty, so that those who are responsible are punished and so that this will never happen again. This will have to wait until democracy comes, until this returns to being a free country as it was years ago. I would like a government where there were no deaths, no tortures, no massacres, where we could be a country of brothers.

---

* An agricultural community formed in the south of Chile by German immigrants after the Second World War. It has always been closed to outsiders, and since the sixties it has been repeatedly denounced for supposed human rights violations.

POOR, HUNGRY, AND OPPRESSED

BLANCA IBARRA ABARCA

AS WE TALK, LITTLE FIVE-YEAR-OLD TANIA TRIES TO SLEEP *in her mother's arms, fondling her mother's breasts. This is perhaps the best image with which to identify this life-giving woman. It's enough to draw near her to feel as protected and coddled as her daughter.*

But Blanca is a strong, vital, feisty, and tireless woman who spreads her warmth throughout La Victoria, the infamous Santiago shantytown that everyone thought would be bombed on September 11, 1973, where repression is intense and young people are beaten up simply for being out in the streets. Here even the children build barricades and throw rocks at the police. A priest was killed here, where they paint heartbreaking murals on the walls, where people are hungry and cold, and where sticking together is the only way of staying alive.

Respected even by the gangs of hoodlums, Blanca Ibarra is a leader of the community. She first took on this role when she dared to offer her house as the site of a soup kitchen, a method of dealing with hunger that the authorities deem subversive.

Her status comes not just from personal characteristics, or from the trip she made to Paris, but from her husband's tragic experience. "When I met him, he was an Alessandrista,"* she tells me, "and I convinced him he should vote for Allende." Now he's in prison for twenty-one years.

September 11, 1973, is an unforgettable date for us. Everyone went out into the street, airplanes began to fly overhead, swooping so low that the tin roofs shook and the noise was deafening. Women began to cry.

People with radios turned them up loud, and everyone stopped in the middle of the street to listen. We heard Allende speaking. He was a very brave man . . . No one has emerged since who compares with him. Everything that he had predicted was happening. The deaths he said would occur, the fight that the neighborhoods would have to put up to occupy the major streets. He had forecast it all in a threatening but sure voice; he knew what was coming.

I was furious. I was crying with fury. I wanted to do something, to fight, but I felt pain and impotence, and I thought I never should have had children, because at times like these children tie you down.

From La Victoria we could see smoke rising where they had bombed La Moneda palace. People stayed out in the streets, and there was a huge crowd on the main avenue. A young invalid with crutches climbed onto a chair and began to yell directions. La Moneda was burning, helicopters were hovering over us, and it began to rain. I'll never forget it: the day started out sunny, but it got overcast and began to rain, and although I've never been superstitious, I've always thought that was a sign. The invalid said that we ought to take over the clinic because there were going to be a lot of wounded, that we should block off the streets to the neighborhood and organize ourselves to fight.

I left my four- and five-year-olds with some neighbors and went to

* A supporter of former President Jorge Alessandri (1958–1964), an independent from the right.

155

the clinic to help. I was so angry and so sad! I was afraid, but I felt I had to do something, I had to contribute. I couldn't sit around waiting for other people to move.

It was cold, and you could hear the shooting. No one knew what was happening. Someone said that General Prats was coming and that the whole army wasn't behind the coup. On television they showed people rifling Allende's house, and on the radio we heard that he was dead, but no one believed it.

The next day, when they were able to leave, the doctors and nurses went home. There was no resistance in La Victoria. I don't think anyone was armed. A few people ran away and were pursued and died fighting on the outskirts of the neighborhood. One day they even put up a barricade and confronted the soldiers, but I don't know if those people were actually from La Victoria. We heard a very loud explosion, and we went to see what had happened. From a distance we could see bodies on the ground, including a woman. The soldiers let them lie there for several days. They took charge of the area and wouldn't let anyone come near; they shot to kill.

At night there was a curfew, and they would set flares that lit everything up as if there were a fire. The children would cry, the women would shout, and you couldn't go out because they would shoot you. Soldiers ran up and down the streets, and a helicopter went back and forth illuminating everything with a big floodlight. The shooting would go on for hours. And one day we saw blood in the streets and didn't know who had been killed or what had happened.

On the fifteenth, for the first time, the soldiers came into the neighborhood during the day. They arrived, firing their guns, at nine o'clock in the morning; they were looking for the priests. These were working-class priests, and they were branded Communists. Hundreds of soldiers were shooting in the streets. The noise was awful. They shot at roofs, and pieces of tin and wood were flying everywhere. I lived behind the chapel; I threw Juan and Mariela on the floor and covered them with mattresses. The soldiers destroyed everything in the chapel. That day made me understand what the following years of terror would be like.

Luckily, at that moment, the priests were out in the neighborhood, not in the parish house. They yelled to them as if they were criminals: "Give yourselves up; nothing will happen to you." When they didn't appear, they shouted more loudly: "Give yourselves up, you Communist bastards!"

At the same time, they staged a siege of the community church. They opened the doors with a grenade and fired inside with a machine gun. They destroyed the pews and the walls. They even broke the pipes in the bathroom.

They couldn't find the priests because they didn't know what they looked like. A crowd had gathered around the parish house and the priests were in the crowd. They were appalled at all the damage the soldiers were doing. Their first reaction was to speak with the soldiers, but people made them realize that it was impossible to have a dialogue with them because they shouted and wouldn't stop shooting. It was totally savage and crazy. They were like wild animals blinded by hate.

I don't know where this hate came from. Most of them were conscripted soldiers—neighborhood people like us, who would return to their families when they finished their military service. I don't know what they were told that made them act like that.

I lived through all of this alone with my children. My husband was a member of MOPARE, the democratic truckers' movement, which supported Allende and continued to drive when other truckers were on strike. On the eleventh, Beño was on his way to Chuquicamata.*

When he was able to return, he drove straight back without even sleeping and arrived with the motor practically in flames. At one of the checkpoints, he saw a truck with its sides up covered by a tarp. It caught his attention because the soldiers had something inside and wouldn't allow the truck to be searched. The police at the checkpoint muttered that it was people they were going to kill. He arrived home on the fifteenth, the same day they came looking for the priests. He was in bad shape. "Is it true that they killed Allende?" he asked me without getting out of his truck, and he began to sob. A hoarse sob. I had never heard him cry before.

---

* A large copper mine located in the north of the country.

Many people didn't come back after September 11. They were arrested in their factories or in the streets, and herded like animals into detention centers. Those who were released from the National Stadium told how they had had nothing to eat for the first few days, how they listened to the shooting at night and heard the cries of people who were hit, how the ground was covered with blood and the smell was unbearable. Soldiers wearing boots jumped on people until they were nearly dead and then shot them.

My brothers worked on the other side of the Mapocho River, and they were forced to walk with their hands behind their heads without looking to either side as they crossed the river. They could still see many bullet-ridden bodies in the water.

That's how we began to learn. And it just got worse. They picked up Señora María, an old Communist leader in La Victoria, many times. They would keep her a few days, torture her, and let her out. She's a very old woman. Once when I went to see her she didn't have any eyelashes or eyebrows; they had come out when they took the adhesive tape off her eyes.

My sister, the only member of our family who was active in a political party, came home crying because her Socialist friends had been arrested or killed. Many of them went into exile. One of my sister's friends told how they had forced keys between his teeth and pulled out his fingernails. It must have been difficult for him because he didn't want to tell us everything that had happened to him. There was a lot of brutality, but the sophisticated torture began with the ghastly DINA. The DINA also came after my sister in '74. They waited for her in her home for five or six days and they wouldn't let the family she was renting from leave the house. Luckily a neighbor told her what was happening, and she went into exile.

A great fear came over this country on September 11. We began to suspect each other. There were informers, and people were arrested on the basis of accusations that had no foundation. You couldn't talk about what was happening; people were arrested even on the bus. They killed dogs because they barked. In the schools they staged military parades so the children would learn how to march.

A FAITHFUL ALLENDISTA

When I first met my husband, he liked Alessandri. Everyone in his family was an Alessandrista and an evangelical. We fought a lot when we were first married because I had always been an Allendista, and I liked to go to the rallies. Beño didn't understand; he said women belong at home and shouldn't get mixed up in politics. His family spoke up too. I would get furious, curse at him, and go out to my marches.

Things began to heat up during Frei's final months. I think we got overpoliticized. I talked about it so much to Beño that by the time of the campaign in '70, he began to go with me to meetings, and he ended up voting for Allende instead of Alessandri. And Allende won!

The period of Popular Unity was the most fruitful era we have ever known. What little we have now, we saved from that time: the refrigerator, the gas range, a twelve-inch television, a washing machine. All of these were luxuries for me. I never imagined my children would each have their own bed! I even remember the prices, because it was very important to me to be able to pay for everything with my money and not buy on the installment plan.

My husband was a truck driver, and he was in charge of an iron warehouse, and we lived very well because prices were fixed and salaries kept going up, so that we were able to acquire more goods. There was a JAP, where they sold everything we needed for the family. Lines would form when merchandise came in, but since we were well organized, everyone got served, and there were no problems with the black market.

But there's no denying that they made mistakes too. There were suppliers who took kickbacks from the Allende government. There was also disagreement among parties. It was the same as it is now: each party wanted power, to impose its own ideology, to have more ministers and more control. Many factories required people to have a party card, which is something I'll never be able to accept!

People began to get active and to choose sides. I think it's legitimate to have different positions, but people locked themselves into particular stances and thought everyone else could go to hell. We even had people who, on the eleventh, played music and danced to celebrate the coup. They had no idea what was coming . . . the hunger that lay ahead.

We've been through a lot of hunger. The trucking job ended and the owner had to fire my husband. There were times when we barely had anything to give Mariela and Juan. Beño would go out early and walk around all day but come home with nothing. He got very thin and would get attacks of nerves.

Things were going very badly. We would try to help others with extra food, but after a while we weren't even able to do that. And they still put Beño in jail for twenty-one years.

WE SIMPLY LET THEM IN

The first two compañeros to arrive came with my sister before she went into exile. The three of them were very nervous. "The police are looking for them," she told me, "and they had nowhere to go."

I didn't know who they were or why they were being pursued. They stayed two or three days; we gave them Juan's bed, and they settled themselves there.

I panicked. I hardly slept the entire time they were there, and every patrol car that went by made me shake with terror. They would sleep, I would look at them, and I couldn't believe it. I couldn't even close my eyes for thinking that they would suddenly be discovered in my house and something would happen to my children.

Since the children always played near the door, we told them to pay attention to everything, and if they saw a strange car or person to let us know. They were four and five years old—still infants.

We never talked about it; we simply took in compañeros who arrived. What we were doing was so little that it would have been disgraceful to say no.

One day my sister brought me a two-year-old girl. Maggie was the daughter of some compañeros. She had a little bag with a change of clothes, a small chamber pot, and a doll that had "Miguel" written on one of its feet. She stayed about a month. We took care of her as if she were our own daughter until some compañeros came to look for her. We never thought that these things might be outlawed by the regime. How could we destabilize the regime by taking in a child?

When my sister had already left the country, those first compañeros came back with others, then those with others, and so on. Sometimes they would come for just a couple of hours. They would take a bath, I would wash their clothes, and they would rest for a while.

They suddenly stopped coming for a year or two, until in '78 some compañeros arrived from Peru. They were a couple, Martín and Chica. They stayed with us for about two weeks, and we became very good friends. They continued to visit us, and at one point stayed with us for three weeks because they weren't able to rent an apartment. Beño shut off part of the dining room and put a bed in there for them. They always went out very early in the morning and returned late at night. We didn't know anything about their activities or even what party they belonged to.

We continued to be friends, and around 1980 Martín began to bring other compañeros again. They would get together, talk, and then leave. He was the only one who ever stayed to sleep. Beño had begun to work as a taxi driver, and sometimes Martín would ask him to take him somewhere or to pick him up at a specific time.

Little by little, we began to realize that he was heavily involved in politics, and we began to get very nervous. We noticed that Beño always had to pick him up at odd hours, but we weren't completely sure, because he told us that he worked for a travel agency and didn't have regular office hours.

We learned the truth when he didn't show up any more. It was at the beginning of '82. Chica arrived with her five-month-old baby and was very nervous. She had barely greeted me before she began to cry. We thought she had been assaulted.

"Martín hasn't been home since yesterday. I know that something has happened to him."

No one was able to comfort her, and she continued to cry. We tried to calm her down but couldn't "They're going to get him, they're going to get him," was all she kept saying.

About a month later she came back, crying again. She showed me a piece of paper certifying that Martín had died the same day he had disappeared. The body had been at the morgue for about a month, and finally some relatives had sent her the paper.

We never found out how he died, but I remember seeing at around that time the news of a confrontation on television and hearing that an extremist had died . . . Still, when the CNI came looking for Beño, we didn't know why.

"Don't get up," they said to me in a friendly way. "We're going to take him in to ask him some questions, and then we'll bring him back."

Tania had just been born. They made Juan, who was thirteen, sign Beño's arrest order.

One of them even shook my hand good-bye. It was the same one who later beat my husband and threatened that he would come after me.

My husband is a super-calm man; he's never argued with anyone. He never goes out at night or varies from his routine. They questioned him and questioned him, and he didn't know how to answer. I think that ultimately they didn't know what to do with him. But they kept him in the local branch of the CNI for five days, and then the public prosecutor put him in jail, in solitary, for another five days.

That was the year it rained so hard the Mapocho River flooded its banks, and I kept walking around the jail with Tania trying to find out what was going on. When I first arrived I was well dressed, but by the third day I didn't even have shoes, and some neighbors had to lend me some so that I could go out again. I had open sores on my breasts, but I didn't have time to go to the clinic. I would have had to spend a whole morning in the hospital, and this would have delayed finding out about my husband. I didn't even know where he was or what was happening to him; I couldn't go to the doctor.

After about twelve days they allowed political prisoners to have visitors, and I managed to get inside the jail. Beño's time in solitary ended that day. I went in hoping to find out what was going on, but he wasn't there.

On my next visit I finally saw him. I had never seen him so white. His whole body was transparent, even his ears. He looked like he was dead! We embraced each other, and I realized that I couldn't cry because I had to give him courage. I cried at night when the children were sleeping.

"They're accusing me of collaborating," he explained to me. "They're accusing me of a lot of things that you know I never did. They've linked me with other compañeros who are here whom I've never seen before. They also claim that I took part in a bank robbery."

Those were the few things he was able to say to me. He had to sign everything the agents wanted because they had put electric prods on him and threatened to come after me and the children. They had blindfolded him, stripped him naked, and made obscene jokes about his body. He never told me much. He would say something, and then he would become very quiet.

In jail he learned that Martín and the others were part of the MIR. His interrogators told him that Martín had been a dangerous extremist, a criminal, and a murderer, that he held up banks and stole money. We never believed it, and we've never been angry with Martín because it's very easy to accuse someone who's dead and not able to defend himself.

It's not Martín's fault that Beño's in prison. It's a result of the decision we made on September 11 to protect and help anyone who needed it.

"We couldn't have kept living," Beño always said to me, "if a compañero had died because we wouldn't take him in."

For a long time we kept thinking he would get out, that there would be an investigation, and since what we had done was so minor, he would be in jail for a few months and then they would let him out. But they kept adding more things: first, he was a supporter of a paramilitary group; then he had hidden people; then he had distributed pamphlets—until in '85 they sentenced him to twenty-one years.

We had already given up hope. I had joined the League of Families of Political Prisoners, and they had told me how these cases went, how people could be held for years without even being interrogated. Now I can confirm what they said because I know there will be political prisoners for as long as this regime lasts.

If I didn't love Beño the way I do, I would not have been able to go on. Whenever I'm about to visit him, I feel as if I can't breathe; I get all upset about how slow the bus is going. I can't take my eye off the time. We've never been able to say everything we have to say to each other.

Beño is the only person I ever dated. I was fifteen when I met him, and now I'm thirty-eight. He is a good, simple, hard-working man. Although he isn't well-educated, he has achieved a lot, and he's always learning new things. We have established a strong family in spite of his imprisonment.

I constantly dream that he has been freed, that he comes home without any notice and calls to us from the gate. Other times I have nightmares. I see him in the jail, but I can't get near him. Hours and hours go by, and no matter how hard I try I can't get in.

My whole life is arranged around visiting days: Wednesdays and Saturdays. I go whether I am sick or not, whether it is cold or hot, even if I have no money for the bus. The only time I failed to go was when I was in Paris.

ONE BOTTLE AND TWO DIAPERS

I went to Paris to take Rey, Martín's son, to his mother.

The household was under control; Juan, Mariela, and I were all taking care of raising Tania, when one day I got the news that a woman was waiting on the corner to see me. It was Martín's friend, Chica. I remember it was May 10, 1983, because Tania had just had her first birthday, and the next day was the first national protest. We hugged each other. She had a bag and the boy in her arms.

"Now they're looking for me," she said, looking at the boy as if to ask what she should do.

I told her to leave him with me and to get away immediately if they were following her. She looked at me and couldn't decide. I explained that since Beño was in jail it could be dangerous for her to stay because they might associate her with us. She cried and clutched the baby. I practically had to pry him from her arms, and I assured her that no matter what happened I would take care of him, that I wouldn't give him to anyone, and that I would raise him as my own.

"We'll see each other again someday," she said and left.

I hadn't heard anything about her since Martín had disappeared, and a world of things passed through my mind, but I didn't say any of them. I explained to Juan and Mariela that we were going to have to raise the boy like one of the family. We were afraid, but what could we do? His father was dead, his mother had to flee, and the child couldn't live that way, being kicked from pillar to post.

I wasn't with her for more than five minutes. I wasn't even able to ask her the child's name. We called him Rey.

He came with a bottle, a chamber pot, a change of clothes, and two diapers. We told the neighbors he was my sister's son, and they helped us take care of him and feed him just as they helped with Tania, because often I didn't have anything to give him to eat. To be safe, we never took him far from the house, and whenever anyone who didn't live on the block appeared, Juan and Mariela knew they were to take him into the house immediately.

At first I didn't tell Beño. When I did tell him his hair nearly fell out. Then, on visiting days, we had to get up incredibly early because we had two babies to get ready. He called Beño "Papa" the way Tania did, and the other compañeros adored him because we told them he was Martín's son.

About six months later I got a letter from the baby's mother from Paris. She was well and had told the United Nations about the boy so that they could send for him. She told me not to be surprised if people from the UN came to ask for him.

Time went by, and one day Father Pierre DuBois, who was the priest of La Victoria, came to my house. He came with a group of people and looked very surprised. He knew me well because I had taken part in community groups.

'Blanca, how many children do you have?"

"Three."

"Then there must be some mistake, because these men from the United Nations have a letter saying you have a child that isn't yours."

I brought them in and brought out Rey. The priest couldn't believe it. They examined him and explained how they had to send him to Paris. After a few days of making arrangements, they told me that I would be taking him to his mother myself, since we had taken such good care of him.

I had never been in an airplane. All the clothes I brought were borrowed from neighbors who had also volunteered to take care of my children.

I got to Paris in January of '84. His mother cried, jumped up and down, and acted completely crazy. I stayed a month and a half. It was very cold. I visited museums and saw how different life was there. Everything was very beautiful. I couldn't believe it when I saw people throwing rugs, televisions, and refrigerators out on the street. I saw a red Italian living-room set that had nothing wrong with it, and I thought about how my house would look with it.

I sold some handicrafts that Beño had learned to make, and with the money I bought shoes for him and the children. Chica also showered me with gifts. She was studying at the university and working as a maid during the day. She looked at her son and saw Martín. She always cried when we spoke about him. She would ask my forgiveness because Beño was in jail, but I explained to her we had nothing to forgive her for because if it hadn't been him it would have been someone else, it would have happened anyway . . .

THE FIRST DEATH

Apart from the trip to Paris, the only times I didn't go to see Beño were on protest days. I couldn't leave the neighborhood, and furthermore, political prisoners couldn't receive visitors on those days.

I'll never forget the first protest, the day before Tania had turned one and Rey had arrived. There was a national call to attend—they even broadcast it over the radio—and everyone went out into the streets. It was overwhelming! At that point fear began to disappear. People joined together, shouting, jumping around; it was as if they had let go after having lived all those years locked up, looking out from behind their windows. There were marches throughout the community. It was like a carnival, and at the height of everything the police arrived.

There were a lot of them, and they came from all sides, shooting and throwing tear gas. We fled to our houses, but they were all full of gas. We had to put the children in the closets. On some instructions they had given us, it said to use vinegar, lemon juice, salt, or boiled eucalyptus to treat tear gas, so all the neighbors got together to improvise and get organized. We were all walking around choking.

At about eight-thirty at night we had the first death of the protest. It was Andrés Fuentes, a boy of nineteen who was in the doorway of his home with his father looking out at the marchers in the street. A policeman came onto the street and began shooting at people in their doorways. The bullet went straight through his head and he died immediately.

Everyone met in the chapel. There was a wake, and they made bonfires in the streets, because during all the protests the electricity was turned off. Early the next day people were out in the street again preparing for the funeral. It was an enormous funeral. They didn't want to let us go on foot, but we went anyway, forming a human chain with our arms, with the coffin in the middle. We carried a hundred Chilean flags at half-mast, shouted denunciations at the police for killing a youngster, and sang hymns. As we got near the cemetery, the police appeared again with clubs and tear gas. People did what they could to get to the funeral.

Father Pierre DuBois had come to the neighborhood in February, and we had found him somewhat tiresome—he was very cold and distant as a priest. But during this first protest we got to know the truth about him. Along with the dead boy, various other people had been wounded, and amid the fighting and the tear gas he put them in his van and took them to the hospital.

Those who were not seriously wounded stayed in the chapel, and we began to organize health teams to tend to them. Members of all the different community organizations came; all of them were very upset about the death of Andrés Fuentes, and we began to realize how important it was to be ready to defend ourselves against what was coming.

In '73 all the social organizations disappeared: neighborhood groups, maternity centers, youth clubs, everything. It was a big change for us, because in our neighborhood everyone used to participate in these things. But as time went on, we were losing all our rights—we couldn't speak freely or even mention certain people.

In '82 there was more hunger than ever, and soup kitchens began to emerge. They were the first real organizations since the coup. After eating, people would begin to talk about the news and current events.

I went out one Sunday, very cautiously, to help with a committee for the homeless that was being established and to help organize a squatter settlement nearby. Some thousand families, many of them young married people living off relatives, set themselves up at dawn. They brought blankets and poles and put up tents with Chilean flags that became a symbol of the settlement. There had been a rumor that this was going to happen, but I didn't think it was certain. As afraid as everyone was, I didn't think anyone would dare to do it—it took a lot of courage.

During the morning, busloads of police arrived. At the time we didn't know what that meant. Women with children went to speak with them and explained that they didn't have anywhere to live. The police responded that they had orders, and that by eleven everything had to be cleared away. People refused, and the police began to throw things around, ripping the flags, throwing tear gas, and arresting people. Everyone who could fled to La Victoria.

That's when the first soup kitchen began. They had taken a pot of beans into the street, and the organizers explained that they were for everyone to eat. People were embarrassed about taking their plates out, but little by little they formed a line and began to help themselves to food. They were about halfway through when the people fleeing the squatter settlement appeared, followed by the police.

The policeman in charge said that this type of thing was prohibited, and he ordered them to stop. They threw the food on the ground! People were furious, and began to throw stones at the buses that went by spraying tear gas. That day people stayed out in the streets very late. They talked on the corners, and many of them said we had to get organized because the police were arresting us and beating us for no reason.

During these conversations, one group decided to continue the soup kitchen so that each of us would have at least one plate of food a day. The one requirement was that you needed the food and that you were willing to help by asking for food in the market or helping to cook. In the beginning people were afraid. The soup kitchens were prohibited because they were considered antigovernment organizations—the government thought they were an attack on their image.

My husband was already in jail, and we suffered from hunger. At times we had only a little tea and bread, but I was too embarrassed to ask for food, and I didn't go to the soup kitchens. One day I got home at about three in the afternoon, and Mariela and my mother-in-law were lying in bed without having eaten anything all day. That made up my mind for me. I threw a pot in my bag so they wouldn't notice and went out. Even though it was late, there was still food left because so many people were ashamed to come. They had started with about fifteen families, and now more than five hundred people ate there every day. I thought it was terrible to be seen in the street with a food bag. I was so furious that I wasn't able to feed my own family!

I began to help and to participate regularly in the soup kitchen until one day they didn't have a place to set it up. I offered my back yard. I was afraid, but I was more hungry than afraid. They ran it out of my house for seven months. Tania's first meals came from the soup kitchen.

All these experiences were raising people's consciousness, and finally, during the first protest, a neighborhood center was set up in La Victoria where all the groups of the parish met.

FALLEN ON THE BIBLE

The priests in La Victoria were a part of the community, and they suffered as much as we did. Pierre was expelled from the country, and Father André Jarlan was killed during a protest.

Once they beat up my son Juan, and André came to see him every day, to talk with Mariela, and to play with Tania. Less than a month later they killed him.

He was a very sensitive man; when things became very bad or someone was severely hurt, André would cry. On September 4, 1984, there was a very large protest. By nine o'clock the police had already come into the neighborhood, breaking glass and stomping on everything in their path. By eleven o'clock Hernán Barrales, a young man who had been standing in the street talking with friends, was dead.

There were no police nearby, just the sound of a bullet from far away, and Hernán fell. "They got me," he said, and at first no one paid any attention. When they got him to the hospital he was already dead. He wasn't doing anything; they shot him just for the sake of killing. Father André was very upset by his death. Hernán was one of a group of young drug addicts that he had rehabilitated.

Since I was a member of the community board, I was in and out of the church many times that day, relaying information or helping one of the many wounded.

At about six o'clock in the afternoon there was a confrontation in the same area where Hernán had been killed. Barricades had been erected, and the police were throwing tear gas and shooting. Father Pierre came out to try to placate people. I was in my house with two foreign journalists, and suddenly Juan came running in.

"The police are coming!" he shouted, and we saw several cars coming into the neighborhood and a helicopter circling very low.

Everyone ran to hide. We heard a car brake, and some policemen threw a tear gas bomb and fired two shots. The people who saw them began to shout insults at them as they drove away. We went out immediately to see what had happened, and they told us that the police had been chasing some journalists who were running toward the chapel. A little while later Pierre arrived with a group of people, went into the house, and asked for André. No one had seen him, and we thought he had gone.

But his beret and bag were on the hat rack. Father Pierre ran upstairs and shouted as he got to the top. André was dead. Shots aimed at the journalists had hit him instead. He was seated at his desk, fallen forward over the open Bible.

Everyone began to cry and shout. We had to calm down the young people, who wanted to kill the police. It was so painful. The people from the board told us how they had to restrain the young people to prevent more deaths.

I couldn't believe that André was dead. Pierre let us go upstairs to say good-bye, and we saw him in his bed full of blood. He had his hands crossed. I wanted to touch him, but I didn't dare. I felt that

André was already with God, and that I didn't have the right. We stopped in front of him and prayed.

It was already about two in the morning. People came from different neighborhoods, singing and carrying candles that they left in the street to illuminate the neighborhood without electricity. They were also meant to illuminate André . . .

We didn't have time to feel our pain. We weren't able to think about everything that was happening. We had to bury Hernán Barrales and at the same time worry about André, because his body had been taken away for an autopsy. The protests continued every day; the barricades had shut off the neighborhood. They buried André in France, but the wake was in La Victoria. We walked in an enormous crowd to the cathedral. It was our good-bye . . . They said we were going to riot in the center of town.

We lived through some very difficult things in those years. A little later they destroyed the barricades, and the soldiers set to work ripping down the posters of André that were up on all the houses.

FROM RAGE TO VIOLENCE

Protests began to be held on the eleventh of every month. During the second protest the barricades were set up. They were a defense against the police, to prevent them from coming in as they had the last time. People took whatever they had—old chairs, mattresses, broken bedsprings, anything they weren't using. Everyone took part —old people, young children, everyone.

At first they managed to keep the police out, but later the police began to armor their cars with steel plates and sweep the barricades away. Then people began to throw rocks and Molotov cocktails. No one hoped to prevent the armored cars from coming in—simply to intimidate them somewhat and prevent the police from coming in on foot.

The violence has become worse. They even say that some people have been armed at the protests, but I've never seen it. Only once did I have the impression that someone was shooting back at the police or the soldiers, and it scared us terribly because they were shooting randomly, and we were all at risk; many people were out in the streets, and our walls are very thin.

Like it or not, if we don't find a quick solution to the situation there's going to be an out-and-out war. I see how the young people are becoming alienated. It's very difficult to show them how dangerous it is to confront oppression. They're so angry about the blows dealt to them, they don't understand that rocks are useless against soldiers or police who are shooting at them. If things continue this way, they're going to arm themselves with something more serious than rocks, so that they're not the only casualties of the confrontations. All the signs that we see indicate that this is where we are going.

I'm terrified by the idea that my son or some other boy could participate in things like that. He could be killed. But we adults have nothing else to offer our children, we have no way out of this situation. As a result, they are turning to violence.

It's become a fact of life that the police come in to provoke and oppress us. Their van comes through several times a day, and a pair of policemen walk around with dogs on chains that turn on the young people when they're simply standing on a street corner. They arrest whoever they want, put them up against a wall, and search them. It doesn't matter to them if you're a man or a woman; they insult everyone. They're very aggressive; they come in looking for trouble. They have a preconceived image of us that we're all bad, all criminals, all armed, and all ready to kill them.

When they catch the kids in a barricade, they strip them, set their clothes on fire, beat them, and make them stamp out the fire with their feet. They have shaved the heads of some children, scalp and all, with their knives.

One day Juan was coming home from school and, since he had his hair too long, the police grabbed him on the way into the neighborhood. People told me that several of them beat him; they ripped his clothing and his notebooks, and then they told him to get lost. They chased him, throwing stones at him until he fell unconscious on the street. People carried him to the neighborhood clinic.

Just yesterday a van full of policemen came, and, as always, the kids began to jeer. Tania and I came out of her school right next to the van. One of the policemen got down and for no reason at all set off some tear gas. My poor daughter turned white and shouted that they were going to kill her, and I began to shout at them. If I could have, I would have beat the bastards up!

Clearly I have become violent, but it's a logical reaction: my daughter is five years old, and she is terrified. These things cause tremendous rage, which all of us here are experiencing together. As a result, if some kid manages to get hold of a weapon, he's going to have a shoot-out with the first policeman who provokes him the way that one did yesterday, and we'll all have to come out and defend the boy. We can't allow them to kill our kids.

THE FATE OF
THE UNION MOVEMENT

MANUEL BUSTOS HUERTA

N SPITE OF BEING A CHRISTIAN DEMOCRAT—AND CONSE-
quently of opposing the Allende government—in September of 1973 he
was arrested and spent three months in the National Stadium. "For being
an asshole," they told him, and, even after inquiries by Cardinal Raúl
Silva Henríquez, no one officially recognized his detention.

Since then he has been followed, threatened, beaten, jailed, and exiled, still
without abandoning the exhausting and frustrating battle that he and other
union leaders have been waging for over ten years. In his opinion the union
movement is practically dead, and he realizes that many workers have stopped
reacting because they fear oppression, unemployment, or finally, the violence
involved in protest.

But he became active as soon as he was released. From his position as a
textile worker, he began the enormous task of reorganizing Chilean workers,
whose demands have played a fundamental role in the country's political and
social development since the end of the last century, and especially since the
twenties, when the workers' organizations were legally recognized. The prin-

cipal parties of the left—Communist and Socialist—emerged from these or-
ganizations, and even though it never included more than 28 percent of the
work force, the union movement is still responsible for the progressive social
legislation that was in effect until 1973.

In his forties, with a little boy's face and the ulcers of a long-suffering man,
Bustos has enough energy and humility to keep going even though he is not at
the head of the movement. When his exhaustive efforts had finally begun to
yield their first fruits, he was not there to hear the applause and take the
credit; expelled by the military government, he was in Italy during the first
national protest against the Pinochet government. From there he watched as
the president of the copper mines, Rodolfo Sequel, a young leader whom no
one knew, took over his post and received the honorary title of "Chile's Wa-
lesa."

That day, like every other day, I got up late and ran for the bus
without even turning on the radio. It seemed odd to me that there
were so many soldiers in the streets and practically nothing was happening.

It was about a quarter of seven; I met some friends from Sumar,
the textile factory where I worked, and we began to walk together.
We had no idea about the coup; we thought it was one of the military operations they were carrying out at that time, searching for
weapons. When we finally got a bus, they told us what was going
on.

A few blocks ahead there was a large group of soldiers with tanks,
and the bus couldn't get by, so we got out and walked. The soldiers
hadn't got to the factory yet, but everything there indicated that
there had been a coup: some radio stations had been shut down and
others were carrying army broadcasts.

I was the president of the workers' union. We quickly organized a
meeting to try to gather information from the supervisor of the
factory, who had had a separate meeting with people from Popular
Unity. No one knew anything. At the meeting some people said we
should go home, and others said we should take over the factory.
Finally, after much discussion, we decided that people should go

home, but that a group of volunteers would stay to prevent any sabotage.

It was about eleven in the morning, and there was a lot of violence outside the factory; you could hear shooting and helicopters and airplanes circling over the area. A lot of rumors were circulating about what was happening in other places. As a result, many people were afraid to go out and preferred to stay. Ultimately, about 200 out of the 1,000 or 1,100 workers stayed.

We kept hoping that the coup would be aborted, but when we saw them bombarding La Moneda palace, we realized that it was for real. On the twelfth, at about six in the morning, the soldiers got into the factory.

It was very violent. They threw people to the ground and made no attempt at dialogue. As president of the union, I took charge of the situation somewhat, and they told me in a very threatening manner that they were going to search everywhere. No one put up any resistance, and no one was armed, so this tremendous violence was not justified. They took everyone out, beat them, put them into trucks, and carried them off to the Buin army base. At about three o'clock that morning, they moved us in buses to Chile Stadium.

BEING ALIVE: A MATTER OF LUCK

As we went in, they beat us. They didn't ask us anything; I guess they were just beating the enemies of Chile.

Inside, they immediately began to group people according to some lists they had. They separated out the union leaders and checked us against their data. I realized they had been following our activities for a while. I showed up as a leader of my union and a leader of the National Workers' Union.

Before they classified me, and after receiving an enormous kick on the way in, I got out of line and went over to an official who was off to one side to ask if I could use the phone.

"Who are you?" he said. "Who do you want to call?"

I identified myself—I told him that I was a Christian Democrat and that I wanted to call Don Bernardo Leighton to tell him I was here. I think I impressed the guard by the directness with which I spoke, because he took me to an office and left me alone to make the phone call.

Don Bernardo advised me to be very patient. "Tranquillity and calm," he told me, "are the only way to save your life."

I hung up the phone and got back in the line where still more people were coming in. Afterwards I realized that I could have left then because no one was watching me. But I certainly would have been killed outside, because it was after curfew.

Don Bernardo's message got me thinking, and I believe it was very helpful. The phone call itself produced a certain calm in me because at least now someone knew where I was.

They began to call people in to interrogate them, but it seemed as if they were killing them because you could hear shots, and no one came back out. When it was my turn, they took me down to a small office, and they hit and kicked me while I was waiting. I heard some shots, but when I went in there were only the three officials doing the interrogating.

The interrogation was very short and very violent; they didn't want any information, they just wanted to scare people. They beat us as if they were taking personal revenge. They even pretended to execute people.

They had information about you on a piece of paper, and they asked me about an interview I had done a little while ago for *El Siglo** in which I had said that I rejected all kinds of dictatorships, military or Marxist. They asked me what kind of dictatorship this was.

"I understand this isn't a dictatorship," I answered them, "and that the military is just going to fix a system that has certain problems. But what I'm seeing here terrifies me."

They beat me again and told me that they were going to kill me, that they were going to shoot me the way they had shot everyone who had come in so far. This scared me terribly because they had machine guns and they were pointing them at me. Ultimately, they

* A Communist Party daily.

let off a burst of gunfire at the ground and then made me leave and go to a different area.

At first I didn't think about death. I never believed that a man could kill another man just like that. But after I saw what was happening I realized that being alive was a matter of luck. They were killing people up in the bleachers. One guy who said something about fascists was kicked in the face and then shot. Other people went crazy and threw themselves off the third level onto the field. When they hit the ground they split open like watermelons.

All this created incredible terror. All the women were screaming. The shouts, the bullets, and the lights had a terrible effect on them. Many of them got their period and stained themselves, but they weren't allowed to leave. It was a truly humiliating situation. What happened in Chile Stadium was awful.

No one spoke. No one spoke about anything. The most anyone said to their neighbor was that they were hungry or cold, but this only happened very slowly. The enormous fear we felt struck everyone dumb.

Every so often, when they authorized us, we could go to the bathroom and drink some water.

It was incredible to see what happened to people. Some had their faces covered in bruises. They had beaten them in an unbelievable way, especially the workers—they were very hard on them.

On the third day, in the afternoon, they took us to the National Stadium. They took us in buses, thrown on the floor in a heap. At first we didn't know where we were going.

TO SAVE CHILE

There were already a lot of people in the National Stadium—all the locker rooms were full, and they left us outside in the bleachers. We were there until September 26 or 27. We couldn't go down, even at night. Actually it was better up there because at least the air was breathable, not like in the locker rooms underground. But at night it was incredibly cold, and we didn't even have a blanket, nothing. The blankets came later, on about October 15—one blanket for two people.

Around September 20 we got some food for the first time. There was one cupful per person, once a day. There were too many people, and we were afraid the crowding was done on purpose to make us try to take some action. They provoked us by not giving us enough food for everyone in circumstances when we were very hungry, practically starving. We were also very dirty. We couldn't wash, we had no towels, no soap or toothpaste, and we had drinking water only when we went to the bathroom, where everyone would push to get to it. Everything was extremely dirty: the bathrooms, the locker rooms, and the people themselves. We slept pressed up against each other for warmth; every bit of space was filled up, and people were getting sick and going crazy. Two friends from the factory went crazy; one died, and the other has suffered from the after-effects to this day.

At night we would be terrified because they would lie to us, saying that extremists were going to take over the stadium and liberate us. They would start shooting outside and shooting inside, and we would have to remain hunched over on the ground. Sometimes, telling us the same nonsense about a rescue, they would take a group out of the stadium to the velodrome, where they would make us sleep on the unbelievably cold ground.

They interrogated me twice. What you saw when you were waiting to be called was as scary as the interrogation itself. We would stand in single file, surrounded by soldiers, and around us in all the passageways were people sprawled on the ground, some of them dead and some of them wounded and crying out in pain. Beaten, tortured people. It was enough to make you cry, because you would be there two or three hours listening to the groans, seeing this spectacle.

While you were in line, a soldier would come and start hitting you for no reason at all. Some people had their ribs broken and couldn't breathe. They punched me twice in the stomach so hard that I had internal bleeding for a week. There was so much pain that after a while you didn't feel it at all. You would forget about it, but from time to time you would notice you were dripping blood.

When you were beaten like that, you couldn't stand up; you would fall to the floor and stay there waiting for your body to react. No one could do anything, no one dared to help. We were all crowded in there, waiting. The only thing that the people near you could do was prop you up to keep you from falling. There was nothing else they could do. They couldn't even get you a little water.

After that, you would go very gingerly into the interrogation. People in civilian clothes did the interrogating. The only thing they asked me was whether there had been weapons in the factory and why I was a Christian Democrat; they didn't seem to need to ask me about anything else. They did more insulting than interrogating.

As they had done in Chile Stadium, they would send you to a different area after interrogating you. Only toward the end of the imprisonment did a few people begin to return to where they had been before.

During the first few days no one spoke; there was a terrible silence. Around the twentieth we began to talk a little. After my interrogation, I was lucky enough to be put in an area with people I knew from a different factory and with some people I worked with at the Sumar factory. Each group was watched by several soldiers, who would stand eight or ten meters away all day long, pointing their machine guns at us. We never spoke with them, we didn't even know who was in charge in the stadium, and we only got to know one low-ranking official who was in charge of our group.

I asked to speak with the soldiers three times. The first time was because we had a very sick person in the room with us. We banged on the door, but they never came to open it. The man shouted all night long, and the next day the Red Cross took him, and we never learned what happened to him.

Another time I tried to speak with the official in charge to find out how I could get in touch with my wife so that she could send me some clothing. The sergeant said that he would ask, and the next morning the captain appeared. He asked who had called for him, and I raised my hand and explained to him.

"Do you bastards think you're in a hotel?"

That was it, but it seems they thought about it, and a few days later the sergeant began to tell us how the Red Cross had delivered washing detergent, how they were going to disinfect the area and things like that.

My wife was never able to send me anything because they wouldn't acknowledge that I was being held. Cardinal Silva Henríquez had made several attempts to arrange my release, but my name didn't appear on the lists of detainees.

The two times that they called me to interrogate me, I asked them why they had me there, and both times the answer was the same: "For being an asshole."

There were some people who came to the stadium and asked for their family members over the loudspeakers. They were desperate! They must have had some kind of friendship with the soldiers because they were allowed to come into the stadium and even to use the microphones themselves so that people would recognize their voices and respond; but as a rule, no one did. They were looking for people who weren't in the stadium. They must have been very influential people.

We had no idea what was going on outside. We knew absolutely nothing, we had no newspapers or radio. We had no explanation for the violence that we saw. The only things we knew were what we heard from the people around us: what had happened in their own factories and how they had been taken.

In that kind of situation you begin to hope for something that you can't identify. There was no information, only rumors and certain things that you saw, like the hooded man. He would walk up and down the stands during the morning, pointing at people who would then be taken away and never return. Some said that they were killed. Others thought they were taken to the islands,* and still others, that they were thrown out of the country. In fact, no one knew.

The only part of the hooded man that you could see was his black eyes. That's it. The first times he appeared he didn't scare me; he seemed somewhat comical. But later, when those rumors began and we didn't see the people he had chosen any more, he began to inspire fear. No one wanted to be near him, though you couldn't avoid it because he went everywhere.

He appeared frequently, and we never knew if he was the same person or if there were various hooded men. After about two months

---

* Rumor had it that there were concentration camps on the islands in the south of Chile.

people began to cheer up; he appeared much less often, and everyone began to breathe more easily.

By that time, also, an official would come in the mornings to read us the paper, but trying to be funny, he would only read the sports.

I was in the stadium until about December 22 or 23; I remember that it was a little before Christmas. Very early in the morning they began to read a list of about thirty people, and I was on it. There were fewer people left by then, but it was still scary to hear yourself named that way. No one wanted to stand up when they heard their name because we didn't know where they would take us.

I went down slowly until I got to the person in charge, who gave us passes so that they would let us through the gates. In a special room they checked us, took our pictures, and lined us up.

An official that we had never seen before appeared. He was very courteous and respectful. He took us outside. It was the first time we had seen the building from the outside in three months. It was completely surrounded by soldiers! This was shocking, and we still didn't know where they were taking us.

At the gate, they stopped us and made us sign a document stating that we had been well treated. It all went very quickly, and the official shook hands with each of us, saying:

"If any of you have had any problems, you'll have to pardon us because this is all to save Chile. In the confusion, some things may have happened for which we, as soldiers, ask you, as Chileans, to pardon us."

Those phrases took away my hatred. I saw in that officer the kind of military I was familiar with, and that gave me faith again.

But we had barely gotten out the gate when I began to realize what was really happening outside. You could smell the terror in the air, and that upset me again. People crowded around to ask whether we had seen or knew anything about their relatives. People were crying, wanting to know about a son or a husband, or even a wife. My wife was there, but there were so many people that we didn't find each other. Although they never officially acknowledged my detention, she had come every day because other people who'd been set free before had assured her I was in there.

NOTHING LEFT

The first thing I did was go to the factory . . . I had to think about my job first. It didn't even occur to me to make myself presentable; I arrived very dirty, with a long, horribly ugly beard.

At the gate I saw that they had installed a military guard. I asked for Señor Uribe, who was the foreman. While they sent for him, they kept me there. Señor Uribe arrived very quickly, and the soldiers stepped aside to let him pass. That seemed a little odd, and it worried me, but in fact he had been named factory manager and at that time was in charge of everything.

He looked very upset to see me, made me come in, and explained that a retired general had been put in charge of the factory. He told me that he had spoken to him about me several times and that he was sure there wouldn't be any problems. We went to see the general immediately, who agreed that I could return to work but warned me there was no longer any union. Just like the official who had said good-bye to us at the stadium, the general insisted that we should pardon what had happened:

"Look," I said to him, "I'm owed three months' salary because I've been unjustly detained in the stadium."

"You have to understand," he answered, "that we have every intention of solving your problems here. Take three or four days off before you come back to work, and tomorrow or the next day we'll talk about your salary."

As it turned out, they paid me for the three months!

But when I went back to work I saw how things were. They had shot and killed about ten workers, among them a woman manager who hadn't been involved in anything. An enormous number of workers had also been fired because it turned out that the security forces had been in place for a while, and they had been keeping tabs on people. All the workers who had participated in the Popular Unity committees and the production committees were noted, and they weren't allowed to enter the factory.

As president of the union, I asked for a meeting, and they said they would receive us and explain to us the new role of the union. I went in very well prepared because I had been in touch with party leaders, and they had told me the government had guaranteed that the unions would continue to function and that the workers were not going to lose their benefits.

In fact, the foreman of the plant was very helpful to us and managed to rehire many people, including the two other union leaders, one of whom was a Communist and the other a Socialist.

At that time, I still didn't appreciate what the dictatorship would mean. Actually, I ran a lot of risks in the factory. There was a major from the army who was extremely arrogant, who walked around with an enormous pistol at his hip, in full view of everyone. I went up to him to talk about our problems, and the guy listened to me. He gave us his guarantee that they wouldn't take anything away from us, and I can honestly say they didn't during that period. The loss of our benefits came later.

At that time, the first problems began to arise when Señor Sumar took back control of the factory from the government and tried to rationalize the business. According to his information, it was heavily in debt and there were difficulties with raw materials, so he decided to change some of our benefits, which he said were illegal. We had several problems then, but at the same time we were able to have a more active and free union because the soldiers had left, and Sumar didn't dislike it. He had always been able to coexist with us, even though he had some pretty tough unions.

Since I had been a national leader of the labor unions, I knew many people, and a short time after I returned to the factory, I began to call them up to find out what was happening elsewhere. I wanted to send a message to other leaders to tell them not to be afraid, to tell them to face the situation. But I began to realize that things were not the same in other factories. In some, leaders were not allowed to speak—they wouldn't listen to them—and in others, there was no one who was able to speak. No one was left.

The first things the government did to reorganize the unions was to pass Decree 198 filling the union posts with the oldest workers available. Since few of them had been leaders previously, at first it was very difficult to make contact with them. It was only at the end of '75 that we began to educate the new leaders through the Cardijn Foundation, an organization supported by the Catholic Church.

That's where groups of workers first met after '73. At first the meetings consisted only of dramatic recountings of what had happened in the factories, of the people who had died, of the security agents who had come and taken somebody away. These accounts began to make people aware that the situation was unacceptable.

During that period some leaders accepted an offer to go to Geneva for the ILO meetings and defend what had happened in Chile. Someone called me from the ministry once to ask me to join a delegation, but I didn't accept.

Those who went argued that they would be able to act as interlocutors for the government and discuss the workers' problems. They acted quite discreetly. I didn't feel strongly, but it seems to me that you can't defend the situation in Chile at an international tribunal when workers' blood has been spilled in the streets and union leaders have been assaulted and killed. They always said that the killings were the result of an armed clash, but I never believed that: it was the result of extremely belligerent action on the part of the military. For this same reason, the leaders of my union didn't go to the meetings that the government organized for May 1 either.

Since there was no progress made toward normalization of the unions' activities, on their return from Geneva the other union leaders decided to stop participating in those meetings also. General MacKay, the labor minister at that time, lied to them. Then a group of leaders from different areas organized the Group of Ten, which coincided with the naming of General Nicanor Díaz as labor minister. General Díaz sincerely believed that it was necessary to normalize the union situation. We insisted that we didn't agree with Decree 198. He didn't either. He actually had a very good attitude, and the Group of Ten began to work with him on reforms in social security and the Labor Code.

Juan Manuel Sepúlveda, Hernán Mery, and I joined the Group of Ten as representatives of the sector that worked under the Cardijn Foundation and that were rank-and-file organizations. We formed commissions to work on the projects that the minister was preparing, and on May 1 General Díaz officially submitted documents with which we were in agreement.

It was a very interesting project, very European in style, with a lot of autonomy for the union; it was much more advanced legislation than what we had before 1973. It simply couldn't happen under a dictatorship, although it had been proposed by a soldier. As a result, within a month, Nicanor Díaz was no longer minister, and Sergio Fernández, who later became minister of the interior, took his place. He shelved all the projects and shut the doors of the ministry for good, subordinating all decisions to the government's economic policy and creating stooge government unions.

That was when we realized that the problems facing us were much more serious than the ones we had faced over the past four years. The Group of Ten adopted a very strong oppositional position, and the representatives of Cardijn decided that it was necessary to enlarge the organization, because originally it had not included any Marxist leaders.

Later, we decided to make public La Coordinadora, which had been functioning for a long time as a coordinator for the several federations and confederations over which I presided. We called a press conference and made our views known, making clear that we were against the dictatorship and that we were prepared to fight both in the area of the unions and in the political arena to reestablish the country's freedom.

UNION ELECTIONS

Before we went public as La Coordinadora as such, we delivered various documents to the government as union leaders.

In '78 we sent one of those documents, signed by seven hundred leaders, in which we asked for higher salaries, union elections, and collective bargaining. The government reacted by sending a group of leaders into internal exile and stripping seven confederations and federations of their legal status. They accused us of trying to provoke a Marxist uprising, of disrupting order and creating expectations that were beyond what the government could offer the workers.

They confiscated the assets of the seven organizations that were affected, they took away their headquarters, and at the beginning, they said they had also stripped all the unions affiliated with these federations of their status. That never really happened, but two weeks later, they announced that there would be union elections within forty-eight hours, and they prohibited the nomination of workers who currently held leadership posts.

Although those elections were announced one day and held the next, in practically all the factories people who supported us were elected, and we were able to keep working despite not being in the leadership ourselves. Two or three weeks later it was announced that Minister José Piñera was preparing the new Labor Code that would lay down norms both for training and for organization and negotiation.

I was no longer a leader, but I helped the people who had been elected, and after my eight-hour shift at the factory I continued to work on training others in Cardijn. At that time I felt exhausted, and I was keen on the idea of turning my energies more to training others, making them aware of what we were going through and what was to come.

But it seemed I was bothering them by advising the union, and the head of personnel, Colonel Zúñiga, decided to fire me on the grounds that my services were no longer necessary. Of the three leaders who had been there at the time of the election, I was the only one who had stayed on; the others had asked for their money and left. They did just what I was thinking of doing when being fired made me start to fight back. I realized that people would miss me, and I felt a need to defend myself and demand an explanation of why they were throwing me out.

I appealed to the courts, because as a former union leader I had job protection for a full year. But before the first hearing took place I took the matter to Alejandro Ales, who had been minister of mining during the Frei government, and who was a personal friend of Sumar. I was allowed to return to work, and since then I haven't had any more problems in the factory. But the union leaders have been much harassed. Even when General Díaz was in charge, they interrogated me a few times in the Tacna regiment. They took me in alone four times, and several other times along with other union leaders. They said that we were stirring up the union and agitating people. What they really wanted was to scare us.

MODERN BARGAINING

A few months later the new Labor Code appeared, and obviously it simply served the government's economic strategy and left the worker with no rights. Still, people didn't protest the new legislation.

We hadn't made any formal wage demands in seven or eight years, and most people were keen on the idea of collective bargaining. Television and the press went on and on about the fact that now the workers would have the ability to negotiate their rights freely with management. When they went to negotiate, though, they realized there was nothing to negotiate. When they made their demands, the factory answered with the polar opposite, and only at that point did they see how bad things were.

Some workers went on strike, but they quickly understood that in addition to its being useless, it was making them lose their salary. People began to see that it was all a farce and that they had no choice but to accept Article 49, which said that if they couldn't reach an agreement and their strike was ineffective, the plant was obliged to maintain their benefits as previously agreed, plus an amount corresponding to the consumer price index. In '82 the government modified this article because it didn't allow them to *lower* salaries, and now even the price index is a matter of negotiation.

The ability to strike is another joke because strikes are limited to a maximum of sixty days, and during that time management is free to hire other people. Furthermore, after thirty days the striking workers themselves are entitled to negotiate individually with the plant.

All of this was designed to protect the economic system. Collective striking is prohibited, and a schedule for negotiations has been established to prevent any major conflict from taking place in a particular area of production at a given moment. Thus, for example, the textile plants negotiate throughout the year: one month they deal with Sumar, and when they finish that negotiation they deal with the Commandari textile factory. It's all very efficient, and within the confines of the Labor Code any action undertaken by the workers is destined to fail.

In spite of their ostensible economic success, the government never had less than 12 or 14 percent unemployment. But up until '81 it wasn't year-round unemployment—the people rotated in and out. Later, by contrast, there was complete unemployment and people couldn't find any work at all. They ate their cars and everything else that they had, and unemployment rose to 30 percent.

Despite all this, many workers still haven't waked up, and have remained passive, terrified by the possibility of unemployment. The reaction has been greatest in other segments of the population: in the middle class, among young people, and in neighborhoods where there are many people out of work. Those people who are employed are too scared and have an immense fear of repression both outside and inside the plant.

IN JAIL

The union leaders elected in '78 held office for four years, and in '82 I was able to run again, and I got elected. But I had not had official union ties for the last four years, and my action within the Coordinadora was questioned by the government, who said that I was a political leader. All of our work had been very difficult; on the one hand, the Coordinadora is considered illegal because it groups together unions from different areas of production, and on the other hand, on a personal level, I have been accused of not being representative.

In spite of the difficulties we faced in '80, we called a conference at Punta de Tralca in which about six hundred leaders participated. This was the first union conference since the dictatorship was installed, and at it we agreed to present the government with a set of demands. We held a press conference to inform people about our demands, which were both economic and political, and within three days the government had thrown us in jail.

I was used to being arrested every year on the first of May. But on those occasions they took us to police headquarters, and this time they put us in jail. Together with Alamiro Guzmán, the secretary general of La Coordinadora, we were in jail for twelve days before they let us out on bail because we had no previous record. Afterwards we were given a sentence of 541 days, but they let us go on parole.

We insisted on presenting our demands because they reflected a resolution that had been taken democratically, and in June of '81 we delivered the document to Pinochet again, signed by more than two thousand leaders. The answer was the same: they put us in jail, this time for six months. They arrested the entire executive committee of La Coordinadora, and they wouldn't let Juan Manuel Sepúlveda, who was abroad, back into the country. They let the majority of the people out on bail after ten days, but they kept Guzmán and me inside. The experience of jail is tough. You feel like you haven't done anything wrong, yet you're treated like a common criminal. It makes you think; you get more committed to the cause than you had been, and your principles are reaffirmed.

'After the first few days, there are moments when you get depressed about being locked up—you feel extremely sad and want to go off somewhere and cry. Everything seems far away, you feel excruciatingly alone, and then you begin to see the world in very morbid terms. The days become very long, above all when they wake you up early to ransack your cell, which happens about once a week. They turn everything upside down, and that increases the sense of depression and anguish . . . There are entire nights when you can't sleep at all.

One of the most humiliating sensations is being taken to the courts in a police van, handcuffed. There are guards who will put the handcuffs on as loosely as possible, but there are others who comply with the letter of the law and tighten the handcuffs on your wrists until they begin to swell up. The majority of guards were very deferential to me. One even called me to the office and let me read some letters that, according to the censorship rules, they couldn't give to me. After I had read them, he threw them out.

At first you think you're going to get out very quickly, but after five months I had given up hope, and I assumed I would be there for a year and half, which was the maximum sentence they could give me.

I was very sad when I couldn't be with my two daughters for Christmas. The first time they came to visit me they cried a lot, and when I explained to them that I was a good person and that I hadn't done anything wrong, one of them asked me, "If they're not going to beat you or do anything to you, why can't you go home?"

On New Year's Eve we were preparing a meal with a group of prisoners when our lawyer arrived and told us we were at liberty to leave.

A USELESS ASIDE

When I got out of jail, I rejoined La Coordinadora, and, fortunately, I still had my job at the factory.

We discussed how to continue our work, and we resolved to hold a new national conference in March of 1982. The government prohibited the meeting after some foreign union organizers had already arrived in Chile, and we had to satisfy ourselves with a lunch with Cardinal Silva Henríquez. It was all surrounded by the police.

Faced with this situation, we decided to decentralize our group and to hold regional meetings which, despite the government restrictions, were attended by 1,800 leaders from all over the country. The majority of people decided that we shouldn't continue to send letters and documents to the government, but that we should work on the idea of large public gatherings that repudiated the political regime, culminating in a national work stoppage. It was decided to hold the first public gathering in the Plaza Artesanos in Santiago on December 2.

On the same day we were informed that we were not authorized to meet. But people knew the meeting would be held anyway, and I calculated that there were about five thousand people there. Still, everyone was very nervous, and most people didn't dare go out into the plaza proper, but stood on the fringes.

There were police everywhere, about eight buses full of them, some armored cars with water cannons, and a group of about fifty policemen in plainclothes, who were brutally beating people. At first only the *carabineros* threw tear gas, but then, while I was speaking to the officer in charge to get permission to tell people to withdraw, the plainclothes police decided to intervene in an incredibly violent way. They beat anyone who got in their way, and the *carabineros* didn't do anything.

It was horrible! A lot of people were bleeding, especially journalists and lawyers. After I saw what was going on and tried to report it, I left for a health center because I had been hit hard on the back and couldn't stand up straight or breathe properly. The doctor sent me home to rest, but first we wanted to go to a union headquarters where we had planned a meeting. In the taxi we realized we were being followed by other cars, and we decided not to go.

I had no intention of hiding, and I went to the Coordinadora to look for my car and to find my wife. I arrived very nervous and tense as a result of what I had seen and because of the beating I had received. I hadn't even been inside a minute when some fifteen police appeared to shut down the headquarters and to arrest me. Outside there was a crowd of cars, and they had blocked off the street.

I was locked up in a cell for the whole night. In the morning they took me to the second floor. They gave me coffee and a sandwich, and after a little while the head of the police, General Paredes, came in. He read me my arrest warrant and told me that he thought things would be resolved quickly, in three or four days.

I went calmly to my cell and fell asleep. Suddenly, at about noon, two policemen appeared and rushed me over to the passport bureau. At that moment it occurred to me that I could be expelled from the country.

They returned me to another office, and after about twenty minutes, the lawyer Roberto Garretón from the Vicariate of Solidarity appeared. "They're being very deferential," he said to me. "The cardinal spoke with the minister of the interior, and they let us come to see you."

"I think they're about to expel me from the country."

"You're crazy!" He didn't believe me. "We'll clear this up very quickly; we believe the government made an enormous mistake in arresting you."

I insisted that they had gone to Pudahuel Airport or somewhere else to complete my passport and that they were going to expel me, but he told me again to stay calm because nothing was going to happen.

Garretón had hardly left when they took me to the basement, put me in a car, and took me to Pudahuel. I found myself on a plane bound for Rio de Janeiro without a single peso because I had left everything at the Coordinadora. I was wearing blue jeans and a short-sleeved shirt. Next to me was a man reading a paper, and there was a very large photograph of me because of the events of the previous day.

"You're not Manuel Bustos?" he asked me.

He didn't believe they had expelled me. He looked at my passport, which I still had in my hand, and realized it had been issued that very day.

I began to explain everything that had happened, and tears started to fall from my eyes . . . I was very upset. The man gave me one of his shirts and twenty-five dollars to call Chile on the telephone. He was a professor at the Catholic University. He was very generous.

I was extremely anxious. I thought about what would happen to my daughters without my salary from the factory, about what they would eat and how they would go to school. I thought about the Coordinadora. I thought how far I could go on those twenty-five dollars.

I had got out of the airplane and was trying to organize what I had to do, when I saw an enormous sign saying "Welcome, Manuel Bustos."

A lot of people were there, and they told me that Héctor Cuevas* had also been expelled and was coming on a different plane. They took us to a hotel, and even before seven in the morning we began to receive hundreds of calls from all over to demonstrate solidarity and offer us whatever help we might need.

The ICFTU sent me a check for a thousand dollars for expenses and a ticket to take me to Brussels, where they had planned an urgent meeting. Furthermore, they had immediately sent help to my wife and daughters. We got more than five hundred cables! The anxiety of uncertainty was diminishing, but the anxiety over being expelled from the country remained. It's very painful. You feel the need to continue fighting, and you realize that you can serve the union movement from outside the country as well.

I left for Brussels to attend the meeting of the ICFTU, where a

---

* Secretary general of the Coordinadora and president of the Construction Workers' Union.

hundred leaders representing 80 million workers from around the world were gathered. They decided to send me to Italy, not as an exile, but as a member of the Italian union movement, and they set up tours to various places, including the United States, for me to speak, denouncing the situation in Chile.

I called thirty-five Chilean union leaders who were in exile. I had already traveled to several countries and seen that they were all slinging mud at each other, breaking up into different factions, which was not helping the workers in Chile at all. All of them came and agreed to create a central organization for solidarity called the Chilean Union Committee. We were received by Felipe González, by the foreign affairs ministries of Belgium, Germany, and France, by the Norwegians, by everyone.

Without question, the most important part of exile for me was my interview with the Pope. The days preceding it were very emotional, and I think they were the only ones in which I was able to forget that I was in exile. I had to wait for about a week before the Pope received me, together with some leaders of Catholic Action.

He spent about ten minutes with us. He greeted me by name and gave me his blessing for the Chilean workers. I felt like I was speaking in tongues. I thanked him for his intercession in the Chilean-Argentine conflict, and I asked him to make a statement on exile. He answered that we would all have to pray for an end to this painful situation, and that he would do so out loud. I also spoke to him about the situation of the Chilean workers and about the significant role that the Church had played.

It's difficult to explain how I felt as a Christian. It was a moment of great happiness, as if I had been near Christ.

In spite of those positive experiences, exile is terrible—it's much worse than being in jail. It causes a tension and anxiety that inspire hate. That's why I was constantly thinking about going back. Even though everyone in my party told me not to do it, I decided to go back that summer, to enter the country illegally and present myself immediately to the courts. I am a Christian Democrat and I have great respect for the party, but that time I was planning to ignore their advice and go back. Finally, however, I was stopped by a letter from my wife.

She is my second wife, and she was expecting our first child. That made me think about things: the time she had spent alone while I was in jail, all the times they had followed me, and the baby. As a result I changed my mind, and she came to Rome. Otherwise I'd have gone back. I wanted to be in Chile, and I didn't care if I was in jail.

One day I was in Rome at a meeting with some workers from the chemical industry when I received a phone call telling me I could return. I received the news, but I didn't have actual written permission, and I went through about ten days of awful uncertainty because you can't take anything for granted with this regime.

When the permission finally came, I left as soon as possible. I arrived in the middle of the day on a Saturday, and it was incredible! I had left Chile alone, surrounded by armed detectives who had put me on the airplane, and when I came back, I didn't even have to wait in line for a police inspection. They stamped my passport with a special stamp and led me to a room where people were waiting for me. I didn't understand what was going on. Outside there were more than a thousand people. They had expelled me from the country for organizing a meeting, and now I was back, and here was an authorized demonstration in which people were certainly saying much worse things than they had said ten months earlier. My exile was one of those useless asides of a dictatorial regime.

THE STREET: THE ONLY WAY

What impressed me most on returning was the general loss of fear, because fear had been the dictatorship's great ally. When they kicked us out, the government thought they had eliminated the danger of people in the streets, but the seeds that we had planted in '75 were already bearing fruit. The protests began to erupt over the course of several months after they threw me out of the country, and the dictatorship couldn't just expel everyone. They put Seguel and some other union leaders in jail again, but only for two or three weeks.

I quickly reassumed leadership of the Coordinadora, and from there I got involved with the National Workers' Command, which had been created to coordinate different unions—both those who were allied with the Communists and those who didn't want to be.

When I got there they were in the middle of discussing the problems of representation, since four of the five members of the executive committee were Christian Democrats and the other was an independent. I was asked to make a study that would lead to reforms, and in March of '84 I proposed an eleven-member executive committee that would integrate all the different federations and confederations. The leaders of the Workers' Democratic Headquarters got angry and withdrew, saying that we were handing over the Command to the Communists because a director of the Miners' Union, who was linked to the Communist Party, had joined the new executive committee.

In fact, this situation made the Command's job easier, because the directors who withdrew were opposed to the idea of popular protest or work stoppages; they had always been in favor of a dialogue—with deaf people, with the regime.

The Command, together with the Democratic Alliance created by the opposition parties, helped organize many protests—the June protest, the July protest, the September protest. But the most important movement we staged was the work stoppage of October 30, 1984, and we did that alone. It was an action of the National Workers' Command organized and effected with practically no money, just by making people aware that they ought to participate. At two in the afternoon, Santiago and the other big cities were empty!

It was a twenty-four-hour stoppage. We had long discussions in the course of organizing it, and for several months possible dates for the stoppage were spray-painted on the walls. A month beforehand, we chose definite dates, and the response was excellent. On November 3, the dictatorship imposed the state of siege once again.

Without the state of siege we would have called a two-day stoppage for the middle of November, and that might have had some effect on the regime, but we didn't dare do anything that extreme because we weren't sure what might happen. All the media had been against us, including the opposition media. The night of October 29, the leaders of the Workers' Democratic Headquarters went on state-owned television to discourage people from taking part in the stoppage.

The parties of the Democratic Alliance didn't support us either. In fact, they had never had much real faith in social mobilization. They had spoken of helping us organize and had discussed giving us support, but they had never really made the political decision to do so. As a result, the stoppage on October 30 wasn't even debated by the political parties. We simply told them there was going to be a stoppage on that day, and most of the leaders had the same reservations as always: "Is it possible to succeed?"

The next day the results were clear to everyone.

I think that all kinds of groups should participate in these social actions: the professionals, the students, the peasants, the politicians, because everyone is harmed by what is going on. They all say that it's necessary to return to a democratic system, and they are convinced that this regime has produced a large number of social and political injustices. That is why we have begun to organize the protests. But the political parties of the Democratic Alliance have been fearful because another political group exists—the Popular Democratic Movement—which includes the Communist Party, and that group has added a violent aspect to social action in the face of the dictatorship's own violence.

The violence of both sides has meant that many of the protests have fallen a little flat, and some have even failed because people were afraid of the violent aspects of confrontation: barricades, stones being thrown, bombardments, light poles being knocked over, and electricity being cut off. The strategy that the Communist Party pursue at their protests has hurt us enormously. It has meant that out of fear many people stay away from the protests, above all the middle class, who have by and large disengaged themselves.

Everyone is nervous when a demonstration is called: we know that anything may happen. The dictatorship has no capacity for dialogue; the only response it has is bullets. We know who is firing, who is killing people: it is armed civil police in trucks who can go wherever they like, or it is *carabineros* who are shooting to provoke people. We have seen this! I have never seen a peasant with a machine gun, but I have seen the police in the shantytowns ransacking and shooting.

Lately I have been very critical of the political groups; I feel that the opposition has committed many errors—the opposition that calls itself democratic as well as the one that has organized popular rebellion.

We lack political decisiveness. It seems as if we want to tease each other. On one side the army tries to trick the population by saying it's going to eliminate the Communists, and that when that happens the country will return to a democratic system. That's a lie. The military know that the day after they leave, be it in '89 or '97, the Communists will return to the country. On the other hand, the Communists also know that it's impossible to eliminate the military, even though they insist that we must engage in armed combat with them. The military will continue to be in Chile, and we will continue to come into contact with them; and the military will continue to come into contact with Communist senators and representatives, who may call themselves liberals, independents, or I don't know what, but who will continue to be Communists.

It's all very aggravating, because the people who take the brunt of everything are those of us who are earning miserable salaries in the factories. In the factories there are hundreds of women who have to let the boss have his way with them in order not to lose a job with a miserable salary. We can't defend ourselves, and while the politicians continue to debate the question of violence and the military keep trying to eliminate the Communists, the country goes to the dogs.

We have tried to get the political parties to reach agreements that would permit them to have a certain negotiating power with the armed forces. If I were a politician, I would call a march or a protest, I would defy the regime somehow. You can't exist by organizing meetings, signing agreements, writing proclamations; you have to defy the dictatorship—in an orderly, peaceful way, but out in the street. When there is no hope for dialogue, meetings in embassies, restaurants, and offices don't work; the only thing that works is the street. The regime has only two options: put you in jail to keep you quiet, or negotiate with you. If you really want a change, don't just keep talking—that's only for people who want their names in the newspapers.

The situation won't last forever, but when it ends, there's going to be a lot of resentment. The distance between the rich and the poor continues to grow. The day the country returns to a democratic system, it will still be very difficult to restore the kind of balance we had until '73.

I see a relatively bleak future, but I have hope. I think that we have a long fight to regain democracy, to make the armed forces come to their senses and go back to their barracks before they have to maintain their hold on power with more blood. I don't want our country to bleed to death.

A "CHICAGO BOY" WITH NO REGRETS

CARLOS PAUT UGARTE

AT THE BEGINNING OF 1984, FINDING A "CHICAGO BOY" WAS like finding a needle in a haystack, and it took me several months to come up with Carlos Paut. Although the followers of Milton Friedman have directed the Chilean economy since 1975, there was one short period—from April 1984 through February 1985, when the economic crisis became so acute that, suddenly, not a Chicago Boy was to be seen.

Some economist friends failed in their attempts to persuade various of their colleagues to talk to me. The majority responded to the very word "interview" with a resolute "no." Those I managed to contact personally gave me one or another account of why they weren't really Chicago Boys, strictly speaking.

One, who seemed to pride himself on his sense of humor, put it like this: "I was among the first to jump ship. The first avalanche occurred in '81, the majority left in '82, and the most obstinate—the ones who seemed incurable —left in '83."

Another, perhaps more honest, confessed that he was too depressed and didn't feel capable of looking back on the past ten years.

Just as I was about to give up hope, Carlos Paut appeared—a commercial engineer, thirty-six years old, married with four children, chief of finances for an insurance company—who, as a disciple and friend of the principal organizers of the economic model, had no objections to the interview. He made no attempt to apologize for anything he had done or thought during the past decade. And he had no problem at all with the label "Chicago Boy," although he had never studied at the University of Chicago.

We "Chicago Boys" are people who think the same way—based on the idea of equal opportunity—and who simply want to do things as efficiently as possible.

We don't have the absolute truth; we preach impartiality. Activities shouldn't develop thanks to special protections or pressure applied by some group. Similar rules should exist for everyone: in other words, we should all have the same opportunities; we all, for instance, should have access to the same credit at the same cost.

Now we're to blame for everything. Still, I think that the net result of what was done is more positive than negative. I can even say that I feel satisfied because any economic policy faced with the kind of problems we had to contend with would have had the same drop in production. At best it would have had a smaller effect in terms of unemployment, but that's a factor of a different nature.

On this point there is a problem of definition, because unemployment is not an economic matter but a social one. You can have a marvelous plant with a social problem: as a plant manager, I may think that the plant is fabulous, while inside things are a mess. These are two distinct things, and it is important not to let economic problems become social problems.

If the decision about unemployment had been in my hands, I might have dared to propose some unpopular measures, such as a mandatory salary cut. There are no miracles here! Chile produces a certain amount, and that is what we have to share. It's painful, but if we don't want to have unemployment, we must accept lower wages. Although this is true, obviously no politician is going to say so because he will never be elected.

In that sense, the new Labor Code was very positive in that it put the responsibility on the workers as well as on the plants. The workers can't ask more than what the plant is able to grant them, because putting the plant in a bad situation in the market means death for everyone. Businesses, for their part, can't afford to ignore the workers either, because they will go elsewhere. This is especially true when there are low levels of unemployment.

Since industry is in real trouble these days, excessive demands by the workers will only lead to collective suicide. Still, the Labor Code offers sufficient flexibility to reach harmonious agreements and to achieve, for example, a lowering of wages to a level at which the plant can survive.

Unfortunately, this Labor Code was adopted only recently, and it's very difficult for anyone to gain significant benefits in a period of recession. You can't ask for a raise in salary when the plant is having problems and when, furthermore, there are five hundred unemployed workers waiting to do your job—and what is worse, for less money.

We may seem very cold because we defend certain ideas that aren't at all popular, but in this case we are really helping the unemployed. From that point of view we are going to seem insensitive, because we are always going to think about those who are worse off and because it's necessary to be cold to benefit the vast majority. Once this is understood, it becomes clear that if one sector comes to ask me for something that is not for the general good, I can't accede to their demands.

What has inspired us is simply thinking about this vast majority that has no representation and no one to defend it. The chairman of the National Planning Office, Miguel Kast, who was one of the great inspirations for all of this, is firmly rooted in this type of thinking: always think of the most underprivileged!

THE LESSER EVIL

Miguel was central to my decision to return to Chile after the eleventh of September. We had both been in the United States—he in Chicago and I in California—and he called me to tell me that I should go back. We had been friends at the university, and I had great respect for him because he was brilliant and had strongly formed humanistic principles, and even greater Christian principles. His opinions had a great influence on me, above all because he had turned down the offer of an excellent job as economic adviser for the government of Mexico.

I had arrived in the United States in August of '73 because I had no job prospects in Chile. I had worked for Assler and Company, but the company had been taken over and I'd been fired. Furthermore, at that time I felt that the country was inevitably headed for a civil war in which many people would die.

I sold the only thing that I had, which was a car, and I left with $1,500, naively thinking that I could set myself up abroad. The idea was to go to Spain, because of the language, but when the coup came, I was still in California with some cousins.

We listened to a Mexican radio station which broadcast news from Chile every day, but that time the news surprised me: they announced that the navy had returned from UNITAS maneuvers and had disembarked in Valparaíso. It was an unconfirmed story originating with Mendoza, but I immediately thought it was something serious because never before had they spoken about the armed forces.

A few minutes later other unofficial sources confirmed that not only the navy was involved: all three branches of the armed forces and police were involved, and they had asked Salvador Allende to resign. It seemed quite serious, and there followed a succession of announcements, including the ultimatum demanding that Allende abandon La Moneda, lists of people who were told to present themselves under penalty of death, Allende's death, and the names of the members of the Junta, headed by Augusto Pinochet, whom I had never heard of before in my life.

I felt a certain relief because, according to the news, there had been a total coup and everything was under control without a civil war having erupted. It was the best thing that could possibly have happened. On the third day I managed to get through to Chile, and since no one had much of an idea of what was going on, I decided to stay where I was for a few months. I took it as a vacation because I had paid my own way through college, and I hadn't had a break for the past five years. Although at that time the universities were free, I felt responsible for not being a burden to my family, since there were five children.

In the end I stayed in the United States almost a year. There, Allende was made out to be a marvelous person, and people constantly made the mistake of supposing that Chilean socialism was like German social democracy; they didn't know the truth about what had been happening in Chile. They couldn't believe it when I told them that my friends from Popular Unity told me that when the revolution came I would be considered an enemy, that the fact of having a car was a sin that labeled me a rich person, and that as a result, I was targeted to be killed in a civil war that the Marxists would win. People in the United States couldn't believe that things had reached those extremes.

They tended to idealize Allende's regime and to see him as a very good person, very concerned with the poor; but they couldn't place all of this in the Chilean context, which is very different from other Latin American countries. In Chile, we don't have just rich people with gigantic fortunes and poverty-stricken paupers the way other places do; here we have people of every economic shading.

Pinochet, on the other hand, they make out to be thoroughly bad. They speak of all the deaths, of the murders, things that I believe did in fact happen . . . I don't doubt that there were plenty of deaths, but deep down I have always thought about what would have happened if civil war had broken out. Instead of mourning 80,000 or 100,000 deaths—I have no idea what the figure is—we would have had a much more painful experience. I saw the coup as the lesser evil, given what could have happened.

I began to see that the principles that inspired the Junta, such as order, were honest principles that I shared. Chile had been governed by a political elite that was motivated more by the interests of the party members than by the interests of the country. I concluded that the soldiers—whose profession is to safeguard the interests of the nation, from a strategic point of view—could offer the same safeguard on another level. But I always viewed it as something transitional, and I continue to see it that way.

Obviously, at the time people looked at things in a very idealistic way, but I continue to share those principles, above all the conviction that this must not be a Marxist society. If you can call me anything, it's an anti-Marxist. I believe in freedom; I like freedom, and as a result, I think that the more freedom you have the more you grow to respect it. But sometimes democratic regimes suffer from too much freedom, and I think we all have to slow down so that freedom does not slip from our grasp; we must preserve freedom, but with restrictions.

When I made the definite decision to go back, I did it in the spirit of contributing what I could, because I actually owed a lot to this country. When I left, I owed it the cost of my studies, which I have always felt should be paid for by the student. I couldn't see the logic in having 600,000 or 1 million workers paying for my studies; I can't take away the poor workers' resources to study for free. I believe that if a student has financial problems, the state should simply make a loan available to him.

In the end, I extended my stay a little longer to take advantage of a law that had been passed permitting professionals to import certain things if they had been out of the country before the coup and had stayed away for more than six months. I was able to pay for some of my trip by bringing back a car, some stereos, and various other little luxuries.

I spent about a year on vacation, leading a kind of hippie life. I'd work for a couple of weeks in my cousin's auto repair shop, and then I'd just hang out. I remember it as being quite pleasant: I was alone, and it was the time in my life when I had the fewest worries. I would get up in the mornings and have absolutely nothing that I had to do.

I had a fleeting desire to stay there, but I thought that I had a profession I shouldn't throw away, and, above all, I felt that I could be much more useful in Chile than where I was.

BAKERS, TO YOUR PASTRIES!

Oddly, when I arrived I did not get in touch with Miguel Kast. After a few days, a friend offered me a job as a financial analyst in the Techno Industrial Company, a producer of refrigerators and other appliances, and since I didn't want to be a burden at home, I quickly accepted.

TIC had been recently formed, and I immediately had to do a study of the merger of two appliance manufacturers who, after having been expropriated during Popular Unity, were being returned to the Javier Vial Group* in the midst of large-scale, worldwide recession caused by the rise in petroleum prices. My job was to come up with the figures and to present the project to the antitrust commission, which was worried that the merger might create a very powerful monopoly that would work against the interests of the consumers. I was supposed to explain that if things continued as they were, the plants were going to be irremediably wrecked, resulting in the unemployment of the 3,500 workers who were there at the time, as opposed to the 1,300 that TIC was planning to let go in an effort to stay afloat.

It was a relatively thankless task, because on the one hand, you had to be realistic about the business, which had run into serious debt, and on the other, to think about the problems of a group of people who would be out of work. After about eight months, I got in touch with Miguel Kast, and they offered to put me in charge of pricing for DIRINCO.†

In May of '75 I became the assistant head of the department of expenses and budgets, supporting the economic minister, Sergio de Castro, who had been a professor of mine at the university. I thought that in this position I would be able to repay part of what I had received from the country, taking advantage of the fact that I was still single, since the salary was quite low. To work in public administration was considered military service.

---

* Javier Vial and Manuel Cruzat headed the principal economic conglomerates that arose after the military coup. Both groups crumbled during the crisis of 1982.

† Organization of Industry and Commerce.

. . . . .

AN ENORMOUS RESPONSIBILITY

I was in DIRINCO until the beginning of 1977. Then I got married and decided to switch jobs, basically for economic reasons. I became the assistant head of finances of Food Cooperative Supermarkets (UNICOOP), which was a good place to be in terms of money, and at the same time, an indirect way to continue to collaborate with government people.

My job was to do a study of the projections for the cooperative, since all the organizations were having problems and wanted the government to lend them $5 million so that they could continue to function. Before making a decision, the authorities wanted these studies, which definitively showed that the business was not financially viable and chose to have the government step in.

Renato Gazmuri was hired as a temporary administrator, and I worked with him in UNICOOP until the end of '78 and then for two more years in IFICOOP, another cooperative the government went into. From there, I went to an insurance company for a while. That's where I was when Renato Gazmuri called me again, this time to work on a big social security reform.

I accepted on the condition that it was purely temporary, for a maximum of six months, because it meant returning to public administration, which wasn't what I wanted to do. I agreed to help install the new social security system, but that's it, because I knew that otherwise I would end up with a long commitment, and I had to think about the economics of it since at that time I already had two children.

I was making 90,000 or 100,000 pesos, half of what I could make outside the public sector. One can contribute to society through public administration or through private business, but with greater personal benefit in one case than in the other.

Together with Gazmuri and Adolfo Rojas, we created all the systems—both legal and financial—to operate the Pension Fund Administration. It was a truly titanic job, and we worked morning, noon, and night during those months to get the project ready by the ordained date.

In the old system there had been about 150 different pension plans, and some were in better shape than others, depending on the pressures that had been brought to bear. Members of parliament, for example, could retire after fifteen years. Faced with this, we aimed to create a system that was fair, that wasn't based on power, but on each person's contribution, measured month by month.

The system was in place by May 1, we saw that it was working well, and in July I left to take a vacation, which I hadn't done in the last four years. I went to the United States with my wife for a month. We had never been there together before. I wanted to show her the places where I had been during my "hippie" stage and also to take advantage of our trip to visit an insurance company in the hope of lining up work for when I returned to Chile.

The little time I had spent working in insurance motivated me because it struck me as an exciting topic that mixed aspects of finance and probability. I was interested in exploring the field, and I accepted an offer from Aetna BanChile.

In the beginning it was a completely unknown company that had relatively modest resources to manage. But by the end of three years it was administering nearly $80 million. As the company developed, its investment portfolio became larger, and, given my previous experience, after six months they offered me the position of chief of finances, which I have held for the last two years.

I like what I do very much, but at the same time it's very difficult. It's an enormous responsibility! In this company, for example, money comes in that must be invested to fulfill long-term obligations for people who are bound to outlive us. It's a very big responsibility, and in my case it has affected the nerves in my back—I'll suddenly go all clenched up and tense . . . Because you're trying to maximize the market opportunities. Economic activity has so many nuances and complexities that you're constantly trying to interpret what's happening.

The competition doesn't bother me much. It's logical and natural, and tomorrow, when someone shows up who's better than I am, I'll welcome him. It's a natural law—because the whole world is like that —and I believe that if you keep that in mind, there's no reason to be afraid of it.

In any case, I don't think I'll end up out of a job. At worst I won't have as good a job as this one, but I think that you always have alternatives. Maybe I won't be the head of finances in an insurance company, but the head of a retail shop. Still, that option always exists.

For now, I feel completely satisfied, and I think I'll be able to continue to do things because I'm not at the stage where my activity is declining. I would like to be a businessman, to do something in some area that would last a long time . . . In livestock perhaps, or some agro-industry. I have a few animals, and I hope to develop something from them.

In '78 I bought six bullocks, which over time have become fifty head. I haven't tried to do the figures because depending on how you look at it, the investment may come out positive or negative. In any case, it hasn't been that good in monetary terms, but from the point of view of development, to start out with six and end up with fifty is good. This is a ten-year project in which I hope to establish a small range for my animals and to increase the number until I have four hundred head.

In any case, I'm not one of those who is indebted beyond his means. We haven't bought ourselves anything special.

WITHOUT A LEVEL HEAD

The only thing that we did was to buy ourselves a larger house than the one we had before, which belonged to my wife. We moved within the same neighborhood, and the loan that we took was for a totally reasonable amount.

There are other people who live happily, buying things on credit, and the open economy has given everyone this option. Still, I think there were people who overestimated their capacity and took on commitments that were beyond what would have been prudent.

Even at the time of the "boom" I realized that things were getting out of hand. I remember that I went down Colón Street every day and saw how they were knocking down houses to put up buildings with apartments valued at $100,000, $200,000, or $250,000. I can't imagine who could buy those apartments because in relative terms I consider myself to have a high salary, and there's no way I could afford a house like that. I thought that someone must have made a mistake, because if there are people who make more than I do, there aren't many of them. Finally, I said to myself that each person knows what he is able to do . . . and if there were banks giving credit for those things, they must see the risks they were running.

In spite of these problems, that was a period of very strong growth beginning in '78 and continuing through '80 or '81, when we felt the repercussions of the recession in the United States. From that point on the recession affected everybody. It affected me directly with a salary cut, like everyone else, and indirectly with some family problems.

My father was left unemployed and a brother, who was very involved with a private transportation business, is doing very badly. These are the natural effects of a recession.

My brother is someone who gets very involved with his job; he was working as a bus driver and mechanic, but he still didn't have enough money to live on. But that has to do with his financing problems, because he didn't put a single peso into the business so that with what he was earning all he could manage was to pay his debts. Someone who doesn't put a peso of capital in simply can't hope to turn a profit! When he finished paying off his debts he was going to have an income both from his bus-driving job and from the business, but unfortunately, the bus was burned during a protest . . . It was just bad luck.

In these ten years, Chile has endured an enormous period of adjustment, and when it began, they said that we were working for the next generation and not for ourselves. But Chileans are impatient, and we want to see results right away. There are many areas of investment—in mining, forestry, and fruit-growing—which will mature in the next five to ten years. And then we will have a different opinion of our economy because these projects, in which Chile has relative advantages, will be in full operation.

Perhaps the international recession can't be blamed for everything, and certainly there were some mistakes made, but you can't say exactly who made them. The responsibility is shared between business, government, and all of us, because I think that a collective error was committed based on false expectations.

To begin with, too many changes were attempted during this period, and there was no time for them to mature sufficiently so that we could measure the results. In that sense, it may have been a matter of irresponsible investments by businessmen. But I don't have the slightest doubt that businessmen and the big finance groups acted in good faith.

Those people were working hard for the development of the country, both Javier Vial and Manuel Cruzat, as well as others who were less publicly known. They wanted growth that would benefit all Chileans. They were handed businesses with thousands of problems, they invested and went into debt, constantly bringing in foreign credits that were designed to benefit others.

I don't think that Javier Vial was thinking only of his personal benefit; I believe he was less interested in filling his purse than in satisfying his ego by arranging things effectively. What he liked, more than ownership, was to have someone bring a project to him and to make it work. The only people who had clearly bad intentions were those who planned in advance to obtain credits and then move their businesses. But Javiar Vial had no intention of hurting anyone.

Now that various executives from the big financial groups are in jail a series of operations are coming into question, about which it is very difficult to know the truth. For example, if the head of a household has run up debts with the grocer, and is suddenly told that this must stop, she can't change her situation overnight. She's likely to pay off everything she owes in the morning, but at the same time to go into the red with the pharmacist, and as a result, her overall debts stay the same. Certainly, a neighbor who is suddenly asked to pay off a debt is going to feel tricked, but everything depends on context.

On the other hand, those groups did not create the country's economic policy. Like everyone else, the businesses were happy while they had the possibility of credit and could continue to grow. But naturally, businessmen don't defend anything beyond their own businesses, and when the problems began, they stopped supporting the Chicago Boys.

· · · · ·

PINOCHET WON'T FALL

It would have been very difficult to apply this kind of economic policy without a military regime, because various groups would have tried to exert different kinds of pressure. It would have been the same as always, and the most organized groups would have walked away with specific advantages. Furthermore, it's very difficult to explain economic problems to the masses, and, as a result, my concept of democracy is somewhat different.

I believe in a democracy in which certain general objectives are submitted to a vote; after that, each matter should be handed over to experts capable of realizing those objectives. In a family, for instance, when there is a health problem, you don't have a democratic vote about what steps to take; you call a doctor, a specialist. In community problems, the same thing should happen, and the idea of "one person, one vote" is fine for general matters but not for specific problems.

This concept of specialists seems tremendously important to me, because, my God, it's easy to make promises without keeping them! In economics there are no miracle cures that take place over night, and anyone who promises those is lying. On this point I think there is a problem of political dishonesty, because politicians make one promise after another, knowing full well they can't keep them.

A politician can stand on a street corner and lie without being punished in the slightest. He can go around creating false expectations that work against the very democracy that we want to defend. As a result, when Pinochet is no longer here, I would like a democracy headed by responsible people, a different democracy that does not contain within it elements that will destroy it. In this respect, I think that freedom ought to be restricted, because it is good up to a certain point and then it begins to endanger society.

When people are deprived of their normal freedom to move around or are thrown out of the country, this is obviously a personal infringement for them. But, on the other hand, what those people do is questionable and reproachable—they're not saints and they don't deserve the same treatment as people who really haven't done anything.

In general terms, dictatorships have a negative connotation, above all when the dictator is bad. Still, when the dictator is not bad, there can be positive results, and I think that is what has happened in Chile.

I don't have any special knowledge about DINA, but if they were really out to find people working against democracy, people who didn't hesitate to kill to achieve their goals, I think what they were doing was good. I'm not one of those who don't believe that there were disappeared persons, because while I was in the United States I heard about all the killings that took place early on, and there must have been a lot of disappeared. Nor do I deny that some innocent people may have died, and that is truly regrettable, but it is very complicated to determine who is responsible. You might be able to determine some direct responsibility, but who is *really* responsible? We could blame a poorly written constitution, a government that made promises it couldn't keep and created false expectations . . . It isn't fair to look for one single person responsible for this situation because, in my opinion, we're talking about a series of historical events in which many people participated.

There are a lot of people today who share with the government certain principles, such as order, peace, and calm, and when we overcome the economic problem—as I hope will happen—the government will regain the support it had in its heyday.

With salary cuts and 30 percent unemployment, they can't expect applause. I figured there would have to be some kind of demonstrations, so the protests didn't surprise me. But no matter how big a mess we are in now, the government isn't going to fall. This isn't a government that responds to that kind of thing; it's an authoritarian government and, if things get really bad tomorrow, I have no doubt that the army will go out into the streets.

I hope that we will be able to solve our problems as fairly and equitably as possible. If we aren't able to look for a rational, humanitarian solution, maybe the best thing would be a dictatorship ten times worse than this one, of whatever party! Because I'm sure that the people who benefit from the protests and the demonstrations are the Communists, never the democratic parties.

THE SOLDIERS' FRIEND

MOY DE TOHÁ

L UCÍA AND GENERAL AUGUSTO PINOCHET UGARTE SEND warm greetings to their distinguished friends Señor José Tohá G. and Señora Victoria E. Morales de Tohá and thank them very sincerely for the noble gesture of friendship they made by leaving the ministerial post.

Lucía and Augusto would like to express their fond feelings for the Tohá Moraleses and hope that they will continue to be considered their friends.

We hope that when Lucía returns we will have the pleasure of seeing you both.

In the meantime, please accept our kindest regards, as always.

SANTIAGO, JULY 10, 1973

She was married to José Tohá for nine years. Her real name is Victoria Eugenia Morales Etchevers, but she is known as Moy de Tohá and is proud to use her husband's name, "because," she says, "if anything miraculous has happened in my life, it was marrying that man"—a Socialist, a high-ranking leader of Popular Unity, a former defense minister who knew the military from up close and who died, after six months in prison, weighing less than 110 pounds.

Moy still has a tender face and a soft, sweet voice which at first conceals the pain and suffering that she carries inside. She sounds convincing when she insists that she feels no hatred, but her face becomes rigid and her age shows when she relates some of what she has lived through in the last decade.

She is inclined to tell her story to make people aware of what really happened: "It mustn't be like what happened with the Germans," she stresses, "where they lived next to concentration camps and didn't know what was going on." According to her, there is no one member of the military who is responsible for what happened; she talks about a dehumanized political system that must be made anathema so that these things will never happen again. "I don't want what happened to me to happen to Pinochet or to Señora Pinochet."

After September 11, 1973, many of her friends asked for her help in facing difficult situations. She was "the soldiers' friend," and she would know what to do. Even Hortensia Bussi de Allende asked her to make inquiries at the Defense Ministry.

She no longer dares to say that she knows the military. She has recently come to understand, she explains, that all military men want to become generals, and for this reason they will never contradict their superiors. She is convinced that not a leaf stirs in the country without the commander in chief knowing about it. She insists that midlevel officers are not to blame, that military men don't act on their own initiative, but follow orders.

When José Tohá died, she went to Mexico with her eight-year-old daughter and five-year-old son. She lived in exile for five years and then returned to a Chile that she didn't recognize. She had no job, no home, and her friends were exiled or dead. She set up a catering business that she later had to sell, but where she continued to work as an employee. Little by little, she became accustomed to the country in its new form, taking part in different solidarity groups that had been created: Committee for the Return of the Exiled, Committee for Children Injured by the State of Emergency, Committee for the Executed, for the Disappeared, Committee for Free Expression . . .

Through them she has continued to fight for the ideals of a Latin American, humanistic, and profoundly Chilean socialism, in which she firmly believes: "The day we have elections, the Socialist vote will be extremely important. I am as sure of what I say as if I had a crystal ball in front of me."

They called at about seven-fifteen on the morning of the eleventh. José got up, got dressed without taking a shower, and called his brother Jaime, who was the minister of agriculture.

"When you get the car, come by and pick me up, because I'm going to La Moneda."

I didn't know what was happening, but it was all very strange.

"There seem to be problems with the navy, because the ships have come back," José told me.

I took a bath and washed my hair. I don't know why; nothing I remember seems to make sense. I washed my hair knowing that José was about to leave, just as he had left on June 29 for the "Tancazo." *

I heard José knock on the bathroom door to say good-bye. "I'll see you at lunchtime," I said. But he kept knocking, so I put on my robe, wrapped my hair in a towel, and went out. He just wanted to give me a kiss. That was the last time José left the house. He never came back.

He took the children and two rifles, with registration papers for the guns, to my mother-in-law's house. He called several times over the course of the morning.

Salvador called to tell me to go out to Tomás Moro, the Allende house, and prevent Tencha (Hortensia's pet name) from going to La Moneda at all costs. As I hurried to dry my hair I began to hear airplanes overhead. They weren't bombing yet, and I didn't know if they were good or bad. Later, during one of his calls, José told me not to go anywhere and to tell Tencha to leave Tomás Moro immediately and to come to our house. It took me a long time to get through to Tencha because the phone was busy. Finally she called me. "I'm under the bed," she told me. "They're bombing us."

They were bombing Tomás Moro even before La Moneda because

---

* A military uprising put down by troops loyal to the government.

they thought there was an arsenal there. I don't know where they got that idea.

At about three-thirty I got a call from Lucho Matte. "Moy," he said, "I have terrible news: the president is dead."

"You're crazy! I just spoke to José an hour ago . . ."

"What I'm saying is the absolute truth. Juan Enrique Lira was at La Moneda taking pictures, and he says Allende killed himself."

That was the version I heard.

It must have been four-fifteen when José called me for the last time.

"This is the last time I'll call," he told me. "Leave the children with my mother for the night and don't let them go out. Don't you leave the house either. They're coming to get me any minute now."

"Where is the president?" I asked him, though I already knew.

"The president is fine, but he isn't here. I'm in the Foreign Relations Ministry." *

I didn't dare tell José that Salvador was dead, but it turned out to be a bad idea because he heard the news in the Defense Ministry from Admiral Patricio Carvajal, one of the principal organizers of the coup.

I had barely hung up before I dialed the Ministry of Defense, and Commander Merrick, a former aide of José's, answered the phone.

"Commander," I said to him, "I want to know what's happening with José, because I was in touch with him by phone, and I know that the president is dead."

"Your husband is walking out the main door of the Ministry of Foreign Relations right now. I can see him from my window . . ."

He listed the peole who were walking with him, which confirmed that he was telling me the truth, because he named some secretaries and government officials like Jaime Tohá, Clodomiro Almeyda, and Carlos Briones, who I knew were with José. I didn't learn anything after that until eleven-thirty that night when I picked up the phone and called Patricio Carvajal at his home.

* The Ministry of Foreign Relations is located inside La Moneda, at the opposite end of the building from the president's office.

Our biggest worry was finding Tencha. Then the phone calls started to come in: Laura Allende* is dead; So-and-So is dead . . . more harrowing things than you could possible take in! So I focused on practical things: Who should I call? Who should I tell? Who should I protect? Who should I ask?

My world before the coup was made up primarily of military people, so naturally that's who I called. The last one I called, who got on the phone only after keeping me waiting for fifteen minutes, was Carvajal. One of my reasons for calling him was that José's name had appeared as "wanted" on the first military broadcast, and I knew that he had been arrested. Jaime Tohá and Orlando Letelier had been on the lists also, and they had been taken into custody as well.

"There's so much to do," Carvajal answered me, "that in the confusion someone must have mixed up his papers." He confirmed that José was at the Military Academy.

"Nothing is happening to him," he told me. "and you know, I have a lot of respect for your husband. He looks fragile, but he's very strong. I'm sure he'll come out of this fine. Right now we're in the middle of too many things, but tomorrow I'll take the necessary steps to get him clothing, medicine, whatever he needs."

"But this can't go on forever! I thought José would be home by tomorrow . . ."

I was very naive. Stupid! The president was dead, but I still wasn't able to see how things were.

I was alone, in bed, when the Junta came on television from the Military Academy. I already knew that José was there, a few yards behind them. What a monstrous situation! Pinochet, with his dark glasses and his horrifying face, uttering phrases that had nothing to do with the man I had known. It was horrible; him, Merino, all of them!

I knew the four of them. The jacket José wore on Dawson Island had been a gift from Leigh†—it was an air force jacket. When I saw

* Senator Laura Allende, the president's sister.

† General Gustavo Leigh, commander in chief of the air force and a member of the Military Junta until July 24, 1978, when he was dismissed for his criticism of Pinochet's policies.

them on the screen I had a sort of pragmatic reaction—something like, Thank goodness I know them and have access to them, so that they can do something! And everyone else thought the same thing. Even Tencha called me for information. To all of them, Moy was the friend of the military men.

NEXT SATURDAY

On Thursday or Friday before the eleventh I was with Carlos Prats at a going-away party thrown for him by the government. We arrived quite late, and we had barely walked in when Carlos called me over to sit at his table. I sat down next to him, on a little stool, and saw that he had a look of deep concern on his face, although by this time the party was in full swing.

Carlos said something to me that I found very disturbing, something like, "What's coming is scary, it's horrible."

"What?" I said to him. "What's coming?"

"Everything that's coming is terrifying. Durán* didn't know the half of it when he talked about blood being spilled."

"You're crazy! How can you say a thing like that? The people in charge of the military realize they can't just crush the workers' organizations, that the people are going to defend their rights."

"It's terrifying. When military men go to war, they go to war."

"But still, Carlos, I think everything is determined by the attitude of the commander in chief. Your attitude stopped things from getting out of hand during the Tancazo and was an example to the officers under your command. I think having Pinochet in charge now is a kind of guarantee, considering his friendship for you, and for all of us."

"Augusto! I've been trying to get in to talk with him for ten days now."

This terrified me, because the two of them were like brothers. They were intimate friends—Pinochet had been his right-hand man.

---

* Radical Senator Julio Durán had made this prediction on a television program.

"How could someone who was commander in chief not have access to the man who replaced him?"

"I call him at the ministry, I call him at home, and nothing. I think Carvajal has converted him."

"What can we do?"

"He likes you a lot—why don't you invite him to dinner at your house this weekend? You can say it's a going-away party for me, to revive the old friendship among all of us when you were at the ministry."

It seemed like a good idea. A little while later I ended up at a table near José and Orlando Letelier. I told them to speak with Prats, because what he said had horrified me. They went to talk with him over in the corner, and they were there for about half an hour.

I was in charge of the pilot program at the Women's National Council, and the next day I called Pinochet as soon as I got to the office.

"Last night I was at a going-away party for Carlos Prats," I told him, "and I felt very guilty because we were so close when José was at the ministry, and we haven't done anything about his leaving. I don't think the time is right for a big party, but why don't a small group of us get together at our house this Saturday? You, Lucía, Sofía, Carlos , Irma de Almeyda, since her husband is away, Isabel Margarita, Orlando, José, and me."

"That would be fantastic," he said, "but you know Lucía has been so nervous and has me so nervous that I haven't been able to deal with this problem of the strike and the shortages. I thought the best thing was to get her and the children away from it all, so I sent them off for a snow holiday. But I'll take a rain check and we can eat together Saturday the fifteenth, at your house."

I was a little uneasy because of what Carlos Prats had told me, but I didn't have the sense that he was running away, just that he had chosen another date. I was completely stupid! I believed a lot of things, and I even continued to believe them after the coup. The coup was on Tuesday; by Saturday José was a prisoner and Pinochet was the head of the Military Junta.

. . . . .

A HORROR FILM

The night of the twelfth Tencha called and asked me to arrange for someone to pick up some things from Tomás Moro—clothing, $150 that she had in her desk, and a gold bracelet with medallions from each of the different posts Salvador had held, which she wanted as a keepsake. She was holding up fairly well. She told me that she had gone to Salvador's burial and that now she was going to the Mexican embassy. It never occurred to her to seek asylum—she didn't realize that the mere fact of setting foot in the embassy would put her in that position. Tencha didn't want to leave.

The next morning I called the Ministry of Defense and spoke with Nicanor Díaz Estrada, who had taken over the position of chief of staff from Carvajal, who had become a minister. I asked him for permission to go get Tencha's things from Tomás Moro.

"Personally," he said, "I would give you leave to go. But I have to get it okayed higher up. I'll call you."

Since he didn't, I called him several times, and he insisted that he was working on it. On the fourteenth, when the curfew had already begun, and after I don't know how many phone calls, a black wreck of a car arrived from the Ministry of Defense. There was a driver, another very large person, and someone who must have been some kind of official who sat next to me. Six or seven years later I discovered that the man next to me had been Pedro Espinoza, one of the people who later took part in the assassination of Orlando Letelier.

I left for Tomás Moro like a zombie. When we got there, an officer camouflaged like a tree appeared and told me I couldn't go in. Pedro Espinoza showed him my warrant from the Ministry of Defense, but he still refused and said that if I would tell him what I wanted, he would bring it to me. A long-drawn-out argument followed, and I saw that the sun was beginning to set. Finally he said to me, "I wanted to spare you, Señora Tohá, but if you insist on entering, I can't stop you. Go ahead."

He opened the front door and there was the same Tomás Moro where roses had just been opening their buds when I saw it the previous Sunday, now torn apart by the bombardment. The tiles around the door had been broken off, the curtains were ripped and falling down. It was as if sixty years had gone by, not five days. But this scene was nothing compared with inside. On the dining-room table was one of Tencha's purses, and the paintings—a Matta, a Portocarrero, a Guayasamín—had been deliberately ripped to pieces with a knife or bayonet. All along the stairs were pieces from two suits of armor that had been broken to bits, the heads ripped from the bodies, the arms thrown farther down the staircase, which was also destroyed. The rug was cut up . . . it was like a cemetery, like a Hitchcock film.

I went up to the second floor, walking between those metal arms and legs, and upstairs there was nothing, because after the bombs, the scavengers of high society had descended, looking for God knows what, and they had taken away every last piece of clothing. The only things left were some suitcases with clothing Tencha had saved from the fifties. All over the floor were miniskirts, gauze blouses—things from another era. I searched and searched and couldn't find anything to bring Tencha except a red dress that evidently no one had liked, and I thought, "How can Tencha arrive in another country wearing red?" The desk had been hacked to pieces, and of course the bracelet with Salvador's medals was long gone, as was the $150 that Tencha was counting on for getting out of Chile.

In Tencha's bedroom even the mattress was split open. The plants had been uprooted, and a collection of Latin American handicrafts had been ruined and left on a table. Nothing was left. I began to fill some cheap suitcases that obviously hadn't belonged to the Allende family but had been left by someone on their staff or had belonged to the police who used to live with the president; I threw in whatever I found: one earring, because the other was missing, a couple of syringes, and a handful of pills. I went down with the suitcases and the officials obsequiously carried them out for me because, of course, they were perfect gentlemen.

What struck me most of all, what shocked me, was that in the living room, in a large yellow chair, the Allendes' German shepherd was giving birth. Amid that profound desolation, where death radiated from the walls, there was life—those puppies were being born. The dog cried, and the pups tried to press their bodies against her in this Empire chair whose joints had been knocked apart by the bombs. I remember that it gave me a kind of happiness to think that, despite everything, there was some hope for life and for what might happen in the future.

Then I went to Salvador's study, which was covered with papers, several inches thick, on the floor—I don't know where they all came from because I don't see how he could have kept that many in one room.

I walked around, picking up some photographs I found. On the back of a chair was a camel's-hair coat of Salvador's, which I put over my arm. The door to Salvador's bedroom was partly open, and since my hands were full of photographs I pushed it with my shoulder, then let out a terrible scream when I saw a soldier asleep on the bed. A soldier with his boots off, half-naked, drunk, with a bottle of Chivas Regal on the floor. When I screamed, the guy sat up and the other officials came running in. They threw him out of the room, cursing at him. It was an awful feeling to see a drunken soldier in that room, the room where the president had slept. The clothes Salvador had taken off when he left—no doubt with the same urgency as José had left my house—were still there. I took the pajamas and the robe and went out panic-stricken. I was eager to close a chapter in my life as I closed the door of Tomás Moro.

At that moment I began to fathom what was happening. I understood what it meant to be hated, to feel that you are an enemy of these people. I saw that the horror was real, that it wasn't just talk or threats or things meant to scare me, but real. That's when the second phase began: the effort to rescue our husbands.

SPECIAL AFFECTION

Early on Monday, September 17, I went with Isabel Margarita to the Ministry of Defense. The entryway was full of low-ranking officers with helmets and machine guns. We presented ourselves and heard someone inside shout, "The wives of Minister Letelier and Minister Tohá are at the door!"

It was as if we had suddenly returned to a past era. An official came out to receive us and asked our forgiveness because he had to search us. We had to leave our identity cards at the door. Inside there was a woman dressed in street clothes, an ordinary woman, who emptied out our purses and searched our things before letting us pass.

From that moment on, we walked around the Ministry of Defense as if we were at home: they didn't ask us anything else, not what we were doing there, who we were looking for, nothing. We wandered around like lost souls, looking for someone to speak with, and it occurred to us to try to find Magliocchetti, who had been Allende's minister of transportation and who we knew was one of Leigh's aides.

He received us with bloodshot eyes. I had the sense that he had been on a week-long spree, or at least that he hadn't slept in days. He was very nervous; he wrung his hands and clearly did not want to talk to us. We were disturbing him and wounding him with our presence. In the back of the room another soldier was seated. He was obviously some kind of security guard, and his presence inhibited Magliocchetti. When we cornered him and tried to get him to tell us what accusations had been made against our husbands, he became so embarrassed that he sent for a prosecutor. But speaking to the prosecutor was about as helpful as speaking to the gardener: he didn't have any legal arguments to make, and all that he finally said was that we should be grateful that they had been arrested, because if not, the hordes would have lynched them.

"What hordes?" I asked him. "The ones from Patria y Libertad?"

"No, the Miristas."

At that point we decided to leave. We continued to walk around the building until we found a small, improvised sign in a corridor saying "Ministry of the Interior." At the door was a young woman seated at an improvised table, and we asked her if we could speak with General Bonilla. She told us that he was in a cabinet meeting, and we left our cards so she could let us know when he would be able to receive us.

We went to another floor, and just then we saw Pinochet coming toward us from the end of the corridor, answering questions from the international press. He was surrounded by cameras, microphones, and lights, just the way I had seen Salvador or Frei a million times. He was every inch a president.

I was completely paralyzed. I couldn't think what to do, and Isabel Margarita, who was at my side, said to me, "Moy, he's going to embrace you."

When we were a few yards apart he moved toward us, and in the next second I saw an image of José in jail with *El Mercurio* in his hands, and on the front page was a photograph of me hugging Pinochet. I put my hands behind me, dug my fingernails into my palms, and must have made some kind of awful face. Pinochet put up his arms to indicate that he wanted the cameras and microphones turned off. The journalists hung back, and he came forward with his arms open, moving more and more quickly until he got to me. He caught me, hugged me, and held me against his chest while I leaned away from him.

"Everything's all right, Moy," he said to me. "Nothing's happening . . ."

"What do you mean nothing's happening? José's in jail, and they're taking him to Dawson Island. I need to talk to you."

"Look," he said to me hurriedly, "come in and speak with Zabala" —Zabala had been an aide to Carlos Prats—"and tell him that my first meeting tomorrow is with you."

He walked on by and the journalists with him. They had turned the lights on again, and he picked up where he had left off, giving explanations about this and that.

We sat down in front of Zabala's office, and suddenly the door opened and Commander Badiola, who had been one of Salvador's aides, appeared. He looked as if he had just seen the devil, because he shut the door with both hands.

Then we went in to see Zabala, who told us—as if it was a big secret—that he had taken General Prats across the border to Mendoza.

"He spoke very fondly of you and your husband," he said to me. "You were very dear to him, and he asked me to do everything I can for you."

We explained to him that we hadn't come to ask him for anything, that the only thing we wanted was an appointment with Pinochet for the next day.

We went home, hoping that something would come of our conversation. We felt as if we had special rights because of our position. A little later, we got a telephone call from General Bonilla's office saying that he would meet with us at noon the following day as well.

We decided that Isabel Margarita, Irma de Almeyda, and I would go to the meeting with Pinochet because the three of us had something in common: each of our husbands had been minister of defense. We thought that each of us would state her personal case and then we would do what we could on behalf of the other people jailed on Dawson Island, who at that time amounted to about sixteen or seventeen men.

We arrived at Pinochet's office at about ten in the morning. We were told that he was in a cabinet meeting and we should wait. About three-quarters of an hour went by, and we saw that soon it would be time for our meeting with Bonilla.

Suddenly Pinochet appeared, a different man from the one who just the day before had been affectionate and caring, like the Pinochet I used to know. He had given me hope that we might have a discussion about what was going on, which was more than any of the other officers from whom I had tried to get news of José had done. Pinochet was someone that I knew well, and I thought he would understand what was happening to our lives. But he was very different that day; he started shouting like a madman when he realized that I was not alone but had come with Irma and Isabel Margarita. He screamed at Irma, asking her what she was doing there, who had invited her. He said we should be thankful that our husbands were being protected by the armed forces because otherwise they would have been lynched by the people. He was shouting outrageously, saying how much worse things would have been if we had been the winners, if we were the ones in power now. Then, I remember, I grabbed him by the coat and said to him, "Augusto, for three years things were the other way around, and I don't remember that your wife ever had to come to my home or my husband's office to ask where you were."

He softened a little, acknowledged that our husbands were on Dawson Island, assured us that they were okay, that they had doctors, and insisted that they were being protected from what would happen to them here. Then he started shouting about Allende and Altamirano again. I asked him if we couldn't go inside his office—

this was all taking place in a hallway—so we could talk quietly and so that the whole world didn't have to be in on our private discussion. We went in, but it didn't help much; he kept us standing and continued his tirade. It was impossible to have a dialogue with him. You would ask him a question, and he would start to yell in response. When we finally left, in single file, I was the last one out. He took me by the elbow and said to me, "Prepare a suitcase for your husband, and I'll send for it so it will get to him on the air force plane tomorrow."

"Only for José? He'd never accept that—it's got to be everyone or no one."

Isabelita and Irma realized what was going on and came back to ask for suitcases for their husbands.

"All right, we'll send each of the husbands a suitcase. But you," he said to me, "are responsible for them—all the suitcases go to your house, and you're responsible for what's inside."

As if we were going to send bombs to Dawson Island!

I realized that Pinochet was not going to help us solve our problems, and that we would have to look for other means. It was the worst experience I have had in my entire life. Because the truth is, I liked Pinochet. I thought he was a little pompous, but a kind, good man with feelings, who had a strong special affection for José. Such a special affection that when the news reached him that Orlando Letelier was going to become minister of defense, he had asked Salvador to return José to the ministry instead. Not because he had anything against Orlando, but because of the soft spot he had for José.

In our meeting with Bonilla, we had to listen to him talk about "Plan Z" and treason against the country, because every time we asked him about the accusations against our husbands, he would answer us with those set speeches. But Bonilla believed in dialogue; he was a Christian Democrat by vocation, with a populist outlook. He was the one most willing to talk to us—or rather least harsh, least rude. He had moral problems in dealing with us, above all with me because we had been through a lot together. He had been in my house, and I in his. He was one of the generals that I knew the best. He was the most humane to us, but he never looked us in the eyes.

He looked out the window, at the ceiling; he seemed very uncomfortable.

We agreed that the first shipment of suitcases would be on September 20, and that they wouldn't weigh more than forty-four pounds each. He advised us that in addition to clothing we should send games for distraction, nonperishable food, sweets and lozenges for the cold, cigarettes, toilet kits, some prescription medicines, newspapers, and books, as long as the books weren't Marxist.

We would be able to send them a shipment once a month, and once a month we would receive letters back.

UNCLE AUGUSTO

I received the first letter from José on October 20. I've kept all of them . . . I read them only once, when they first arrived . . . I haven't been able to read them since. I didn't want to get letters. They were painful—it was too cruel, they expressed a certain calm that was not what I was feeling at the time. I ran around as if I had been injected with the drug they use to make horses run faster, and I kept it up until José died. I would fall asleep in a hurry, and wake up in a hurry the next day . . . the Red Cross office, the Committee on Human Rights, the lawyers, the United Nations High Commission, the U.N. Economic Commission for Latin America . . .

The children had a terrible image of me during that period. José took fatherhood very seriously, and he worked at it. He was very entertaining with the children, and they loved being with him. His absence alone was traumatic for them, and this was only aggravated by my absolute inability to assume a double role, to be tender, kind, and relaxed and at the same time to make the children understand what was happening. No one ever explained anything to them; they just felt the impact of what was going on around them as they were bombarded by news from the television and radio.

The day the first suitcases were ready to go to Dawson Island, an entire battalion of soldiers came to pick them up at my house. Little José was very upset by the goings-on, poor thing. While the soldiers went through the contents of the suitcases, he showed up with a plastic machine gun and confronted a sergeant with a "Hands up!" The sergeant, instead of playing along with a little five-year-old boy, pointed his own machine gun back at him.

"Throw it on the floor," he said to him. "We're the only ones allowed to have guns around here."

José just stood there looking at him, half-terrified, half-surprised, until he finally asked:

"Listen, are you a good guy or one of my Uncle Augusto Pinochet's guys?"

One of my Uncle Augusto Pinochet's guys! Commander Merrick, the officer in charge, realized what was going on and ordered the sergeant out of the house. What was true for José was true for all of us—for us, he was Uncle Augusto Pinochet. He wasn't a good guy any more, but he was still part of our lives.

I couldn't really read the letters that came from Dawson Island. It was too awful knowing that José was living through such horrors, especially in light of the pampered existence he had led until then. He came to socialism from a relatively well-to-do family and economic well-being. He was a deeply sensitive man, with a tender spirit. He was tender to the whole world, even to animals. This came through in his letters, and that's why I didn't want to see them. I just wanted him to write "I need this or that" so that I could get started and put my energies into getting him what he needed.

I knew all about Dawson Island because the island had been turned over to the navy due to José's own efforts. In September of '72 he went to Punta Arenas with Admiral Montero*—I don't remember if Merino, who was a squadron chief, went also—to transfer control of Dawson Island, the same island that was now his jail. I had photos of the ceremony, and I knew that the wind there can reach a hundred kilometers an hour and the temperature can go several degrees below zero.

As time passed, we also began to learn how they were treated there. They would go to the bathroom with a guy pointing a machine

---

* Admiral Raúl Montero, commander in chief of the navy, who did not support the coup and who was replaced by Admiral José Toribio Merino.

gun at them, and they weren't allowed to shut the door. They were subjected to all kinds of abuse—they were forced to work, they were threatened, they were given a daily newspaper collage that was specially made to show only the number of deaths, the bodies found in the Mapocho River, and other things along those lines. We found all of this out from some young men who were sent to that region in the course of their military service and then came back to Santiago. They were struck by what they had seen and wanted to talk to us. Some of them even smuggled out letters for us. We didn't really know if they told us these things in good faith or if they had some ulterior motive, but we later found out they had told us the truth.

No one could ever deserve that kind of treatment, not even the people who were inflicting it on our husbands. Before, when I would sympathize with the Vietnamese or with people who were tortured in Brazil, in my heart I felt that their stories were a bit exaggerated —how could they not be! But when we began to experience all this horror, I understood that it had all been true, that these things really do transpire between human beings.

I felt that we were in the hands of butchers, whose irrationality couldn't be predicted, calculated, or controlled. And all within the courtesy that soldiers show to women. To them, we are second-class beings, fragile and delicate, who must always be treated with respect. That's how it was every time we had to speak with them. Of course, I'm speaking only of women who are not imprisoned, because they had no trouble giving us three weeks of house arrest so that we weren't free to move about.

At the end of November the International Red Cross called us because a delegation had made a tour of the country's concentration camps. Various family groups went, and they would call us in to give us reports. The Dawson Island women received little boxes made of matchsticks, with an ordinary, everyday black stone inside on which our names or initials had been scratched. The stones had been engraved for us by our husbands with a bent, rusty nail so that each of us would have a Christmas gift.

After delivering the gifts, they began to give us information about our husbands. They were Swiss, and I've always had a profound respect for Swiss workmanship, but they were as cold as a cuckoo clock. They would recite in a monotone: "I saw Bitar,* he weighed so many pounds, he needs this or that; Letelier had a problem with a tooth; another one has headaches; you must send them aspirin and a lot of vitamin C; they 're all cold, they need windbreakers because even now during the spring the cold is intense, they need rain boots and work gloves because they're carrying posts and building sewers . . ."

When they got to José, they told me in the same tone that he was no longer on the island but had been transferred to the Punta Arenas hospital with a diagnosis of acute malnutrition—acute malnutrition!—due to lack of food. Then we discovered that their diet consisted of one plate a day of beans, chick-peas, or lentils, without a single piece of meat or a drop of oil—nothing. After two months, they were given permission to walk on a stretch of beach, where they were able to find shellfish washed up on the rocks. Of the packages we sent them, half the contents were stolen when they were opened for inspection.

José lost forty-five pounds his first month on Dawson Island. He was naturally thin, six feet four inches tall, and weighed 165 pounds. But when he got to Punta Arenas he weighed 120 pounds, and when he died he was just under 110.

I went away from the Red Cross meeting crazy with pain and a terrible feeling of impotence. I walked to the home of a friend who lived downtown, and when I finally recovered from the news I found I had been asleep on her bed for over an hour. I began making desperate phone calls to the Defense Ministry, to the Center for Detained Persons, everywhere. I finally got in touch with a naval commander who was an aide to Patricio Carvajal and who had worked in the ministry with José.

"Señor Tohá was never a heavy man," he told me. "Of course he would be malnourished! I'm not going to pass your message on to Minister Carvajal. He has plenty of more important things to worry about than Señor Tohá's health."

I went back to the ministry and spoke with an air force officer

* Sergio Bitar, minister of mining during Allende's government.

named Rojas. I explained to him what was going on and told him that I had to go to Punta Arenas to see José. He acknowledged that what was happening was terrible and promised to speak with Carvajal and call me back. After twenty calls on my part, I got his call informing me that this was not something that came under the admiral's jurisdiction; we would have to take it up with the minister of the interior or of national security, or with members of the Junta. They passed the ball back and forth.

Then I called Espinoza, who was at the Center for Detained Persons.

"How could you even think of going there?" he asked me. "Absolutely not! If there's anything that can be done, the doctors are doing it, and if nothing can be done, let me assure you that we will personally deliver his corpse."

It occurred to me to speak with Magliocchetti, Gustavo Leigh's aide. In fact, since the speeches on the eleventh of September, Leigh was the person I trusted least in terms of sensitivity. Magliocchetti advised me to write a letter and promised to give it to Leigh and petition him to let me go to Punta Arenas. I brought the letter to his home, and the next day he called me with authorization to travel immediately.

A DEVASTATING VISIT

I landed in Punta Arenas about the twentieth of December. I immediately went to see the officer in charge, General Manuel Torres de la Cruz. A dear friend! He was one of those who used to send me boxes of toffee, which I never ate myself but passed on to Salvador, who was a fiend for toffee. It was like arriving at a tea salon: "How lovely to see you! You haven't changed a bit, as beautiful and young as ever!" I explained that I had come with authorization to see José, and all his amiability disappeared.

"That can't be so. It's absolutely forbidden to see the prisoners."

"I have authorization from Gustavo Leigh."

"But he has nothing to do with this; he can't give you authorization. It's a matter for Carvajal."

After a long discussion he decided to be generous: "Look, breaking all the rules, and committing the most exceptional irregularity" —for which I was supposed to be very grateful—"I am going to let you go in, but for only fifteen minutes, and that's it."

"I'm not going to see José unless I can see him every day that I'm here, until I can say 'I'll see you tomorrow.' "

At that point he decided to call Santiago, but since he couldn't get in touch with anyone, he told me to go to the hospital, and he guaranteed that I could honestly say "I'll see you tomorrow."

I left for the hospital. I took a bag of things with me. I had been living for the past few months on the money I got by selling my Fiat 600, and with the little money that was left I had ordered a track suit, some heavy sweaters, and wool-lined gloves. I also had with me letters from the children, photographs, and everything I could think of that would help him, after all he had been through. At the entrance were three guys, one with a scar from the corner of his eye to his mouth. He asked me if I was Señora Tohá, and they made me go into a room and get undressed. They took apart my shoes, dumped out my purse, and damaged the photos of the children. They were very, very strange people—like aliens.

Finally, we began to walk down a long corridor until we got to a room with a window and a hospital bed. I waited about fifteen minutes until suddenly the door opened and José came in, walking between two soldiers with machine guns. His pants flapped around his waist. It was scary to see someone that thin. I always said José couldn't get any skinnier than he already was; he was as thin as possible for someone his height, and now he weighed forty-five pounds less! His hair looked as if it had been cut with a lawn mower. I hugged him; I hugged him and it was like hugging little José, my son. He had always stood very erect, but now it was difficult for him to walk; he was extremely pale, and he had already spent two weeks in the hospital where, no matter how bad the food was, it had to be better than at Dawson Island.

Before José arrived, my escort had warned me: "Conversations between visitors and prisoners must be strictly about family matters. You may not speak of politics; you may not speak of friends or of illnesses. You may tell him about your children, what you have seen at the theater, books you have read, that type of thing and nothing more."

I knew that if I stuck to that it would destroy him, so in my mind I put together a conversation that they wouldn't be able to prevent. We sat on the bed, I took his hands and began:

"Yesterday I visited Pinochet. I brought you some cigarettes from Admiral Montero; I spoke with Magliocchetti; Leigh let me come; I met with Urbina . . ."

I created a sense for him that although he was on Dawson Island, reduced to the least possible degree of human dignity, in Santiago the machinery kept working and he continued to be a real person. I set up this entire scenario for him, knowing that the soldiers watching us wouldn't interfere, because they function in terms of authority, and even if I wasn't talking about family matters, I was talking about their superiors. Also, in some sense the conversation protected me.

That's how we spent fifteen minutes. It was awful. At the end, I wanted it to finish, to be over, because it was too destructive. José reacted well. He only broke down when he spoke of Daniel Vergara,* and told me that the press had been completely ruthless.

We had four visits, each one very different from the others and all designed to destroy us psychologically. Everything was unexpected: I never knew if I was going to have five minutes or an hour to spend with him; our talk was never natural or easy because there was so much to say; and we never knew how much time we could count on. In their efforts to break José down, they hadn't counted on his wife coming to see him. That helped him, and they didn't want him to be helped. They had no intention of letting him stay alive.

The second day they gave us an hour, during which José kept repeating, "There is nothing that you can do for me personally, don't even think about it—even less for me than for anyone else. I don't want you to make any separate efforts on my behalf, without the other wives. You may not use my position to get any better treatment for me than for anyone else."

---

* Undersecretary of the interior and member of the Communist Party.

I told him about the invitations we had to go to Caracas, Mexico, Spain, and I realized that José wouldn't want to leave. It was a question of principle—the only way he would leave here would be with a trial. I told him about the children, and that was the only time I saw him smile. Carolina had made him a box out of ice-cream sticks to keep his cigarettes in, which they had practically destroyed when they searched my things. But José fondled it, and he stroked Caroline's little face in the picture of her with a dog.

While he spoke to me, José looked at the soldier in front of us as if he were mesmerized. When he told me about the bombing of La Moneda he was overcome with deep emotion . . . it was like a suppressed sob, not of tears, but of great pain.

As time went by I learned how much they had tortured him. They kept him for forty-eight hours with 200-watt spotlights in his eyes. During the trip from Dawson Island to Punta Arenas, they had tied him to the deck of the ship. He lost consciousness twice, and when they knocked him down with a rifle butt he passed out again. In the hospital they told him they had to ascertain whether he had cancer because he was so thin, and they put him through horrible tests. Three aides carried what was left of him back to his bed.

On the third day they also gave us an hour. For the last visit, just before Christmas, I had ordered a cake to be made. I bought a roast chicken, a Christmas cake, and some drinks, and I put it all in a basket with a big ribbon and some Christmas decorations. They tore it all apart. They stuck a knife in every part of the cake and reduced the Christmas cake to crumbs.

That day it took José longer to come to the room, and while I was waiting for him the guy who accompanied me said, "You know what, lady? I've grown to like you these past four days. What do you do about the sex problem? I tell you, the men have a hard time of it; sex is the worst problem for all of them."

"Look," I answered, "I have so much respect for the intellectual greatness of the men that you have imprisoned here that, though that might be a problem for most people, I think that these men's anguish and their problems lie elsewhere. I also happen to have a lot of respect for their wives."

At that moment José came in, and knowing how sensitive he was I didn't want him to know what had happened because it would have made him very uncomfortable to hear me defend him on this point. But the guy changed the topic:

"Listen, I have plans to go to a movie this afternoon, so I'm giving you fifteen minutes, and that's it"—at a time when we had thought we would have an hour again—"and since your wife is such a friend of the Communists, she's welcome to spend five of those minutes visiting with Daniel Vergara and Silva instead."

There were four prisoners in the hospital: José, the two he mentioned, and Osvaldo Puccio, who had had a heart attack. I accepted his offer to spend five minutes with Vergara, and the guard announced that he had a Christmas present for us as well.

"With respect to this sex thing," he told us, knowing that José hadn't heard anything about it, "you have one minute to make love."

He left the room, and that was the only time we had alone. We had so much to say to each other that we didn't say a word!

The minute ended, and he opened the door again.

"Now we'll bring a record player so you can dance, because here come the Communist and Silva."

The two of them came in, along with Osvaldo Puccio and his wife, who had also gotten permission to visit him. I embraced them; we exchanged a few words and ate some of the things I had brought until the soldier began to hum a farewell song.

"OK, that's it. I have to get to the movies, so go on and say good-bye."

A MATTER OF LIFE AND DEATH

The night I got back to Santiago I began writing letters to everyone under the sun—to Carvajal, Arellano, Bonilla, Pinochet. I informed them of the state in which I had found José and held them responsible for whatever might happen to him.

At this point all the women knew that we were no longer seeking fast and fair trials for our husbands, but their very lives. Our actions determined whether they would live or die, because if they were left on Dawson Island for the winter, they would all die.

My letters had some effect. A couple of days later José was re-turned to the island with a chicken in his hands, and while the others ate beans, they let José have his chicken. He never ate the chicken, though, but shared it out among the others.

I continued to plead his case at all different levels until, on January 30, Carvajal's aide called to tell me that José was back in Santiago. He told me José had been diagnosed as severely malnourished and that he was being put on a special diet at the military hospital.

On the island they had told José that he would be taken to the military hospital for a complete check-up and that then he would be taken home and put under house arrest. They say that José looked at them and didn't say anything—that he went into his room, shared out all his possessions, and walked in silence to the ship that was at the shore. He didn't say good-bye to anyone.

They gave us permission to see him on February 2, and I gave my place to my mother-in-law, who hadn't seen him since September. She came out with her face contorted with anguish. "I don't know if he will be able to walk in the state he's in," she told me, and I couldn't imagine him any thinner than I had seen him in Punta Arenas.

We were allowed to visit twice a week, always with the unwelcome presence of a guard. I went alone on the second visit because I had asked permission to bring the children and other family members on the sixth, which was his birthday. José was sitting on his bed. He had on a hospital gown, and when he saw me enter, he moved to-ward me, supporting himself on a dresser and a chair. I had the sense that he was having trouble focusing his eyes, although he'd never had problems with his sight before, but now he had lost some of his vision.

The day of his birthday I brought him a cake with a little candle. The hospital was full of soldiers from the intelligence branch, and Colonel Aguirre, an insolent man who smoked a pipe, grabbed the cake to search it and stuck his fingers in it. When we arrived with the children, my mother-in-law was already there with José's sisters-in-law and other people. José's meeting with the children was very emotional; they climbed onto the bed and asked him a thousand questions. José was choked up with emotion; he lost his voice, and all he could do was hug them to him.

That day they gave us an hour, and we tried to make the get-together as light-hearted as possible, although it was interrupted several times by intelligence officers. They forbade me to bring in a bunch of things that had been sent to José, and they made a terrible scene over a gag on a card sent to him by his niece. It was a card with a picture of a sick person on it that said, "Even though everyone else wants you to die, I hope you get better soon." They took this as a remark directed against them, and they threatened to arrest all of us the next time something like that happened. They said all this in front of José, my mother-in-law, the children . . . the whole situation was like Kafka.

One or two visits later I remarked to José that he had put on a little weight and that surely they were going to release him. His answer was so terrible that I assumed it was a product of his imagination or a psychological effect of being imprisoned: "I'll never leave here."

The next time I went with one of my children, because they wouldn't let me take both of them; an official was waiting for me at the door: "Señor Tohá is not here any more."

"And where is he?"

"I'm not able to say where he is, but they took him away this morning."

From the nurses, who had grown to like José, I learned that they had taken him to the air force hospital. They had him in the basement, in rooms that weren't finished yet, where they also had Edgardo Enríquez, the former education minister, and General Bachelet.

I went back home in despair and called the Ministry of Defense. I spoke with Colonel Ibáñez, who made some inquiries and was able to confirm that José was at the air force hospital and to tell me that he was being interrogated by Attorney General Oteíza, who was a dog trainer for the air force.

The next day, I managed to find Oteíza. In addition to acknowledging that he was interrogating José, he told me that the doctors had authorized him to take José out of the hospital. He refused to tell me where they had him, but I found out that he was at the Air Force War Academy.

I was so upset that I decided to call the government building and ask for a meeting with Pinochet. They told me that all his appointments were filled for the next six months, and although I insisted that it was a question of life or death, I was convinced that he wouldn't see me. Nevertheless, twenty minutes later they informed me that Pinochet would meet with me at five that afternoon.

It was over five months since I'd been inside the building where I had worked for more than a year. It was changed; it had an air of luxury that we had never had, and it seemed vulgar to me. Magliocchetti had heard that I was there and made me come up to his office on the floor just below Pinochet's.

I told him the story and he couldn't believe it. He felt terrible. I don't think that he was too closely allied with the system; he was there out of opportunism, for business and other reasons, but I don't think that he was emotionally comfortable with or completely aware of what was going on. When I told him that Oteíza was a dog trainer, he tried to explain to me that public prosecutors can be any kind of people, not necessarily lawyers. Then I pointed out to him that it wouldn't look very good in the history books that the air force had chosen a dog trainer to interrogate former ministers. After fifteen minutes an aide to Pinochet called to say he was waiting for me.

He met me at the door to his office. "Madam, may I help you?" he said.

"Excuse me, but I have not come to speak with the president of the Junta, but with Augusto Pinochet, whom I have known for quite some time."

A conversation followed that was like fingernails on glass. He was evasive, jumping from one topic to the next: Tencha was to be declared "stateless," and things like that. He insisted that I should be grateful to him for seeing me in less than twelve hours.

"You never had to ask for an appointment to come to my house," I reminded him. "You came to our house as if it were your house, even before you became commander of Chile's army. You were always received warmly; we were kind to you and considered you our friend."

I asked him to tell me what had happened to José and to return my husband to me.

"You can't ask that," he answered. "I can't do it, because the army has nothing against your husband, but the air force will surely have charges to bring against him."

The minutes went by, and while I kept trying to make him understand the seriousness of the situation, he went back to the theme of how ungrateful I was. He said that in spite of being a Marxist-Leninist, I was free, that thanks to him José had been moved to the Punta Arenas hospital and then to Santiago.

"If I do anything," he said finally, "I will do it for little José and Carolina, because those children are not responsible for what has happened, and because all children deserve a father."

This made me angry, and perhaps I wasn't thinking straight when I answered, "If you do anything, you'll do it for the relationship you had with José, for what you knew about him as a human being, for the friendship that José gave you and that you gave him. You won't do it for little José and Carolina. I can take care of my children myself."

He looked at me surprised and continued to pace back and forth. "I promise to speed up the legal proceedings, but that's it. I'm not promising anything else."

The meeting must have lasted about thirty-five minutes, and in spite of everything, I left with the sense of having accomplished something positive.

The next day, in our lawyer Alfredo Etcheverry's office, I met with General Bachelet's wife. She advised me to speak with General Berdichevsky because he was the judge in the "Bachelet et al." case for which they were questioning José.

I knew Berdichevsky very well. He had been the air force officer in charge of the Punta Arenas air base when José delivered Dawson Island to the navy. He received me immediately and showed surprise at my story, because, according to him, there was no charge against José in that case. He called Oteíza on the phone while I sat there, and stated for him the accusations that I had raised. I don't know what they said to him on the other end.

"But that doesn't justify it," he said. "You have to wait until he has recuperated before you start interrogation."

He hung up and told me that in five days José's incommunicado status would be lifted. "What's happening is that his name has come up several times in the course of the trial," he added by way of justification.

His words had a great effect on me, or maybe I needed to react positively to someone, needed to believe in something at that point.

At the end of those five days José would be able to receive a visitor. I gave my place to his brother Isidor, who is a doctor. He had also been arrested twice, and he got special permission from the public prosecutor's office in Chillán to come to Santiago and visit his brother.

I don't know what happened in the Air Force War Academy, but I was shocked by what my brother-in-law told me. José had said to him, "If they're going to kill me, I'd rather that they did it quickly," and he explained that they were going to execute him as a murderer and a thief.

After twenty minutes Oteíza had come into the room.

"Don José," he said, "I know that it's a great bother to keep questioning you in writing, but we have a job to do. I'm leaving you four questions to respond to, and I'll pick up your answers in the morning."

"I have no trouble responding to whatever accusations you want to make," José answered, but he looked at his brother to indicate that it would be better if he left because Oteíza wanted to speak to him in private.

Isidor said good-by to José, and it was the last time he saw him.

On the next visit I discovered that he was incommunicado again. They wouldn't let me see him. Another two weeks went by.

I called the Ministry of Defense, but I couldn't get anyone. Those were terrible days because little items began to appear in the papers saying that José's health was very precarious. The nurses would call me and tell me to come see him, or at least to let him hear my voice in the hall, because one of the means they had of torturing him was to tell him that I wasn't coming to visit because the children and I had been put in jail too. They also had a psychiatrist, who evidently interrogated him using pentothal and hypnosis.

Those were terrible days. On Saturday, before March 15, the Ministry of Defense advised me that I could go to see him and that I would have an hour alone with my husband.

I hadn't seen him in almost a month. I left full of hope, with my hair freshly done. I stopped in the doorway a few yards from the bed. He was lying down with one leg raised as if to prevent the bedclothes from touching his body. And he couldn't see! From a distance of a few yards he couldn't make out the person in the doorway.

"José, it's me."

He had been trying to sit up to see who it was, and when he heard my voice he fell back and stared emptily into space.

"They're going to kill me."

I lay on the bed, took his head and put it on my shoulder to hold him. He was reduced to skin and bones; his body was as thin as a corpse. I tried to lift his spirits by telling him that they were going to send him home any moment now, that we had a new invitation to go to Venezuela and for him to teach at the university. It was useless.

"I'll never leave here because they're going to kill me. They stand at the foot of my bed and make fun of my helplessness. I just want this all to end as soon as possible."

I insisted that he had to think of the children and the fight we were all putting up. I spent an hour using all the means I could think of to reassure him. "I have to write," he kept repeating. His condition was such that he should have been in a sanatorium, on double food rations, all relaxed and calm. But instead they kept squeezing and squeezing him until nothing was left, when it was perfectly clear he had nothing to give them. It was enough to see José's statements during the trial to realize that.

An officer came to tell us that we had five minutes left. José pressed my hand with all the strength he had left. When I got up to leave, he wouldn't let me go, and I went back to give him another kiss.

"You have to pull yourself together because they're taking you out of incommunicado, and I don't want the children to see you like this. For them, you're a film star, and they would be very upset to see you this way."

"The children are never going to see me again," he insisted. "They're going to kill me."

I went back home in despair. All the Dawson Island women were waiting for me there because we had become a true sisterhood and we all shared whatever happened to each of us.

"José is dead," I told them. "He's still breathing, but he's dead. They're murdering him."

They made me see that I had to say something to Colonel Ibáñez, who was the one who had told me I could go to the hospital. I picked up the phone and called immediately.

"Colonel, I've just seen José for an hour, and I'm telling you that José is dead. He's dead! I'm absolutely sure they're going to kill him."

That's the kind of pressure we were living under! It's an oppression here, inside the skull, that actually made me lose consciousness several times during those months. It's a feeling of total powerlessness—you feel things slipping through your hands, and there's nothing more you can do about it. You've knocked on all the doors, rung all the bells, opened all the windows, resorted to all the people you are able to resort to. And, as if in a masquerade, everyone appears to be helping, when in fact they are murdering. They're murdering! Out one side come the kind words, the gloss of education, gentility, a little coffee for madam . . . while with their other hand they're wringing the neck of the person you're trying to rescue. This was the sense I was getting as time went by, with those nightmarish transactions, in that masquerade where people told me one thing while something entirely different was going on.

PICKING UP THE BODY

General Bachelet died on Tuesday. I found out in Etcheverry's office. I was overcome with despair, didn't know what to do, and so I went to the hospital. I didn't know if José knew the news or not, if he had heard it on the radio and television. I bought a newspaper to find out what it said, and there was another article about José: "Ex-Vice-President of the Republic Gravely Ill in the Military Hospital."

I got to the hospital and they wouldn't let me see him because he was technically still incommunicado. Some nurse suggested that I send a note in to him, without letting anyone see, so that he would know I was here. I left reassuring myself because José had asked me to come back the following day and to bring him some deodorant. I knew that he didn't really need any but that he wanted me to know he was all right.

Because of the newspaper article, I spoke with the hospital director, Dr. Patricio Silva, who during this entire time had done nothing but put obstacles in my way. He assured me that José was fine, that that's just how newspapers were, and that as soon as the incommunicado status was lifted, José would recover completely.

The next day I went back to the hospital, and then I went to Bachelet's funeral. It was awful. Some soldiers came and tried to take the urn, the women grabbed it away from them . . . we sang the national anthem. During that whole period, that was the only time I broke down. I felt that I couldn't stand any more, I was going to die. It was as if everything I had held in, compressed in my chest, suddenly exploded, like a pressure cooker when the valves are opened. I thought I would fall over from crying so much—I was hysterical. It was an enormous relief. I think tears are the best medicine human beings have, and I regret not being able to cry more readily.

The next day I went to the hospital again with pajamas, towels, simply excuses to get near him.

Friday, March 15, to distract myself a little, I went to the market with Isabel Margarita. We bought some clams and sat on my terrace for lunch. We were about to start eating when the phone rang:

"This is Colonel Aguirre. I'm calling to tell you that your husband has died and that you may come to pick up the body."

. . . Isabelita says that I called him a hyena, that I told him he was inhumanly cruel . . . that I called him every name I could think of . . .

I hung up and called Colonel Ibáñez at the Ministry of Defense.

"Colonel, I spoke with you after I had spent an hour with José and told you they were going to kill him. Don't tell me I was wrong, because they have killed him now!"

I did some positively stupid things . . . I was like another person . . . a mindless being. I moved around the house without knowing what I was doing.

We got to the hospital, and Aguirre was there with his pipe and his impeccable jackboots. "You may go up alone," he said. "The other woman can wait here, because both of these rooms are reserved for you while you are picking up the body."

We went up. Aguirre walked ahead, chatting away with an aide who must have been from the intelligence agency. The hallway was endless. At the end was a screen, and behind it I saw three nurses, leaning against the wall, crying.

I went into José's room. He was naked, covered with a sheet up to his waist, with his arms out forming a cross. His eyes were half open, his mouth was shut, and a small thread of blood was coming out of the corner of his nose.

I began to talk to him, to tell him everything . . . everything that they hadn't let me tell him during the six months this agony had lasted.

"Have you finished making your speech, madam?" Those were Aguirre's words.

"No," I answered, "and I'll never be finished with this speech."

"Well, before you finish—and not wishing to interrupt your momentum—I'll tell you that it was his decision, not ours."

I looked and saw that at the base of his neck, José had a red line. Aguirre handed me a belt as if in proof.

What Colonel Aguirre didn't know was that I had spent ten years of my life as a police expert. During those years I had seen hundreds of cases where people had decided to put an end to things with a belt around their necks. And there's no mistaking the body of a hanged man: his face is purple, his mouth is open, his eyes bulge out of their sockets. José had the most peaceful face in the world . . . How he actually died, I don't know.

When they killed Orlando Letelier, I remember saying to Isabelita, "We were lucky. We had a body, we buried it, we know where it is."

ABOUT THE AUTHOR

Patricia Politzer studied at the University of Chile and lives in La Reina, Santiago. She was one of the first journalists to speak out against the Pinochet coup in a national radio broadcast in 1978, and she has a weekly political interview column in the opposition newspaper *La Época*.